DITCH YOUR CUBICLE: NOT YOUR LIFE

DITCH YOUR CUBICLE: NOT YOUR LIFE

BECOME A FREELANCE INSTRUCTIONAL DESIGNER IN 7 MONTHS

PARKER A. GRANT, Ph.D. &
ANDREA DOTTLING, M.Ed.

979-8-9868320-0-5 Trade Paperback
979-8-9868320-1-2 eBook

Library of Congress Control Number: *to come*

Any references to historical events, real people, or real places are used fictitiously. Names, characters, and places are products of the author's imagination.

Book design by Glen Edelstein, Hudson Valley Book Design

Printed in the United States of America.

First printing edition 2023.

IDLance, LLC
680 E. Main St. Unit 501
Stamford, CT. 06901

CONTENTS

INTRODUCTION

WELCOME TO OUR BOOK. And by "our" we mean Andrea 'N' Parker's book. No, not THAT Andrea N. Parker, the American film and television actor who is known for her roles on ER, The Pretender, Less than Perfect, Desperate Housewives, and Pretty Little Liars. We know, we know, that mix-up happens all the time. But yeah, we're Dr. Parker A. Grant and Andrea Dottling.

And we're the Head Honchos of IDLance! We're here to help you break outta that cubicle/open floor plan/glass-walled office situation and live your freelance instructional design dreams!

Why did we write this book? We wrote this book so that instructional designers who want to gain full control of their time (and their lives) have a friendly resource to help them along. When we each went freelance, we were kinda lonely and overwhelmed and sometimes even confused by all the conflicting information out there. We also felt like we had to kiss a lot of butts just to learn the basics of the freelance ID industry. Not to say our industry isn't friendly, but there's a lot of top-down ish going on like, "I'm an expert and I do everything the exact right way and thus you must say and do exactly the right things to receive the sweet manna from my heavenly lips." No thank you.

What is this book even about? Well, we're gonna lay out a 7-month plan for you to prepare for and actually make the leap to freelance freedom in the instructional design world. This includes everything from cultivating the "right" mindset, to preparing your personal finances, to finding your people, making your portfolio, and finding clients. All that stuff and more. Basically, how to start and run your own instructional design freelance business. Our emphasis is on your business. In these forthcoming pages is a step-by-step process for the 7 months before you go full-time freelie. We can't tell you exactly how many steps right now because honestly, we're still writing the rest of this book as we write this intro. And, also, counting the steps was Andrea's job and math is not really her strong suit so… just know there's enough steps to get ya where ya need to go - in the direction of your ID freelance goals! Along the way there will be some fun doodle illustrations to hammer the important points home and give your delicate little eyes a break from the mountains of text. Did you know that Parker LOVES doodles? As simple as they may be, he knows they can pack a punch with learning tips!

What is this book NOT about? This is not a book about "how to be an instructional designer" or even "how to be a 'good' instructional designer." There's a lot of stuff out there for that already. So many free and paid materials at your flamin' hot Cheeto-coated fingertips. Maybe we'll write about that someday, but today is not that day. And, this book doesn't cover in-depth details of writing proposals or contracts. There are a thousand versions of these, and you'd be better off asking ChatGPT to write drafts for ya – according to your OWN specs! Really, our focus is helping you make the leap to freelancing. There are a ton of emotions to deal with, so we'll do our best to prepare you. Okay, now that we got all that out of the way, it's time to get a move on!

7 MONTHS BEFORE YOU DITCH YOUR CUBICLE

AS THE BEATLES said, "I get by with a little help from my friends." Now, they also said they do some other more nefarious things with a little help from their friends, but that's for another book. Also, wow. We did not see quoting The Beatles in our very first chapter since we don't even really like them that much (except George - he seemed alright), but life is full of surprises, innit?

(Disclaimer: Please don't let any disagreement re: The Beatles deter you from perusing the rest of this book.)

Anyway, "a little help from your friends" is what Step #1 is all about!

Join Your Peeps

Congratulations! You've made the decision to start your freelance journey. To some, this may seem like a scary or isolating experience. To others, it may feel like a long time coming. Either way, it's mega exciting! As exciting as the time you figured out you could take the silverware compartment out of your dishwasher and keep it in your sink to collect cutlery in between washes. Basically, pretty life changing.

Whether you're just starting out or making a career pivot, it's important to know that you aren't alone! Joining a global ID community is a terrific way to feel grounded and find support in your journey (quest).

STEP #1

WHY SHOULD I START BY JOINING A GLOBAL ID COMMUNITY?

Joining a global ID community can help alleviate some of your fears of the unknown in going full 'lance. So, what exactly is a global ID community?

- A global ID community is pretty much just like it sounds. It's made up of a group of people (e.g., instructional designers, instructional developers, teachers, project managers, video creators, friendly interweb garden gnomes) that are currently freelancing as a side gig or (like you) working on a full 'lance ID career.
- Because it is a "global community," meetings are usually held in a digital/virtual space. No, not one of those metaverse Second Life-looking pixelated "office" spaces decorated with soul-sucking NFTs. Just like, text, video, and voice chat and stuff.
- These communities provide an opportunity to collaborate and connect with other like-minded individuals going through similar work (and sometimes life!) things. (Anyone else have a partner who puts ketchup on their pizza?? Anyone?)
- Some ID communities provide their members with the ability to find or share open gigs.

Now that you have a basic understanding of what a global ID community looks like, let's take a deeper dive into a specific community: IDLance (Ooh! Ooh! We know that one!)

IDLance is a global ID community we started in 2020. IDLance's mission is all about supportin' freelance instructional designers and those who need them - in all kindsa ways. We cultivate and mentor a community of freelancin' "fiends" who are focused on the instructional design industry. And it just so happens that we tap into that community to staff and run ID projects for organizations big and small. As of the publish date of this book, we've worked with the Fortune 50 companies, restaurant and hospitality industries, financial literacy non-profits, major internet communication platforms, clinical social outreach programs, higher ed, major ad agencies, the food industry (this is the industry that Parker *ahem* loves… hey, who doesn't love Kellogg's cereals?), and more.

Slack serves as the virtual meeting space for the IDLance community. It's an online messaging service that enables users to connect via their phone or computer to communicate as a group and one-to-one. The IDLance community has a number of channels that enable users to talk about all the things that are important to growing a healthy and happy life as an ID freelancer.

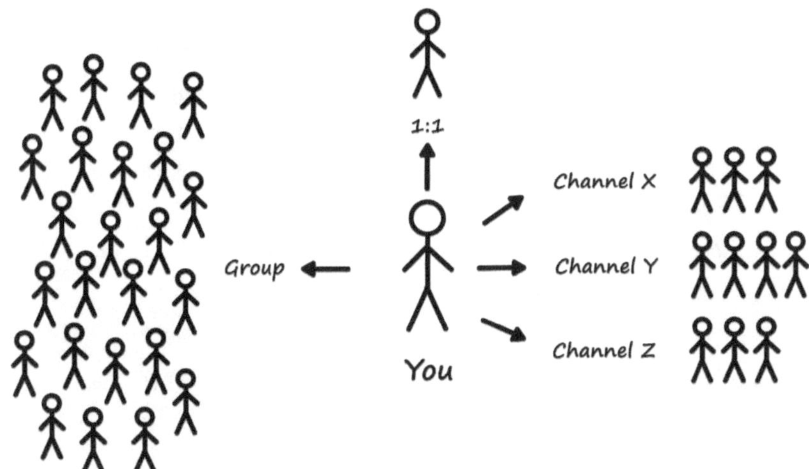

Whether you are in a Slack community or a social network, use a multi-prong strategy to connect with your network via groups, channels, and one-on-one. This approach increases your chances of finding new gigs (even before you ditch your cubicle)!

Here are a few of the most popular IDLance channels:

- **#ChitChat:** Have a question about how to interact with a
  client? How do you add text-to-speech in Articulate? What

are your favorite open-source sites to get images and audio for your eLearning projects? Have you read the latest article from Forbes on the challenges and opportunities of upskilling a workforce? These are some of the types of questions that are shared on a daily basis in the #ChitChat channel. What better way to find out you're not alone, then to post a question and multiple responses filled with fellow IDs eager to help, collaborate…and sometimes even commiserate!

- **#SoRandom:** How do you like your coffee? Have you seen the latest manatee eating lettuce TikTok? Do I really need a standing desk? Check out this accidentally obscene drawing from my kid! This is a lighter channel that allows members to share what makes them laugh, cry, and remind us all that we are all in this together.

- **#CheckThisOut:** Updating your portfolio? Working on a cool new eLearning in Storyline or 7taps and need a second set of eyes? This channel provides members the ability to share and garner feedback from the IDLance community. Your project doesn't have to be completed or finished. Different perspectives inspire us and get us all back on the path - even when frustrated.

- **#TeachersLounge:** A great community made up of current and former teachers from elementary, secondary, and post-secondary institutions. The lounge is a great place where teachers can talk about how to take what they have done in the classroom and translate it to ID projects. You can also use this space to argue over who had the better Harry Potter themed classroom. (Sorry not sorry, Sammy's "Platform 9 ¾" into the bathroom wins.)

- **#Gig-Alerts:** IDLance has a channel devoted to assisting its members in finding new gigs or projects. Members have the ability to share opportunities that they have heard about and are unable to take on. In addition, as we said before, we have projects that we fill using members from our community. These are especially helpful when you are trying to find your first projects.

Starting your freelance ID career doesn't have to be lonely. A global ID community like IDLance can be there for you every step of the way. Just like your favorite tv show that you keep on while working to keep you company!

STEP #2

HOW WOULD JOINING THE IDLANCE COMMUNITY GET ME STARTED?

In Step #1, we gave you our viewpoint of what the IDLance community can offer freelance IDs. In Step #2, you'll hear from some of our members. We reached out to seven of our peeps to provide us with "their story." They shared their inspiring journeys to becoming a freelance ID and their (consensual) relationship with IDLance. We hope that you find their insights as valuable and ego-stroking as we did!

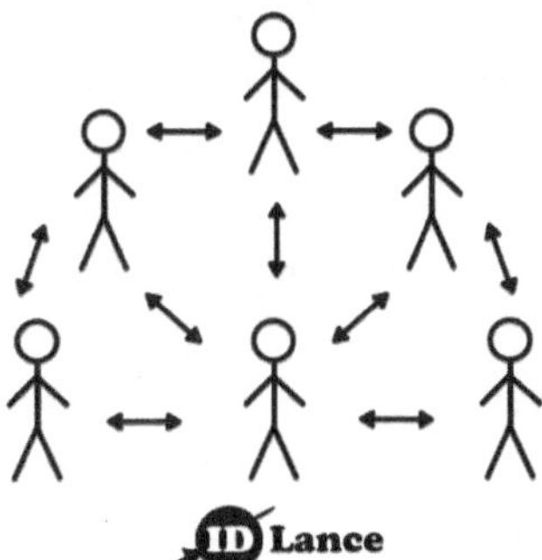

Networking in the IDLance Slack community allows IDs connect with other IDs who are in the same journey of starting, maintaining, or growing their freelance businesses. This connection, in turn, fosters the learning process and the business growth!

What was your background before becoming a Freelance ID?

Five of our seven interviewees were former teachers. The other two were more corporate-y.

- *Before becoming an ID, I was a teacher. Some of those years were 7th grade English. Some of those years were served as an instructional technology coach. I even had a 6-month run as an assistant principal!* - Alex M.
- *Before becoming a freelance ID, I was a secondary social studies teacher and adjunct professor. In addition to my teaching job at the high school, I was the technology integrationist - in charge of developing, writing, and facilitating training for my staff of 75 and a student body of 1,000 students.* - Craig M.
- *Prior to joining the wonderful world of freelance I worked full-time as a Training Developer for Chipotle Mexican Grill. Our team created all training materials (digital and print) for over 1800 restaurants. Specifically my role was to design, develop and test eLearning courses and training materials such as recipe cards, facilitator guides, manager training programs, onboarding programs, etc. Prior to Chipotle I worked as a Graphic and User Interface designer for a variety of corporations for 8 years.* - Yanna R

What made you jump into the Freelance ID world?

- *I taught preschool for 15 years. I adored teaching but needed to make more money.* - Star P.
- *I would love to mention that one of the best things about freelance is your opportunity to say "no" to a project. In a corporate setting you often can't say no. In the world of freelance you get to map your own journey. If a proposed project is not a good fit, you don't need to take it :).* - Yanna R.

- *I worked in mostly global corporate L&D departments as a learning technologist. I was laid off and unable to land another corporate role.* - Tasha R.

- *I stumbled across a job opening for "instructional designer" - which I had never heard of - and got curious... Very quickly, I realized that this role pulls together many of my strengths! So I dove into learning the craft.* - David B.

- *I wanted to get out of academia for a bit! I heard about instructional design, and with my background as an educator in K-12 and higher ed, it seemed like an awesome fit. I landed my first ID job at a Fortune 200 company and had an amazing team and manager who supported my professional development. I became one of my team's top Storyline developers in a fairly short time. I loved being an ID and all the responsibilities that came with it.* - Allie Y.

How did you find out about IDLance? What made you want to join the community?

- *I learned about the IDLance community from Andrea. We had worked on an earlier project together and she gave me a heads-up about the community. I was still green in the freelance world and was looking for a place (community) to bounce ideas off of and to help mentor me on my freelance journey.* - Craig M.

- *I discovered IDLance through LinkedIN a handful of years ago. I interviewed for a gig with Andrea, and we just hit it off immediately. I didn't get that gig, but Andrea and I have worked together quite a bit over the years and have remained good friends and colleagues even outside of work instances. When I found out there was a community of even MORE cool folks who share the same passion for this job, I jumped in with both feet.* - Alex M.

- *I was first introduced to Parker Grant though a dear friend Patti Bryant (who is also a pioneer in the ID community). We originally spoke about working on a project together, but IDLance wasn't officially launched at that time.*

- *A year later Parker and Andrea launched IDLance and approached me to work on my first project. I joined the community to stay up to date on project tasks and project related communication. At that time I didn't realize IDLance was a robustly growing community with many fans and talent! I feel like many subscribers of the IDLance community are true fans. IDLance has found their niche, their tribe - that's pretty incredible. - Yanna R.*

How do you engage with the IDLance community?

- *IDLance's Slack channel is a very supportive community to tap into for peer-to-peer tips, tricks, job leads… you name it! An excellent resource for new and veteran IDs alike. - David B.*
- *I post gigs when colleagues need an instructional designer and I'm not able to take the job. I also ask for advice on a regular basis. I love being able to tap into the collective wisdom and experience of this great community of instructional designers! - Star P.*
- *I currently engage with IDLance community in many ways! I love our Slack channel. I like to give advice, seek advice, and celebrate people's successes. I've also found a handful of gigs through the community, which is awesome! - Allie Y.*
- *I love engaging with the IDLance community in every way I can. When I'm stuck, I ask the community a question. When I have answers to others' questions, I chime in. Sometimes we vent. Sometimes we get a little random. But overall, it's like having a whole training department within arm's length. We may all be working on different things for different clients, but we all just "get it" when we discuss our working lives with one another. - Alex M.*

How has IDLance impacted your freelance career?

- *IDLance has provided me the opportunity to spread my freelance ID wings. They provide me with the opportunity to help design and create engaging eLearning experiences. The nudge and vote of confidence have made me more confident in my abilities and always quick to say "yes, how can I help" when they are in need of freelancers.* - Craig M.

- *IDLance has made me feel much more confident as an instructional designer, because I can get advice from more experienced people about working with clients. They also gave me some of my very first instructional design gigs! Having that work on my resume helped me get other freelance jobs. I learned a lot from working as a junior instructional designer and eLearning developer through IDLance.* - Star P.

- *In a world where I work alone, I get from this community a sense of validation, that I'm on the right track and doing well. Sometimes when we operate in a vacuum, we have no idea if we're doing good, or bad. And we typically are our own worst critics. I've learned that my innate strategies have been pretty much on track. But, I'm able to get support with roadblocks, and in a timely manner.* - Allie Y.

- *They have helped me to feel like I am not alone and that I have resources to contact when I have run into a question that I don't know how to answer.* - Tasha R.

- *The freelancing side of my life would have probably fizzled out without IDLance. I probably would underprice myself, be missing huge chunks of freelie knowledge, and feel as though I lacked support without the community. IDLance is such a wealth of information and camaraderie that helps keep that freelance fire burning. In short, without IDLance, I wouldn't be the ID I am today!* - Alex M.

VISUALIZE YOUR INCOME AND EXPENSES

Having a community is great, especially when it comes to embarking on such a crazy - um, we mean fun! - journey. You're on the path and ready (well, ready enough, right?) to start your majestic quest to become a freelance instructional designer. Yes, it's great that you've found something you (potentially?) love and yadda yadda, but let's get down to the nitty gritty right away. Let's talk about the thing that enables you to buy those vintage 90s Littlest Pet Shop toys on eBay for your kids. The infinite holiday-themed beds in every room for your fur babies. The plethora of plant spawn to maintain your desired house vibe. The green rectangle stuff that you can use to obtain all the (possibly vegan) bacon and eggs the diner has...

STEP #3

WHAT DOES IT TAKE TO EARN SIX FIGURES IN MY NEW FREELANCE BUSINESS?

So let's do it. Let's talk about money.

You're more than likely in a full-time job. Your employer sets the parameters, goals, and details for your daily work. They determine if you are a salaried or an hourly employee and what kind of health insurance, bonuses, or paid time off you deserve. They dictate the hours you work and whether you have to work in the good ole office or can work from home or that new coffee shop downtown. You know the one, with the choco-chip croissants and inconsistent hazelnut mocha lattes (but when they're good, they taste like liquid Nutella manna-from-heaven!).

When you're salaried, each of these variables is set by your employer and largely out of your control. It sucks to think of it this way, but this kinda means someone else is deciding how to structure YOUR life. That's so NOT Raven.

As a freelance instructional designer, you can take back control of your (literally precious) time and earning potential. This book will provide you with a guide to do that. Well, that's what we're attempting to do, at least!

So, go grab the snack of your choice, maybe a lil drinky drink, and we'll begin our journey talking about the path to a six-figure income as a freelance ID. Yes, that's right - this journey has a destination of six figs. Who's gonna stop us?!

NERD ALERT! There will be some math ahead. Don't worry though, we got you. Well, not necessarily all of "we," but those of us on the team who are "math people." *cough...Parker... cough*

As a freelance ID, you'll often have an hourly rate that you'll charge clients. Did you know that your hourly rate can give you an INSTANT estimate of your annual income? Here's a great trick to use:

Take an hourly rate, double it, and add 3 zeros.
Let's break it down:

- Your hourly rate: $50/hr
- Double it: 50 x 2 = 100
- Add 3 zeros: $100,000

Voila! It's a very crude and quick way to estimate an annual income assuming 40 hrs/week and 52 weeks/year. The exact math is $50/hr x 40 hrs/week x 52 weeks/year. That's $104,000 per year. Slightly higher than the crude estimate... but close enough!

What if you charge $65/hr?

- $65 x 2 = $130
- Add 3 zeros: $130,000

Approximate Annual Income

$$\$37/hr = \underline{\hspace{4cm}}$$
$$\$48/hr = \underline{\hspace{4cm}}$$
$$\$62/hr = \underline{\hspace{4cm}}$$

Use this activity to quickly estimate the annual income for each hourly rate given. Remember to double the hourly rate and add three zeros. The annual income assumes 40 hrs/week for 52 weeks/year.

Now that we know the math to get to six figs, we can come up with a super actionable plan to achieve that goal. In the next step, we'll chat about estimating your income for the first year of sweet, sweet freelance life.

STEP #4

HOW DO I ESTIMATE MY INCOME FOR THE FIRST YEAR OF MY SWEET, SWEET FREELANCE LIFE?

So, we already did the math on how to get to a six-figure income. (Some of us here are trying not to have nightmares from all that arithmetic... *cough...Andrea...cough*).

Now, we can help you estimate your first year's freelancing income. So exciting! In this step, we'll look at the two main factors: your employment status and your desired hourly rate.

Employment Status: Some people decide to remain in their full-time or part-time job when they start freelancing. That's totally ok! This provides them with peace of mind as they start side-gigging and developing their freelance career. If you can manage this for a while, this can be a great thing. It's kind of like the song that one of our niece's Miley Cyrus dolls would sing (over…and over… and over:)

(You get) the best of both worlds!
Chill it out, take it slow!
Then you rock out the show!

You can be Miley Stewart by day doing your "day job" and then turn into the fabulous freelancing rockstar Hannah Montana at night (or whatever hours you end up 'lancing)!

Other people decide that they're DONEZO being tied to a company or cubicle and are ready to become their own boss ASA(F)P.! (Guess what the F stands for??)

Unlike Taoism, there is no One True Way. Mix and match, go back and forth, do whatever you need to do for yourself and your household.

There are pros and cons to each strategy, of course. Having a full or part-time job may provide a nice lil security blanket when it comes to knowing you've got a regular income coming in. But, being "tied down" may also limit you from taking on certain gigs due to time and other constraints. It can also be a recipe for major burnout. But, on the other hand, maybe your "day job" is kinda cushy and you have the time! If you want to make the "full leap" ASA(F)P we have some advice for you to make that transition as smooth as possible. All you have to do is… read the rest of this book (lolz).

Here are some questions to ask yourself if you are trying to decide if staying in your current role could be the right option for you:

1. Am I ready to just say YOLO and make the leap to freelancing?

2. Do I have enough emergency money to help pay my bills for 6 months in case I have trouble starting out on my own?

> 3.   Do I have the confidence, talent, and related experience to become an ID freelancer?

Chew on these for a while.

Hourly Rate: Your hourly rate will help determine your earning potential as a freelance ID. Remember, way back when, a few pages ago, when we did that math equation to figure out a possible yearly income?

Your natural next question is probably: "How many years do I need to work to finally afford my luxury yacht?"

No? Oh, right. Then we bet you're wondering: "How do I know what my hourly rate should be?"

Well, luckily for you we at IDLance have just the thing to help you with that! Please see below, dear friends.

Table 1: Suggested ID Freelancer Rates Based on Experience

	Experience	Rate (USD)
Starter Rate	0-1 year	$35-45/hr
Growth Rate	1-2 years	$45-60/hr
Experienced Rate	3+ years	$60-75/hr
Entrepreneur Rate	Varies	$75-140/hr (often built in fixed project rate rather than using hourly rate)

These guidelines are based on real life experience. Some may say they're too low or too high, but we're here to give you realistic and actionable info, here. Sure, you can start out charging $90/hour on day 1 of your freelance career but... well, good luck with that. Save us an invite for your yacht party!!!

Let's break down each of the levels to gain a clearer picture.

Starter Rate – $35-45/hr (0-1 yr of experience): When you're a new freelancer (even if you've got some ID chops from your salaried work), your number one focus should be grabbin' as many new clients as you can handle. One way to increase your chances of landing a gig at first is to use a lower hourly rate. If a client sees you can do great ID work AND you can offer them a competitive rate, you have a better chance of getting the gig.

If you're gonna charge a lower rate, be sure to let the client know you are capable of doing the work. You don't wanna come across as a bumbling fool saying, "Hey! I'm cheap! Hire me!" But instead, let them know you're offering a discount rate because it's such an "amazing opportunity to start working with you."

Growth Rate – $45-$60/hr (1-2 yrs experience): As you gain clients and experience, you'll keep building a portfolio of glorious real-life projects to showcase to other prospective clients. We will talk more about building a portfolio in Step #16.

NERD ALERT: Make sure you have permission to share your client's work in your portfolio. Get in the habit of ALWAYS asking and getting approval in writing (if the project went well, of course). There are some *non-shady* ways to get around them saying "no" - we'll cover that in the portfolio section, too.

Experienced Rate – $60-75/hr (3+ yrs experience): Over time, you can act like a Jefferson and move on up in your rate structure. The first three years are your opportunity to quickly get clients under your belt, build up a portfolio, and upgrade your resume and curriculum vitae (CV).

Entrepreneur Rate – $75-140/hr: When you get to this level, don't be surprised if we're coming to YOU for tips - heehee. But actually, in this category you'll often want to quote projects at fixed project rates rather than an hourly rate.

Back when IDLance was in its early days, one of our contacts from Andrea's solo freelancing days came to us with a client that seemed like it could be a good fit for baby IDLance. We shared our mission 'n' our skillz and landed the gig! It was a moderate contract at first, but then one of the people involved has since led us to some other amazing opportunities. As we pursued these leads, the web just kept growing and growing! Yes, sometimes it's about good luck - but we also made it a point to meet with as many people as possible. The more people you meet, the more opportunities you see! Infinite monkeys, infinite typewriters, and much more. Never say no to a conversation!

Need a nap yet? We may have taken 2-3 already in between writing spurts. It helps the brain!

As you saw, there's a lot that goes into estimating your income for the first year of freelance freedom. Will you continue with your current job on a full- or part-time basis? What will your hourly rate be as you start to build your freelance ID client base? These factors will help provide you a clearer picture as you move ahead in your journey.

Your Desired Annual Income	Your Estimated Hourly Rate
Example: $80,000	$40/hr

Use this activity to quickly estimate your hourly rate if you know your desired annual income. Write down your desired annual income in the left column. Remove the three zeros. Then divide by two to get an approximate hourly rate. This is, of course, assuming you work 40 hrs/week and 52 weeks/year. If you work less than that, then you would have to increase your hourly rate to reach your desired annual income.

Now that we have an idea of the income possibilities, it's time to look at everyone's favorite Destiny's Child Song: Bills! Bills! Bills!

Once you know your expenses, you can paint a clear picture of how much you need to earn as a freelance ID to keep afloat. Hey, the good news is that when you're working from home without a commute, at least your "auto-mo-bills" should be way less, right?

STEP #5

HOW DO I ESTIMATE MY INCOME FOR THE FIRST TRIMESTER (AKA 3 MONTHS LOL) OF FREELANCING?

So now you're asking yourself, "How much cash monies can I *really* make in my first few months as an ID freelancer?" Sorry, bud, but you're going to be annoyed by the answer: It depends. Don't cry, boo. It's the same for everybody.

Here are some factors that influence the first three months and beyond of your freelancing income.

FTE vs. Freelancing Income: When you're in a full-time role, you've got a set salary and/or guaranteed hourly rate. That rate is usually consistent until some kind of performance review from your manager (gross). This may be after 90 days, a year, or maybe you'll end up like Milton from Office Space - stuck watching the squirrels get married and guarding your office supplies until someone notices you're there.

Freelance income works differently (you probably guessed that). Lil old YOU are responsible for finding and securing gigs, all the time. Sometimes it'll seem like you are blissfully drowning in a sweet milk chocolate river of possibilities and potential clients (thank goodness for those Oompa Loompas!). Other times it'll feel like you're moving slower than the butt of a disappointed child stuck on a poorly designed playground slide in the middle of summer (we still remember the sound). Before we go too far down daydreaming of either scenario, let's keep our focus on the first three months.

The First Three Months: Slow and steady wins the race. One of our kids' favorite stories is the tortoise and the hare. Before you start groaning, HARE us out! So yeah, yadda yadda, the rabbit and the tortoise are going to have a race. The rabbit brags like a jerk and talks about how much faster he'll be than the tortoise. The tortoise keeps his focus and doesn't pay attention to the rabbit. Meanwhile, the rabbit stops for TWO vanilla iced lattes with restretto shots (how basic!) and lingers at a boutique for a new pair of Balenciagas. While rabbit trots back to the trail, the tortoise, in his classic and understated yet efficient Adidas Sambas, slowly and steadily wins the race.

That's the same story you remember, right?

The same analogy can work for your freelance career. (Bet you didn't see that coming!) You may need to take it slow and steady starting out, either out of necessity or just plain practicality. Gather those building blocks!

Before you make your freelance leap (aka quit your 9-5), it's ideal to have a gig or two or a handful lined up. This is the beauty of the seven-month plan. You can have a target date or time period set in your mind of when you would like to begin your freelancing career - and plenty of time to prepare! So much time you can sneak a trip or five hundred to Taco Bell along the way! It's a fact: cheezy gordita crunches help you plan better.

Yes, there's some legwork to prepare for that moment. But it's worth it. eLearning agencies and/or your soon-to-be former employer are two great resources to assist you in finding your initial gigs. We will talk more about eLearning agencies and getting gigs from your soon-to-be former employers in later steps. We know you're waiting with bated breath to read about it!

Unlike your first middle school dance, set yourself some reasonable expectations. When you're starting out, don't expect that you'll be getting a 40-hour/week contract from one client right away. That is pretty rare. But, you might get a 10-15 hr/week project from one client and something similar from another client, and maybe something else a few weeks later. When starting out, aim to fill at least 20 hrs/week with contract work. Don't worry, there's a lot you can do with the rest of your "normal" work-week time, both personally and professionally. We'll let you come up with your own ideas for personal stuff (please keep them to yourself, we barely know you!) and leave the professional ideas to us (in a later page!).

So, with that being said, let's see what your income could look like in the first three months as a freelance ID:

- Hourly Rate: $45
- Projected Weekly Income: $45/hr x 20 hrs/week = $900
- Projected Income 3 Month Income: $900/week x 13 weeks = $11,700

Growing Your Freelance Income: As we talked about earlier, being freelance is (thankfully!) unlike your FTE gig where you have to wait patiently or "play the game" for your boss or manager to give you a raise. When we were full-time employees, we kinda felt like one of those golden retrievers balancing a treat on their nose, drooling for the moment our owners say we can flip it into the air and MAYBE catch it. As a freelance ID, you hold the power in increasing your income. Here is how you can give yourself a 25% raise during months four through six.

While you're working in the first three months, keep pounding the virtual pavement to find more gigs. Try to increase your number of project hours from 20 to 25 hrs/week. The extra 5 hours a week may not seem like a lot, but it can go a long way to helping you realize your financial goals. Kind of like when you follow that advice to declutter your home 10 minutes a day. It all adds up! Take a look at the numbers:

- Hourly Rate: $45
- Projected Weekly Income: $45/hr x 25 hrs/week = $1,125
- Projected Income 3 Month Income: $1125/week x 13 weeks = $14,625

You just gave yourself a 25% increase in quarterly income! Way to go! HUZZAH! WOOP WOOP!

Repeat for your 3rd and 4th quarters. Maybe try for 30 hrs/week in Q3 and 35 hrs/week in Q4. If you pull it off, you'd get $17,550 in Q3 and $20,475 in Q4.

Let's see what your first year's income could be based on these projections:

Table 2: First year's income by quarter

Quarter 1	$11,700
Quarter 2	$14,625
Quarter 3	$17,550
Quarter 4	$20,475
Total Income:	$64,350

$64,350. That is a very nice start to the year, and you aren't even working 40 hrs/week yet! It can be tempting to pile on as many projects as possible, but you don't want to get overloaded with work JUST yet. Try and take on work similar to the technique we recommend using to fill your plate at a Golden Corral. A couple of chicken tendies, a small plop of mashed potatoes, a lil bit of mac n cheese - enough to survive, but with plenty of time and space in your belly to make sure it's safe to eat without needing to run to the bathroom every 5 minutes. We recommend not over-committing in the beginning while you're still figuring out how to navigate contract client relationships, juggle multiple projects and their priorities, and cultivate a livable meeting schedule. Plenty of time for "overloading" your plate later when you've got a subcontracting plan B in place.

Year 2 Income Growth: So, as you can imagine, you can boost your income for Year 2! Increase your hourly rate to something like $55/hr (growth rate). By year 2, let's say your average week is 30 hrs.

That's $55/hr x 30 hrs/week x 52 weeks/year = $85,800.

NOT. TOO. SHABBY!

Year 3 Income Growth: What happens in Year 3? Try $65/hr for 30 hrs/week. That's your six-figure income, baby. $65/hr x 30 hrs/week x 52 weeks/year = $101,400.

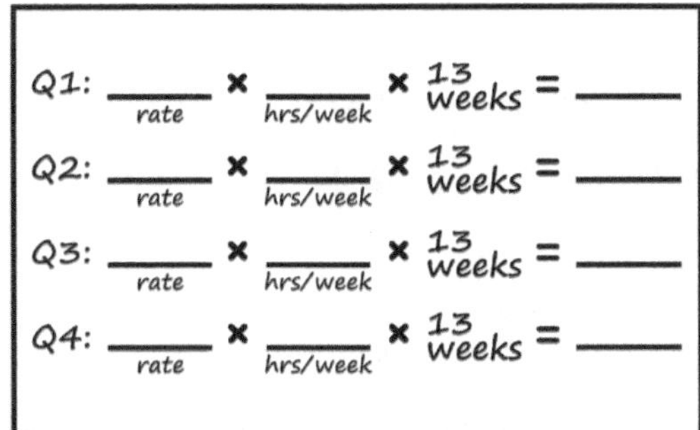

Write down your target income per quarter and then add the four quarters up to estimate your target income for the year. Think of this as a financial goal worksheet. No one can truly predict a freelance annual income, but having a target income is a great start!

From Year 1 to Year 2, you gave yourself a 33.3% raise (that's unheard of in a full-time job, right?). From Year 2 to Year 3, your raise was 18.2%. Let that sink in. YOU gave yourself that raise. Unless you're on some soul-sucking fast-track ladder to corporate executive salaries, bonuses, and stocks, you won't find those kinds of raises in any "normal" job. But you CAN in freelancing! All without ever having to play Boar on the Floor! (Succession, anyone?)

Year 2 & Year 3 Income Estimate

Now that you have estimated your first year's target income, estimate your Year 2 and Year 3 income. Increase your hourly rates and possibly your labor time (hours/week). This is totally up to you and your desired lifestyle. Remember, you have no limit on your income. You're the boss… so give yourself a raise.

STEP #6

HOW DO I ESTIMATE MY MONTHLY EXPENSES AND REDUCE THEM BY 30%?

We've looked at how much money you could potentially earn in your brand-new freelance ID gig. Now, it's time to chat about your monthly expenses. Hey, wait where are you going? Come back!

...you there?

Ok, great. It's time to, as infuriating infantile grown-up culture says, "start adulting." Which means, it's time to start thinking about the monthly expenses you have now and find ways to reduce them. Ideally, you'll want to cut them down by 30%! The first step is to get an overall snapshot of your current expenses and how much of your income they eat up. Your expenses are like lil Mr. and Mrs. Pacman and their hungry kids gulping down your funds, dollar by dollar. Once you know how much you're spending, if you're willing to put in some effort, you can start saving money post-haste!

Why does it matter? The less you NEED to spend, the more you can save, and the less pressure you have on yourself to work like a dog (no offense to dogs) just to break even.

First, visualize your income and expenses. It's easy to bury your head in the sand when it comes to spending money. But sshhh ssshhh, it's alright, little one. We'll try to make this as painless as removing a band-aid SHOULD be. (How is band-aid removal pain still a thing? We can put a man on the moon and plan a Mars civilization but can't figure this out?)

Ok ok, here are a few simple steps to help get you started.

1. **Log into your bank account:** Online banking makes this gloriously convenient. Once you're logged in, you'll be

able to see your month-to-month expenses and browse through your statements. Find your recurring payments and average monthly expenses.

2.   **Check your credit card(s) statement:** Some of us have only one credit card, others are like the Edward Scissorhands of cards (that makes sense, right?). This would be a good time to look at the statements and see how much you are spending on food (groceries and eating out), gasoline, entertainment, subscriptions, and any other expenses you have. If you pay any bills like internet and your phone through cards, note those, of course! Just because you're getting cash back or reward points doesn't cancel out the spending! (Booo!)

3.   **Income:** How much money do you have coming in every month? How much are you raking in at your current job? Do you have any other forms of income? If you have an OF, no judgment here. We chatted about projecting your income in the first three months of your life as a freelance ID. This projection is important to make sure you can cover your expenses, or, if you may have to cut more than 30%, or tap into savings for a while.

4.   **Create your visual:** You need to SEE for yourself how much money is coming in and out every month. Get out a pen and paper, open up Excel or Google Sheets or download one of the many apps. The point is you need a spot to track and see for yourself what your monthly budget looks like. You truly won't believe it until you see it. It's amazing how many late-night Amazon orders we forget about. We know, we know - you REALLLLLLY needed those llama keyboard key covers you saw on TikTok!

Take a peek at what you're spending now and estimate your monthly expenses. Be honest with yourself. Don't pretend like you can live without that iced Mayan mocha latte every day.

Knowing your total (average) outflow can only help you later as you figure out your goals.

Top 7 Monthly Expenses

1. Rent:	$1250.^{00} (E.g.)
2. Utilities:	
3. Eating Out:	
4. Phone:	
5. Netflix:	
6. Groceries:	
7. To Savings:	
Total:	

Write down your top seven monthly expenses. Examples include: mortgage/rent, electricity, auto, oil, credit cards, insurance, cable TV, student loan, groceries, etc. Then, review your list of expenses and challenge yourself to reduce this by 30%.

Know your number now? Ask yourself: how can I reduce this by 30%? That may seem like a lot, but here are ten ways for you to reduce your expenses in the next 30 days.

1. **What's on TV?** Do you have cable? How many different subscription services do you have? Cable and subscriptions services can add up quickly and without even us realizing it. Here is a look at how we cut our monthly "TV" budget by 52%. Do you really use ALLLL the subscriptions all the time? Come on, let's be real. You're only watching la creme de la creme: Discovery+. Another proven fact: watching "Seeking Sister Wives" while making storyboards makes you a better writer. Science says so.

Old Plan	Before	New Plan	After
Cable: America's Top 120+	$85	Sling Orange + Sports Extra	$46
Subscriptions: Disney+, Discovery+, Netflix, HBO Max	$39	Pick one: Disney+	$14
Monthly cost:	$124		$60

2.   **Learn to make that cup of coffee.** 54% of Americans over the age of 18 drink coffee everyday. A ⅓ of which consume specialty drinks like lattes and cappuccinos. Wanna know about how much money you can save by brewing your coffee at home vs. buying the specialty coffee from your local barista? Check this table out. For all you caffeine guzzlers out there… stay home with your office brewer! Yeah, they have iced coffee makers now, too! And milk frothers to get yourself that vanilla sweet cream cold foam you lie awake at night thinking about!

16 oz. Cups / Week	Weekly Savings	Monthly Savings	Annual Savings
2	$2.60	$11	$132
5	$6.50	$28	$336
7	$9.10	$39	$468
14	$18.20	$78	$936

3.   **Refinance your mortgage.** If you have one and the current interest rate is on your side, doing this could reduce your monthly bill by $100-200 a month. You've got nothing to lose by looking into it.

4.   **Insurance stuff.** Hire an independent agency to shop for the best rates. They can sign you up for a more cost-effective, auto and homeowner policy that meets your needs. Don't worry, the insurance companies pay the

agencies, not you, so it's a win-win for everyone! By going this route, you might be able to shave off $100-300 per year. Honestly, we recommend doing this every time your policy is up for renewal.

5. **Hire help.** There are companies out there that can negotiate things like your internet or cell phone bill for you. You only pay them a percentage of what you save if they can get you a lower price. Billshark is one of our favorites. Again, something to try at least once a year! Nothin' to lose here, either.

6. **Sell your new car for a new (pre-loved) car.** If your car is relatively new, get rid of it! You won't be commuting anymore, anyway! Purchase a decent used car that has less than 150,000 miles. This could cut hundreds off your bill per month! The nice, pre-loved vehicle still gets you from point A to point B – and you'll pay a lot less per month. As a freelancer, you'll probably be working from home a lot anyway. Check out Facebook Marketplace or local listings and buy your used car privately – stay away from pricey dealers and shady characters! If it seems too good to be true, it probably is. Or, you might even wanna check out something like Carvana - they vet the cars pretty well. Not only should you shop around for the best price for your new (used) car, get multiple quotes when selling your old (new) car!

7. **Use coupons.** They're not just for grandma anymore. Use sites like RetailMeNot, Rakuten, and Honey to find discounts at pretty much any store. Some of them have tools for your web browser that automatically search for discount codes and give you cash back as you're shopping online. Chances are your local grocery store has an app that makes couponing easy, too. Believe it or not, this can yield at least $50 per month and can be very addictive. If you make it on Extreme Couponing, please give us a call.

Love that show. If you're really dedicated, apps like Fetch Rewards can give you money back if you snap pictures of your receipts. It's probably witchcraft and we have no idea how it works, but it exists!

8. **Shop smart.** Do the math and figure out if there's a delivery service that actually helps you save money. For Amazon Prime people, you can get a discount on recurring orders of household essentials. Grocery delivery places like Imperfect Foods can help you save up to 30% because they deliver you "ugly" produce that's perfectly fresh and delicious. C'mon, who doesn't love carrots that look like grumpy old men (or even Parker at 5:00am)! We even found that if you're terrible and indecisive at grocery shopping like some of us (*ahem*… Andrea), meal services like HelloFresh actually can SAVE you money and food waste. Again, do the math for your specific lifestyle!

9. **Conserve energy.** Optimize your heating and cooling in your house or apartment. Use a programmable thermostat to do the work for you. Unplug unused electronics because even devices, when turned off, still consume electricity! Use natural light during the day instead of artificial lighting. Every kilowatt counts!

10. **Consolidate your debt.** Do you have a lot of credit card debt? Sometimes you may seem like you might be snowed under and never pay off your cards. Personal loans can help you consolidate your debt and offer you the opportunity to repay at a lower interest rate. Putting more money back into your pocket over the long term.

We know it's a challenge to estimate your monthly income from freelance gigs, so we're going to go a little easy on you here. You can't predict the future, but let us ask you this: do you have an idea of a target monthly income for the first 3 months yet?

Will you increase your target for months 4-6? Give it a shot. Be reasonable, but optimistic. If you will it, Dude, it is no dream.

If you don't think you'll get enough from freelance gigs in the first few months of your journey, do you have other ways to earn money for the time being? Do you have savings? Can you tap into your retirement account (be aware of the fees!)? Sell a kidney on the black market?

Sell some stocks? Turn in the savings bonds you got from your Nana? Cash in the life insurance policy your parents had on you as a kid? Maybe rent out a room in your house for $500 per month?

You could even consider driving for Lyft, being a shopper with Shipt, or being a dog walker with Wag. Make ends meet, meet new people, pet some doggos and get out of the house.

So: are you comfortable with your financial outlook? If you are, keep going! Do it!

If you're not, hold off on making the leap – but continue with the rest of these steps while you keep your day job. Moonlighting is a beautiful thing. It absolutely can't hurt to start getting the "gig experience" and can even make you feel less stressed out about your traditional gig. It's almost calming knowing you are actively working towards better days ahead. Tuck away the extra dough to have on reserve when you make the big change.

You have your finances in order now (maybe?), and so it's time to keep movin' on down the line of preparation.

TAKE INVENTORY OF YOUR PREFERENCES AT WORK AND IN LIFE

What Do You Rock At? Now that you have decided to make the leap into freelance life, the world is your oyster. The instructional design industry offers a variety of different opportunities based on your skill set. Each role is aligned to and complements an individual's skills. In this step, we will have you evaluate your skills and interests and provide an overview of the types of roles that make up the instructional design industry.

Chances are (and 30 Helens agree), doing something you like also means doing something you're good at. Of course, it's possible to like doing things you're terrible at, but those things aren't the best choice for your new venture.

We love that show where people who like to bake but can't even mix buttercream frosting compete and make a lopsided Mt Rushmore out of cake as much as the next person. But unfortunately, in the real world, there's not usually a $10,000 prize to be had from being awful but loveable at your job.

Just sayin'.

STEP #7

HOW DO I FIGURE OUT WHAT I'M GOOD AT IN THE INSTRUCTIONAL DESIGN INDUSTRY?

Alright. Let's get down to the nitty-gritty.

What are you good at? Surely, you have strengths deep within you somewhere that you've developed over the years through school, work, or play. Let's break this down so we can help you identify a few areas that you're "more better" at than others. In each possible area of expertise in the table ask yourself the corresponding questions. You can use the back of an envelope, napkin, or someone's shirt (with their consent)!

Has what you found pointed to two, three, or eight possible areas of interest? If so, maybe this is a good starting point to think about what type of freelance role you're meant to play.

If not, just give it some time and a good think over the next few days.

Instructional Design Skill-Based Assessment. Let's get crunchy and turn inward. It's time to reflect and evaluate your skills... nunchuck skills, bow hunting skills, or those skills that will help you land your freelance instructional design gig. We've identified nine of the most prominent instructional design skills: writing, visualizing, communicating, listening, planning, problem-solving, researching, and educational technology. Take some time to self-evaluate your interest and aptitude based on the following three responses:

- Nope. Not interested. Next!
- This is interesting. I need to learn more!
- This sounds like me!

Once you're done, you'll have a nifty inventory of your skills and interests. This will be useful when we start to look at the buffet of instructional design gigs.

1. **Writing:** How does your writing measure up in the following areas?

	Nope. Not interested. Next!	This is interesting. I need to learn more!	This sounds like me!
Clarity and consciousness			
Active voice			
Attention to detail			
Believable conversations			
Humor			
Engaging stories			
Step-by-step procedures			
Analogies			

2. **Visualizing:** How well do you visualize data and ideas in
    the following areas?

	Nope. Not interested. Next!	This is interesting. I need to learn more!	This sounds like me!
Static graphs			
Photography			
Typography			
Layouts			
Infographics			
Color schemes			
Animations			
Motion Graphics			
Video production			

3. **Communicating:** At which kinds of communication do you excel?

	Nope. Not interested. Next!	This is interesting. I need to learn more!	This sounds like me!
Verbally			
Visually			
Physically (e.g. body language, facial expressions, hand gestures such as the eloquent middle finger)			
With technology			

4. **Listening:** What kinds of listening do you do well?

	Nope. Not interested. Next!	This is interesting. I need to learn more!	This sounds like me!
Noticing patterns			
Identifying the underlying simple components of complex concepts			
Identifying theories and ideas			
Spotting what works and what doesn't			

5. **Planning:** What strengths in project management do you have?

	Nope. Not interested. Next!	This is interesting. I need to learn more!	This sounds like me!
Estimating project timeline			
Estimating project scope			
Estimating and adhering to budget			
Stating goals and objectives			
Organizing resources to do the job			
Identifying contingencies			

6. **Assessing:** How well do you design measurements in the following areas?

	Nope. Not interested. Next!	This is interesting. I need to learn more!	This sounds like me!
Cognitive understanding			
Behavioral achievement			
Business performance			

7. **Problem-Solving:** Which of these problem-solving skills are you great at?

	Nope. Not interested. Next!	This is interesting. I need to learn more!	This sounds like me!
Asking the right questions to identify the real problem			
Pinpointing what measurements or behaviors have to increase			
Identifying what measurements or behaviors have to decrease			

8. **Researching:** Are you above average at any of these research skills?

	Nope. Not interested. Next!	This is interesting. I need to learn more!	This sounds like me!
Identifying the Who, What, Why, When, Where, How			
Finding and citing reputable sources			
Categorizing and chunking information			

9. **Educational Technologies:** How well do you work with the below technology?

	Nope. Not interested. Next!	This is interesting. I need to learn more!	This sounds like me!
Rapid authoring tools			
HTML5 and CSS			
Graphic editing tools			
Video editing tools			
JavaScript			
Learning Management Systems			

> **Your TOP THREE Skills:**
> 1. ____
> 2. ____
> 3. ____

> **Skills You WANT to Develop:**
> 1. ____
> 2. ____
> 3. ____

> **Skills You DON'T WANT to Develop:**
> 1. ____
> 2. ____
> 3. ____

With the inventory of skills you identified in the previous tables, choose the top three skills you already possess. Pick three skills you want to further develop. Then, identify the three skills you do NOT want to develop. Your inputs here will help increase your focus on a path to success in your freelance career.

Types of Roles: Now that you know what you're good at, it's time to think about what you're interested in. We're not just talking about passive interest here. We're not asking, "What's been your favorite Netflix show about chefs?" We're asking, "What are you interested in RIGHT NOW that you can see yourself doing well enough to make a living?"

There are many roles in the L&D industry. Below, we've focused on 8 of the common ones. For each role, we've given you a short summary and the skills associated with each position. Check out LinkedIn or other job-board sites for job postings and summaries related to each field.

Instructional/Learning Designer: Instructional designers are experts in learning theory and are responsible for designing and developing courses and curriculum.

- Writing
- Visualizing
- Listening
- Communicating
- Problem-solving
- Researching
- Working with ed tech
- eLearning developer
- Visualizing
- Communicating
- Problem-solving
- Working with ed tech

UI/UX Designer (mainly for custom eLearning solutions): A User Interface (UI) or User Experience (UX) designer is responsible for creating learning experiences that are usable, enjoyable, and accessible to help to meet user's needs.

- Visualizing
- Communicating
- Problem-solving
- Working with ed tech

LMS Administrator: A Learning Management System (LMS) administrator is responsible for maintaining a client portal or LMS. They are responsible for managing the content to support various business goals.

- Planning
- Assessing
- Working with ed tech

Accessibility Expert: An accessibility expert is responsible for making sure that websites and other content are accessible, or usable, by as many people as possible. Accessibility can cover individuals with disabilities to users using mobile devices or slow internet connections.

- Listening
- Problem-solving
- Working with ed tech

HTML5 Developer: An HTML5 developer uses HTML code and debug websites and is responsible for troubleshooting errors and conducting performance and usability tests.

- Visualizing
- Communicating
- Problem-solving
- Working with ed tech

Project Manager: A project manager is responsible for planning, organizing, and directing a project. They are responsible for making sure deliverables are on time, within budget, and within scope.

- Communicating
- Listening
- Planning
- Problem-solving

Copy Editor: Copy editors review text for errors in grammar, punctuation, spelling, and may also look to see if brand guidelines are being followed.

- Writing
- Communicating
- Researching

Assessment Writer. An assessment writer is responsible for writing formative and summative assessments based on content and learning objectives.

- Writing
- Communicating
- Researching
- Assessing

Congratulations! This was a big step with a lot of information. It was important though because it was all about YOU! We encourage you to continue to revisit the self-evaluation skill summary and role description as you move closer to launching your freelance career. Good work!

STEP #8

HOW DO I IDENTIFY WHAT I REALLY LOVE TO DO IN LIFE?

What is love? Baby don't hurt me. Baby don't hurt me… wait, Night at the Roxbury came out in 1998? Sorry, we had a moment and now that song will be stuck in our collective heads the rest of the day (week/year). You're welcome.

What do you love? What is your passion? How is what you love and what you are passionate about connected to your work? Those are a lot of questions, but how often have you thought about connecting your love and your work? We checked in with a few IDLancers who have connected their passions to their work.

- Craig is a lacrosse coach and fan of the game. Although his skill for the game has never matched his love for the game, that has never stopped him from sharing his passion. In addition to his freelance ID life, he works as a freelance writer covering Men's Division 1 Lacrosse. The lacrosse side gig has helped him hone his ID writing skills. Win-win-win!

- Jessica loves to travel with her husband Brian. She has been to all seven continents and collects Starbucks cups wherever they travel. (She is still waiting for that first Starbucks to open in Antarctica.) Jessica's travels provide her with a broader and diverse perspective of people and cultures around the world. She enjoys working on projects that call upon her to take a more global approach to learning design. She's da "cultured" ID living the digital nomad dream.
- Rebecca is a former high school physics and calculus teacher. Her analytical and process-oriented mind loves a good math or science problem. Rebecca is now a K-12 and Higher Ed freelance ID. Her specialty is making eLearning modules that showcase her love of STEM along with areas like social studies, the humanities, and language arts. The ultimate teacher transition!

Lots of us may like what we do, but what if we love it and are really into it? That is where the magic happens (in a way that doesn't make you feel overwhelmed and burnt out trying to monetize your passion). Think about those three freelance IDs above who are able to blend their passions with their work. Don't take it from us, take it from John Ruskin, a 19th century writer and philosopher.

"When love and skill work together expect a masterpiece."

Ole Rusky was talking to you! Yes, you, specifically!

What happens when you combine what you love to do with what you are good at? It's your niche (as long as you have a market for it) - and it's your masterpiece no matter what!

Ok so you just finished breaking down your skills in the last step. Now we want you to do something similar to reflect a bit more on what you may love.

What do I love to do in my free time?	What would I do if I won the Powerball?	Out of all the jobs I have held, I really loved doing these tasks:

Now that you know what you're good at (Step #7) and what you love, you can carve out your own lil niche. A niche is a specialized market. Think about Craig writing about lacrosse, Jessica using her travels and understanding of culture, or Rebecca building STEM-based eLearning courses. Each of them found their niche and that is where the masterpieces are designed, developed, and implemented time and again. Does this mean that Craig ONLY writes about lacrosse, or that Jessica ONLY takes on global culture-y projects, or that Rebecca REFUSES any project that isn't about STEM? No, of course not! Finding a niche just means knowing what you LIKE to focus on and leading with that focus.

STEP #9

IS THERE A WAY I CAN FIND A NICHE IN MY FREELANCE CAREER?

A niche doesn't have to be a subject area - it could be a skill! Your niche could be video editing, storytelling, creating scenarios, building games in Articulate Storyline, or many other things. Whatever it is that you like to do but that you're ALSO good at and feel confident offering those services.

Finding your niche enables you to become a specialist in your L&D field. Finding your niche starts with knowing *what you're really good at* (Step #7) with *what you really love to do* (Step #8). Once you have these two components, you're able to find *a sweet sweet and maybe even spicey slice of the L&D marketplace* to call your own.

You may have a background and passion in Aviation Engineering or advocating for LGBTQ+ populations, or maybe you just REALLY love making learning videos. As you take on more L&D projects in a specific field over time it can provide you with a competitive advantage over other freelance contractors.

As a generalist, you may be able to research, design, and develop a learning experience for the client. It may even be pretty good. If you are a specialist in the area, you may be able to dig deeper into the learning and make connections for the learner that may not have been clear on the surface.

In this step, we will break down the process of pulling a Dumbledore and finding the wondrous magic of your own L&D niche. (Author's note: Parker was a magician in his teen years. His favorite trick was making food disappear! He had to figure out how to make magic happen with his future business... now that was more challenging!)

The road to becoming a specialist. You've identified your skills (Step #7) and what you love and/or are passionate about (Step #8). Now, it is time to find the magic, or your niche. Let's start with a visual of what we are talking about and then break it down.

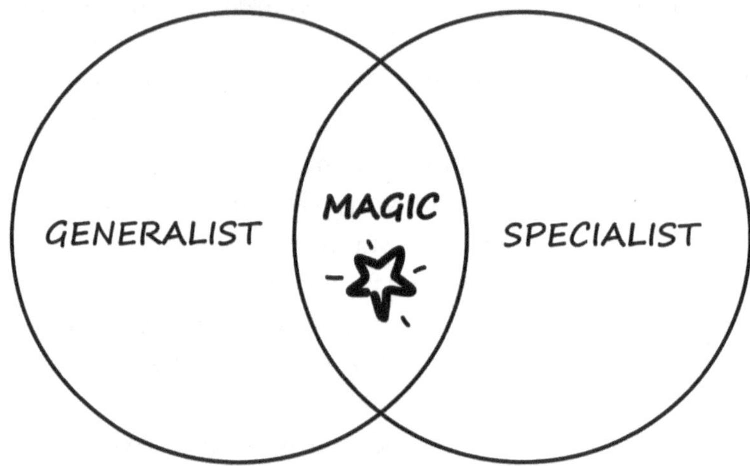

Magic is at the intersection of being a Generalist and a Specialist. Start learning as a Generalist. Then try a few paths as a Specialist. In this journey, you'll discover your magic. This is where you can make your freelance career take off (without the fairy dust).

Water water, everywhere… aka so many positions, which one is right for you? You identified your skills and the corresponding roles that you might be interested in Step #7. You are on your way, bb! You know the roles you are ready for. Your resume is clean (umm, well it will be soon) and the portfolio (wait, don't worry we will get to that, too) is ready to be shared with potential clients. A quick LinkedIn job posting search for roles here in the US will show you the market is hot 'n' ready like a Little Caesar's extra most bestest pie for people with your skills and interests:

Job Role	LinkedIn Results
Instructional/Learning designer	5,619
UI/UX designer	13,113
LMS administrator	43,817
Project manager for learning projects	266,691

Did you say you wanted to be a Project Manager? It seems like they might be hiring. But before you start furiously applying, let's take a pause for a sec.

You may have the skills to qualify for one or many of the jobs listed, but are you ACTUALLY interested in ACTUALLY DOING the work? This matters. You don't want to create the same situation as you have in your salaried role over and over with each contract.

One of the reasons you may be jumping into freelance life is you are tired or bored or feel like a 9-5 prisoner at your current job. Sure, you're probably a "company rock star" and know the ins and outs of the position. (Fun fact: people considering freelancing are often over-achievers!). But maybe you're just going through the motions lately. The work doesn't put a spring in your step, and you hate being stuck in one place for most of your life. At the end of the day, week, or month, you're left wanting more.

This is why we didn't stop at Step #7. It's "easy" to identify the skills and roles you may qualify for. The freelance challenge is to go out and match those skills and roles to what you are passionate about. The reason for this isn't what you think. It's not so that "every day you work is a pleasure" or that whole "If you do what you love, you'll never work a day in your life" crap. It's because as a freelancer, your career is UP TO YOU. If you're not motivated to keep doing what you're doing, or full of excited energy to keep pounding the virtual pavement to find gigs and grow your client base, you're not going to be a freelancer for very long. Them's the breaks.

Disclaimer: We know not every contract you land is going to be the epitome of what you'd like to be known for in your life's work (unfortunately the economy isn't doing well enough to support you recreating 80s workplace training videos with opossums full-time…yet). But knowing what IS your epitome can provide enough excitement to keep you focused, fueled, and ready to keep growing your biz.

Go for it. You can find your niche at the corner of Happy and Healthy… jk… it's really at the corner of *what you really love to do* with *what you're really good at.* This is prime real estate to find clients that need your services, with projects that excite you either because of the subject matter or the method of instruction! You'll be getting paid to do something that you love (at least some of the time), and, hey, that's nothing to thumb your nose at. Being able to do what you "love" even part of the time is not something to be undervalued… like Three Musketeers bars unfortunately often are.

STEP #10

HOW DO I DECIDE IF I SHOULD FREELANCE AND QUIT MY 9-TO-5?

Should I stay or should I go? Not only was this an overplayed hit song from the early 1980's by the Clash but could very much sum up where you may be in your decision to jump into that freelance life. Maybe you feel somewhat committed to making the leap. A bit lukewarm like eating a room temperature paella. It seems kinda good but also like it could just as likely be a pretty bad idea that could mess you up for days. Maybe you're still wiggling and hopping back and forth in indecision like Justin Timberlake trying to dance in khakis in 2022. Or maybe you can't wait to get the f*** out that way-too-heavy office door and leave behind the smell of stale non-dairy creamer in the mini fridge.

Wherever you may be on the commitment scale, we're here to help you kick it up a notch (ya know, only if you want to).

Getting to the promised land will take some hard work, street smarts, a steady dose of resolve, and many, many submarine sandwiches. Luckily, this lesson can help you with that last one. Um, we mean, the second to last one.

Note: We know we said we don't like the whole "I'm an expert" thing, but we do happen to be experts on submarine sandwiches. So if you need a list of recs for your tri-state area, hit us up.

Anyway, believe it or not, there are some techniques you can use to maintain the determination and focus you'll need to make the leap into full-time freelancedom.

Just know this: the more committed you are, the smoother your transition will be. Sort of like learning to do any one of those X-Games sports. Have you ever seen someone half-ass dropping into a half-pipe? It ain't pretty. Onward and forward!

Quit playin' (mini) games and start setting mini goals. We know that your goal is shedding your "normal" 9-5 and going freelance. That's a big goal! It's a doable one…but big. It's easy to be overwhelmed by such a goal, tbh. To save your brain from exploding, we recommend breaking down your Moby-Dick-sized goal into smaller, more manageable, goldfish sized pieces.

Make sure that your mini-goals are specific! Specific goals will tell you what you need to do to consider it complete. They are kinda like learning objectives, right? (You know all about those!). Unspecific goals can be very overwhelming and confusing. They're also more likely to discourage you or make you think "I can just do that later." Incorrect, young padawan. The time is now!

Let's say for example you set out a goal to "get your finances in order." A brilliant idea. Knowing how much money is going in and out of your back account every month. The problem is that this goal is vague and nonspecific.

To some, getting your finances in order would mean creating a budget and tracking your spending, while to others it could be making a pretty collage out of your credit cards.

"Getting your finances in order" needs to be specific and measurable. Let's rework this good idea into something specific. Something like, "create a Google Sheet that tracks my income & expenditures for the last six months to come up with an estimated monthly budget." This is a specific and measurable goal because you are:

- Looking at a specific time frame (6 months)
- Doing something with the information (creating a budget using a Google Sheet)
- To achieve a specific goal (estimate your average monthly income and expenses)

Write your goals on paper. Have you ever tried to do a small DIY project at home? Anyone who has taken up the task knows that any project, no matter how large or small it will involve at least three trips to the hardware store and at least one additional trip to their competitor when they are out of that thing-a-majig. And probably at least 14 minutes each trip spent looking at plant babies and/or holiday decorations.

One of the reasons it may take us multiple trips is that we make a list in our heads of everything we need to complete the project. Inevitably, we see a bright shiny object and forget the one or two important things on our list. If we had written it down, we could have checked or crossed off each item as we got it and saved ourselves a trip or two. The same logic applies to writing your goals on paper.

Writing your mini-goals down is an explicit, intentional action. The process helps you articulate exactly what you intend to do AND it plays a part in motivating you to complete the tasks to achieve it. Doing this also gives you the opportunity to strategize, ask questions about your current progress, and brainstorm your plan of attack.

There was a fancy study done that suggests you're almost 50% more likely to achieve a goal if you write it down. Talk about a life hack!

Share your goals. Humans are social creatures, and peer pressure and vanity are real. So use them to your advantage (for once)! No one wants to feel like a failure (or an @ss).

Here's the problem though. You might not want your current employer to find out about your grand plans at this point, right? So how do you share your big picture goal or mini-goals if you don't take this public on social media (or behind the podium at the White House Rose Garden)?

We have the solution.

Call us old-fashioned but talking (offline) with your most trusted friends and/or family can do the trick! You might want to skip that one weird uncle who's golf buddies with the CFO of your company, tho. However, the rest of your peeps probably won't tattle to your boss. Heck, they probably don't even know your boss' name!

Even if you talk with only one other person about your goals, your commitment will be much stronger than if you keep it to yourself. So if you're nervous, just start with one person. When you're more comfortable, keep sharing the news with more trusted friends, siblings, cousins, shamans, ferrets, cashiers, and milkmen. You'd be surprised just how much one of the co-head honchos has shared with her local Publix's and Michaels' cashiers. They're so friendly, encouraging…and efficient!

After you share your goals, you will feel the need to be seen by those others as a "responsible" person. If you say that you will do something, there is a higher probability that you will really do it. Yay for shame and responsibility and commitment tactics and psychologically tricking ourselves!

Revisit your goals frequently. Have a space where you will keep your goals. Maybe it's in a journal you keep at the house. Or a collection of sticky notes you have on your bedroom mirror, or a dry erase board. Probably best to keep these things at home, the boss may get huffy seeing the grand plans to 86 your current job.

It isn't one of those things you just write down once, tell once, and then forget about it. No, you need to revisit your mini-goals enough times (like… um… daily) so that thinking about them becomes a habit. When you revisit each mini-goal, it's an opportunity to reflect on your own progress toward it. You can ask yourself about what actions you can take to get even closer to achieving your goal. You'd be surprised with how many new ideas or methods of tackling the goals you may come up with when you force yourself to think about them over and over again. You may feel stagnant for a few days (weeks) and then one day… BAM! You'll "Emeril Lagassi those goals" (yes, we're using a person as a verb) to make a delicious gumbo of accomplishment.

Revisiting your goals enables you to track your progress. An important note, this is not like in high school where you got one shot to solve for X in Calculus using a tangent of matrix. (Hey! We promised no more math talk!). Success and progress may not be linear, in fact it will probably be like Andrea's college physics grade… messy! That's what happens when you have no problem explaining the theory of relativity but every problem in the universe involves plugging actual numbers into $E = mc^2$ and doing any actual arithmetic. Go figure!

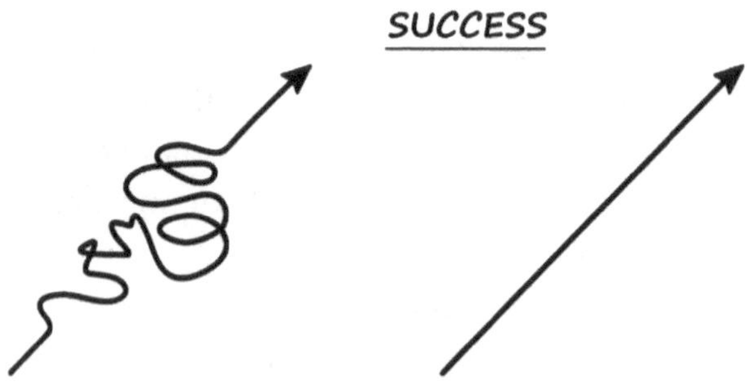

Success is not a straight line like many people think. Success is a messy path that goes up, down, left, right, and every-which-where. But that messy path DOES go up. So, don't give up. It's all about deliberate practice, persistence, and consistency.

If you're not making much progress, then think of some specific actions to take so that you CAN get closer to the goal. Every little, tiny bit helps. Did you know that jogging just 5 minutes a day gives major health benefits? Similar concept.

- What can you do TODAY that will get you even just a centimeter closer? Chances are, there's something. You can even multitask. Take a walk and make a call, google stuff while on the throne, connect with people on LinkedIn while gawking at that season of The Bachelorette with TWO Bachelorettes.

- Don't be afraid to bounce ideas off a bestie or (trusted) colleague, if you want to. You could even write an idea on a piece of paper, tape it to one of those oversized swirly balls that are always at Wal-Mart, and literally bounce it off the family member of your choice!

- Ask for some professional help if you can. Sometimes we can be in a mental "rut," and we just need human interaction and assurance that you're not crazy from an "authority" to get over it.

It's incredibly hard to do this alone – we get it! We've been there. Anytime someone offers to help... take it! And do not feel guilty. There will be a time when you can return the favor, no doubt. Because you are going to succeed, and you are amazing! You're good enough, smart enough, and gosh darnit...people like you! Ok, ok, take it easy making out with that mirror, weirdo.

On the flipside, if your mini-goals are being reached pretty quickly, that's DEFINITELY okay! But, don't rush it if it means you're not absorbing what you're doing and just half-heartedly checking off the box. A spreadsheet of expenses with tons of math errors and wildly guesstimated amounts is not going to help you. But, if you're moving right along and demolishing your goals left and right in an acceptable fashion we'd like to say...

Just keep on keepin' on!

Another one bites the dust!

A rolling stone gathers no moss!

Etc.

Etc.

And...good work!

Use even more ways (to the max) to achieve your mini goals. When it comes to fostering your commitment to the cause, it's not just all in your head. Taking physical action can help grow your attachment and help you keep your promise to yourself. Toiling towards your goal will be embedded in your daily life and before you know it, you'll be there chillin' on freelance beach with the rest of us. Don't worry, it's not a nude beach. Our greatest fear was being on Naked and Afraid, remember? *shivers*

Set routines. We know, how boring. Routines aren't just for toddlers. Routines are HARD for a lot of people, yet some people thrive on them. Try to think of your routine as a way you can stay centered and grounded in your daily life. Variety is great, but routines can provide the control and structure you need to achieve your goals in this crazy world!

Even though sticking to routines can be a bit lackluster, they can help you make the transition to the freelance world. Just make sure they're positive routines. You know, the kinds of routines that get you closer to your great escape from the corporate world! An example of a routine could be:

Every morning, we wake up and we choose one thing from our to-do list that we will accomplish by lunchtime and another that we will accomplish (or start) before dinner. Really, it can be that simple.

Successful freelancers didn't get to where they are by winging it. There's a time and a place to do your YOLO thing, but this isn't it. Forming good habits, being disciplined, and following routines are usually actions that most successful freelies have in common. This takes time, but it's well worth it. But don't freak out! You're not re-creating a 9-5 prison. Your routine doesn't have to be all-or-nothing, and it doesn't have to stay the same forever. The best part of your routine is that YOU create it!

Things like this are what set you apart from the rest. Did you know Jerry Seinfeld sits down to write every single day? Yes, even at his most famous. And look how he turned out (pretty sure he has a yacht and a few nice cars... and unlimited free coffee). We mean, sure, he's still neurotic but he sorta kinda seems happy most of the time?

Only you can figure out what routines work for you. Are you a rooster? Or nighthawk? Figure out the best times to work on your transition plan (composed of all those mini-goals you set up). Know the best times you can get some rest, too. And don't forget to take breaks! All work and no play makes Jack a dull boy, amiright?

Whatever works for you, just be consistent and persistent! Get an app that gives you lil rewards or badges for following through - if that works for you (Have you heard of Habitica?).

In the end, you'll get better results. Some days it might start out feeling as torturous as a hangnail, but just push through and you'll surely find your flow. Also, don't forget to moisturize else you'll be living that age-old warning.

It gets the lotion on its skin...

Er... nevermind.

Get an accountability partner. This period is going to be one of the most exciting – and scary – times you'll face in your life. When you're standing at the edge of the chasm between your old salaried life and your freelance life, pondering how to cross it, you'll need some help and old-fashioned inspiration.

Find yourself a buddy who will hold you responsible for your progress.

Getting someone officially on your side, a partner who BE-LIEVES in you, can help you stay on track. This is a time where it's okay to give into your competitive spirit or social guilt from not living up to a promise. This is your future we're talking about! Having someone or something to answer to is a powerful motivator, and the best accountability partners are also trying to achieve their own goal.

Maybe it's a friend who has already made the leap and is working to expand their own business. You could check in on each other every week to see where you're at in terms of meeting your mini-goals. Or maybe it's someone who will be your business partner and is striving to make the same leap as you! Twinsies!

Whoever it may be, stay in touch as often as possible. Talking once a month ain't gonna cut it in terms of keeping each other in line. You need someone to check in at least 1 or 2 times a week – throughout the WHOLE journey. Someone who is committed to helping you as much as you're committed to helping them. Get your text on.

Make it a habit to keep each other's noses to the grindstone. You and your accountability partner will inevitably encourage each other to step outside of the box and try new techniques to meet your goals. Beautiful progress!

There will be challenges, but you'll be in it together. Over time, you'll develop a stronger work ethic because you've used all of the above techniques to keep your commitment game strong.

Way to go, freelie!

6 MONTHS BEFORE YOU DITCH YOUR CUBICLE

EXPAND YOUR SKILLSET

We like cookies. In fact, one of us staged a protest when her high school cafeteria started making their cookies smaller. For years, the cookies were able to sit securely on top of a styrofoam cup without falling into the Mountain Dew and then one, sad day they started getting smaller and smaller and then PLOP. Cookies soaked with Mountain Dew. Gross.

What kind do we bake? Well, chocolate chips with extra chocolate chips and a scoop or three of peanut butter. Do you know the hack to keep them soft? (Besides eating them all in one sitting). Well if you have a few left, throw a piece of white bread in the cookie jar. The white bread will soak up the moisture, keeping your cookies soft. Now if you'll excuse us, we have cookies and a glass of milk waiting for us.

Delicious! You may be asking what cookies have to do with ID hacks and, more importantly, where is my cookie? Life hacks are fun. They provide us with little efficiencies to help make our days run smoother and keep our cookies soft. We have come up with a list of nice hacks that will bring some welcome efficiencies to your freelance ID life. With all the time and sanity they'll save you, these hacks will enable you to buy or bake your own cookies!

STEP #11

WHAT ARE THE ESSENTIAL ID HACKS
I NEED TO KNOW?

Solid understanding of learning models. We said we wouldn't talk about "how to be a good ID" but bear with us for a lil bit. We're cutting to the chase of what pages and pages of instructional design theory boils down to when it comes to what you ACTUALLY need to do on freelance ID projects.

So, what makes for a good learning experience? How do adults learn? How is designing for in-person training different from developing virtual training? Depending on your background these questions may have never crossed your mind.

These are the sorts of questions that instructional designers have to ask on a daily basis when they are researching and creating a learning experience. Having a solid learning model foundation is key to helping answer these questions. There are a number of models that instructional designers follow or subscribe to. We would like to dig into one that has been beneficial for us, the Experiential Learning Cycle.

Developed by David Kolb, the experiential learning cycle is based on the belief that learning is the process through which knowledge is created through the transformation of experience. Here are a few key takeaways to get you started:

- As we learn new ideas, we modify and get rid of old ideas.
- Learning is a life-long process, with no finish line.
- When learners and the environment interact, both are changed. We need to recreate it to respond to our needs and help shape our understanding.
- Learning isn't uniform. Each field has its own set of skills and processes to follow.

Still have questions? Good. That is another great ID hack. We encourage you to look closer at and research the Experiential Learning Cycle as you dig closer to making the leap. Just understanding the cycle is a hack in itself that bypasses all the other models out there in the industry.

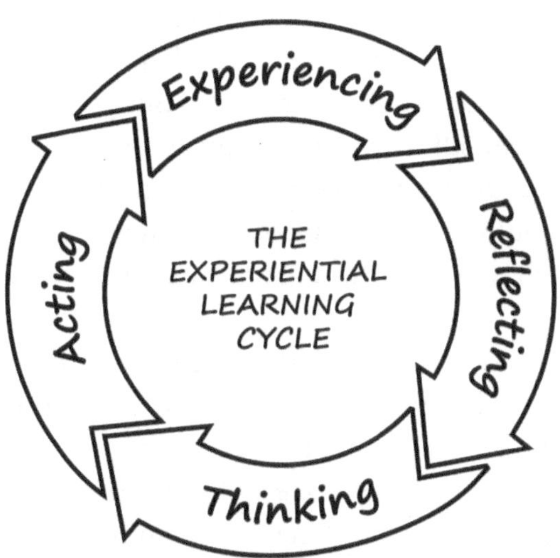

The Experiential Learning Cycle is a learning process that begins with an experience, which is followed by reflecting on that experience. Then, abstract thinking helps you to form new concepts and meaning as a result of the experience. In turn, this leads to your decision to engage in deliberate practice and try out what you've learned.

Cultivate Communication. This seems obvious, but good communication is an essential ID hack. And it's not as simple as you think. Good communication takes adaptation and, as Timothy Olyphant aka Nick in "A Perfect Getaway" would advocate for: situational awareness.

Communication presents itself in many different forms as an ID. You will be collaborating with fellow ID, GDs, PMs, and all other sorts of acronyms. Your viewpoints may not always align. How and when you communicate your thoughts and ideas will shape how far you can go.

When you're actively on a project, a great way is to stay in touch with the client at least once a week via a live meeting or recap email to give them updates. Pay attention to how the client likes to communicate. Everything in email? Text message? Face to face? Collaborative documents? Instant message? Casual? Likes an agenda? Find out what makes them feel comfortable and supported and...well, support them.

Communication will also be vital when looking for new gigs. After a project is done, check in with your client every so often to say hello. LinkedIn is a great way to connect and showcase your latest and greatest projects. If you connect and remember something about their life or likes, ask how it's going or let them know about that new show starting with Vincent D'Onofrio as the villain.

These are just a couple of the main ways communication is important for an ID freelie. We could go on and on about it, but we have to finish the rest of THIS book.

Writing skills. Let's be honest. We need and love our copy editing and QA people. They help us reign in our ideas when we see a squirrel eating a meat pie in a tree (RIP) or some other distraction while writing. They're also important in helping to make sure that our content aligns to the brand standards set forth by our client.

We've used these opportunities not to think about what we may have done right or wrong; instead, we view them as learning opportunities. For example, what terms are bolded or not bolded when writing a job aid? It may not be so obvious. How do you write in a "down-to-earth-yet-professional-way" specific to a certain company? It takes practice! And, turns out, we learned that when it comes to writing, we could always use some more "learning."

There are some neat tools that can help you write better. Grammarly is a cloud-based program that assists with spelling grammar, punctuation, and clarity. It's great at finding words or phrases that spell check may have missed. Once we have all the commas and em dashes in place, we sometimes put everything into Hemingway. Hemingway assists you in making sure your writing is bold and clear. They provide a reading level and measure the complexity of your sentences. For instance, this paragraph is at an 8th Grade reading level! Yay middle school, the universal language!

So whether your QA person is real, live human, an artificial flesh-colored cyborg, or you use a cloud-based service, these practices will help to ensure that your writing is in tip-top shape. And remember that just like when you started trying to shred "Through the Fire and Flames" on Guitar Hero, practice makes perfect!

Learning technologies. As an instructional designer, you'll be asked to research and design learning solutions for your client (hopefully this is not a surprise??). Knowing how to bring those learning solutions to life (and not just boring spoken or on-screen text) is a hack that can separate you from the competition.

The top two learning technologies out there are Articulate Storyline and Rise. While the license fee may be steep, knowing how to build and design in these environments is crucial. When you're writing storyboards or visualizing content, you'll know what's possible in the platform and how to use all the features. A lot of the time clients will have these two tools in mind when looking for freelies.

Having your own license may also help you find more gigs! Some gigs may not need you to research and build a storyboard. Some projects just need developers who can build in Storyline or Rise. Know what we did when we started out? We used one of those no-interest credit cards to purchase the license and paid it off over time as we got more gigs. WHAT'S IN YOUR WALLET?!

You'll also be able to transfer the educational technology skills to other learning development software that may come up from clients.

Time management. So much time, so little to do. Wait a minute. Strike that. Reverse it! At least that's what that hottie Willy Wonka said. (Oh, you don't think he's a hottie? He's just a child-endangering monster? We are not the same.).

Time management is an essential skill when you are living your best freelance life. Whether you use a paper calendar or planner or the latest and greatest app, you'll need a way to keep yourself organized. Especially when you're juggling three projects, two kids, a dog, and those plants you got that always seem either too dry or too thirsty.

When are you most creative or productive? In a traditional 9-5 job, the thought may have never crossed your mind - because you didn't have a choice! When you're a freelance ID you'll have more freedom to set not only where you want to work, but WHEN you want to do your "actual work." Use your most "alert" time of day to do your ID, writing, storyboarding, development - whatever you have going on at the time. The other times of day to do your (insert "life" stuff) and whatever else. This whole process is finding out what works best for you! Take advantage of it!

Here's a typical schedule for one of our Head Honchos:

- **7am-8am:** Get the kids ready for school and drop them off. (But let's be real - one kid wakes up between 5:30am-6am EVERY DAY but they've been trained to watch their iPad and eat pretzel chips until 7am.)
- **8am-10am:** Take the needy dog for a walk and do some development work if there is any. For some reason "building" right in the morning (or late at night) is when we're best at it. If there's no dev work, we do chores.
- **10am-1pm:** Time for meetings! We try, if possible, to keep them in a block for productivity and sanity's sake.
- **1pm-3pm:** Working lunch.
- **3pm-5pm:** Do some more focused work, impromptu meetings, and swim in the pool for exercise while watching Welcome to Plathville or a murder documentary.

- **5pm:** Pick up kids or take fur kid for walk.
- **5:30pm-8pm:** Dinner, "family time" (aka watching tv while eating dinner), bath & bedtime for kids.
- **8pm-11pm:** Could be any mix of hanging out with spouse, doing work while hanging out with spouse, doing work alone, watching tv, doing some sort of art project solo, showering, taking a bath, crying in the bathtub, or going to bed early.
- **11pm-2am:** When it's really busy work, yes, we do work until late at night just to get ahead on some things, so the days don't feel so stressed. Especially when it's a meeting-heavy week!

There is also an alternative schedule (on a day with less meetings) where we go to a coffee shop in the morning until about 1pm. Then, we come home and do house stuff until school pick-up. For some reason, working at a coffee shop gives us more bang for the buck in terms of work accomplished.

(There is also an alternate-alternate schedule from when our kids were under 2. Contact us for that one!! We labeled it the "Hold Onto Yer Butts" schedule. But honestly, it wasn't THAT bad. Let's chat!)

Visual design for non-designers. We all know what good design looks like, but does it look like C.R.A.P. (Contrast, Repetition, Alignment, and Proximity)? This framework (Williams, 2015) enables you to develop consistent, visually pleasing designs. Here's how:

- Contrast asks, how are you grabbing a user's attention and focusing their attention? This can be done in font style/size and color.
- Repetition provides consistency with the user, so they know what to expect. Like using icons and imagery that "goes together."
- Alignment organizes information for the user - for both images and text.
- Proximity looks to group text, images, and content that go together.

Gig searching. We'll get into other ways to find gigs later, but the biggest "hack" we can give ya is to become a LinkedIn content marketing type person. You can build a personal brand and share your content with the world about anything remotely work-related that you wanna talk about. Project management strategies? Tips for working parents? (Hint: Watercolor paints and ice keep them occupied for a long time!) Favorite Articulate Storyline tricks? The only key (and this is the hard part) is that, for this to work, you have to be CONSISTENT and PERSISTENT for at least 18 months. 3 or 4 times a week. Why? Clients will come to you, and you'll make connections to other IDs and freelies who may need help or know of some gigs that will fit you like a wax glove - but less painful. Fun fact: One time one of the Head Honchos was in Niagara Falls as a young child and did one of those Ripley's Believe It or Not "Make a wax mold of your hand!" things. Well, they didn't hold her hand in the ice long enough to numb the skin, but still dipped her delicate little 8-year-old hand in hot wax. Pain and sorrow and extreme red handedness ensued while a wax figure of Marilyn Monroe looked on with a threatening grin.

Anyway, content marketing is kinda fun and sure beats having to knock on doors all the time to find new gigs and meet new people.

Keep up with trends. Be on the lookout for new technologies and trends in the marketplace and brush up on skills to meet the demands. Example: When Rise first came out, not many clients were adopting it. Now, it's one of the most used tools for many organizations due to its simplicity and ease of use for making nice-looking things quickly. Another example: TikTok is increasing its hold in the microlearning market. Do you know how to make TikTok videos for educational purposes? More importantly, have you heard the corn kid song? Or are you familiar with 7taps or Arist for other types of microlearning? Get with it, dude! The best way to "keep up" is by staying engaged in those global ID communities and, of course, LinkedIn.

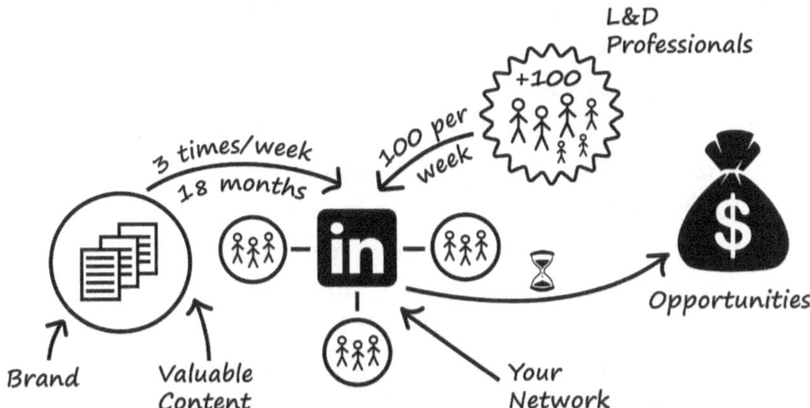

Here's one of the secrets to have clients find you. Post original and valuable content on LinkedIn 3-4 times each week for 18 months. Develop a visual brand around your content. Be consistent and persistent with your content in terms of both substance and visual design. Also invite 100 L&D professionals each week to your network. Watch what happens over time...you'll be amazed!

These are just a few of the hacks that can help separate you from your freelance ID competition. Don't worry, you don't have to master them all now (wooooosahhh). Through practice and repetition these hacks will become part of your process.

STEP #12

HOW DO I LEARN TO USE THE AUTHORING TOOLS AT NO COST?

We love movies. Especially funny ones. One of our favorites is Young Frankenstein starring hottie Gene Wilder (again, if you disagree, it just means you haven't fully matured yet. It'll come.). Besides having a number of funny one-liners, it has a famous scene where the monster first comes "alive." Dr. Frankenstein (pronounced Frank-en-Steen) is so proud and excited as he shouts...

It's Aliiiiiiiiiiiiiiiiiiiiiiiiiiiiiiiiiiiiiiiive!

That same feeling is shared by all the IDs out there with authoring tool skills.

Authoring tools enable IDs to bring their research, learning theories, and storyboards to life. We talked about this a bit earlier, but let's act like our brains watching Reading Rainbow and expand. The purpose of this lesson is to help you find your inner Dr. Frankenstein aka the developer/creative side of ID.

Authoring tools are designed to help instructional designers create professional, engaging, and interactive eLearning content for custom training courses. Some IDs find their niche by doing this exclusively. One of the IDs we work with is a magician (not the creepy kind) when it comes to authoring tools. She is able to take our storyboards to create good-looking and engaging eLearning experiences that are easy to follow conceptually because of the way she visually organizes the information on screen.

Her tools of choice are Storyline and 7taps. As you probably know, Storyline is the industry standard when it comes to authoring tools in the L&D space. Through Storyline she is able to create almost any eLearning experience we can imagine. Do you want to sling shot Bob Ross' head onto a canvas to learn about what happens when certain colors mix? Storyline can do that. Do you want to use a Tetris-type game to discover how amino acids link together? That's also possible. Or do you want a simple drag and drop to add items to your cafeteria tray while you try and build a nutritionally sound meal? Yup! (Hint: Half the tray should NOT be deliciously soft chocolate chip cookies. We're sad, too.)

Now, onto 7taps. 7taps is one of the world's leading microlearning tools. Plus, as of the publishing of this book, you can get an account for free (at first)! Microlearning is a "newish" trend in the L&D industry. Microlearning chunks and breaks learning into very small, digestible pieces. 7taps is a portrait-style mobile phone experience where you can insert text, videos, short quizzes, and even generate AI talking heads to narrate your stuff. Some of them are freakily convincing!

So, what are the next steps? Well, go on out and explore, little explorer! There are plenty of YouTube videos, websites, and eLearning communities out there to support you on your journey. Just gotta gather up that courage to make that first move and try 'em.

One tip to quickly learn an authoring tool of your choice is to use two monitors. Use one monitor to view your authoring tool. Use the other monitor to show a tutorial of how to use the authoring tool. In the freelance world, time is of the essence. Learn quickly so you can land those gigs!

Here is a quick overview of some common authoring tools to help you start your new journey! Take advantage of their FREE TRIALS. You know what that means? You can start learning WITHOUT paying for the subscriptions (yet)! Happy exploring!

Articulate Rise 360. Rise 360 is a web-based application that allows you to build eLearning courses efficiently. Rise courses are all built on the web. One of the coolest features of the app is that the courses automatically adapt to the user's device. Rise is part of the Articulate 360 suite and requires a yearly subscription. They do offer a no obligation free trial to help get you started! The free trial is plenty of time to get acquainted and make some portfolio stuff.

Articulate Storyline 360. As we spoke about above, Storyline is the industry standard when it comes to authoring tools. Storyline is part of the Articulate 360 suite and requires a yearly subscription. Check out the free trial (same account used for Rise 360) to help you get started. Articulate has a great community, E-Learning Heroes, to assist you in your process.

Adobe Captivate. Captivate is pretty well-known in the authoring tool market. It offers templates to assist you in getting started. It requires a subscription to use and does offer a free trial for you to get started. Adobe offers users training and certification programs to help you in your journey, too.

Arist. Arist is on the leading edge of microlearning. Their learning solutions come with three main components: content, questions, and feedback. And they're all delivered one text message, instant message, or email at a time! They offer pricing based on an individual or team basis and provide users with an opportunity to demo the product before they begin. You can see it in action for free which will give you a great idea on how to design courses if the platform comes up in your projects.

7taps. As we said, 7taps is a web-based microlearning authoring tool. 7taps provides users with four user interaction pages: cards, quizzes, audio, and links to create courses. 7taps enables designers to deploy the learning to users and uses tracking to measure user performance. Get a free account and start exploring!

H5P. If you want to get super creative with your knowledge checks and interactions, but don't want to be tied down to an "authoring software," H5P is an amazing free playground for making interactive web activities. It can be a great sandbox to practice designing things like branching scenarios, quizzes, interactive videos, and drag and drops. Plus, if you end up designing for platforms that take HTML5 activities (like Canvas, Moodle, or Blackboard), you'll have a leg up!

STEP #13

HOW DO I HONE MY WRITING SKILLS (QUICKLY)?

Writing is hard. But, alas, our content must be engaging and understandable by our audience. What will keep the learners from falling asleep or tapping away to go into a TikTok hidey hole? How do you say things in a concise way while still keeping it lively? Along with keeping interest, you have to worry about spelling, grammar, and clarity! After all, which of these courses would you trust more: "How to Draw Blud From Patience in Four Eazy Steps" or "Introduction to Phlebotomy: How to Safely Draw Blood in a Hospital Setting."

Anyway, in this step, we will look at some strategies to hone your writing skills. The first one is simple, keep writing.

Find your passion project. Gotta write to get right…are we right? But about what? It's up to you. That's the best part. What are you passionate about? What do you want to rant about? Do you love food (like Parker does?), traveling, sports, or binge-watching your favorite HGTV or Bravo shows (Bring! Back! Southern! Charm! Savannah!)? The point is to find something you enjoy and commit to writing about it on a consistent basis.

Then, get some feedback! Share your thoughts on social media or via text or email to some pals. Sometimes it's scary but mostly, if you have the right pals, it's just fun.

Use active voice, not passive voice. With active voice, you put the subject first. Whereas with passive voice, you put the verb first.

- **Sentence 1:** IDLance creates the best L&D content in the industry. (Aw, shucks!)
- **Sentence 2:** The best L&D content in the industry is created by IDLance.

While both of these sentences are true and describe the same action, one packs a more of a punch. The first sentence is active voice. A sentence that utilizes active voice is direct, clear, and easy for readers to understand. Passive voice adds an unnecessary layer of complexity and usually extra weeny words. As an ID, every word matters so you need to be efficient with your message before BOOP a squirrel comes along to distract your learners.

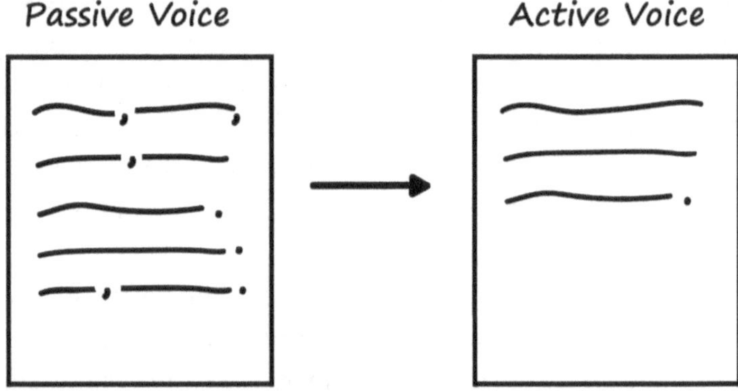

As a freelance ID, start writing as you normally would, which will likely be in passive voice. But then go back and rewrite it in active voice. Practice makes permanent as they say!

Check out Grammarly. Have you ever found that spell check in Word and/or Google Docs misses errors? Grammarly is here to help. Grammarly is a cloud-based program that gives you a shortcut to correct spelling, grammar, punctuation, and even clarity.

There's a free version that assists writers with spelling and grammar, but also will offer suggestions to make content clearer and more concise. For a monthly fee, users can upgrade to a Premium or Business version. These versions offer additional selections to enhance concision, engagement, and delivery. Grammarly is a great resource if you do not have a dedicated Content Editor to review your work before it goes to the client. It's like having a gentle, kind copy editing wizard living in your browser.

Simplify with Hemingway. One of the challenges of writing is to convey your message in a way your learners can understand easily. Hemingway assists you in making sure your writing is bold and clear. It's a must-have resource to improve your writing. It provides you with the readability level, estimated reading time, and word count of your piece.

It's also a great learning tool for writers seeking to find where they can improve. Hemingway uses AI to color-code and check your writing for adverbs and passive voice. It even offers suggestions for simpler phrases and points out if a sentence is "hard" or "very hard" to read. Hemingway is like having a writing coach waiting for you every minute you need it.

Writing can be challenging but words are pretty important to instructional design! If writing isn't your forte, or if you just want to keep improving, these tools can help. There, now you have no excuse but to be the best writer you can be!

Butterfly in the skyyyyyyy, I can go twice as highhhhhhh-hh...

STEP #14

HOW DO I DEVELOP VISUAL DESIGN SKILLS THAT WILL WOW CLIENTS?

When was the last time you were wowed? You stopped. Took a moment to recalibrate. For us, it's every time we come across the Halloween decorations second at a well-kempt Michael's craft store. Not the corny "Football, Friends, & Fall" autumn decor with leaves and pale orange pumpkins. We're talking the fortune teller-themed, spooky skull candles where the wick lights the brain on fire, the glowing crystals, and LeMax Spooky Halloween village displays. That sh*t rules. And when you're at a "good" store, the level of detail and display arrangements make you want to stop, look at, and buy E.V.E.R.Y.T.H.I.N.G.

This should be the goal of visual design. Engage the audience. Keep their attention long enough to get the message across and make them want to take action. Have a cohesive theme that's not too "busy." Make them wanna buy your dish.

"Good art inspires; good design motivates." Otl Alcher, a German graphic designer and typographer, said that.

"I'll let you be in my (visual design) dreams if I can be in yours." Bob Dylan said that.

"Give me liberty AND give me a Canva license." We said that.

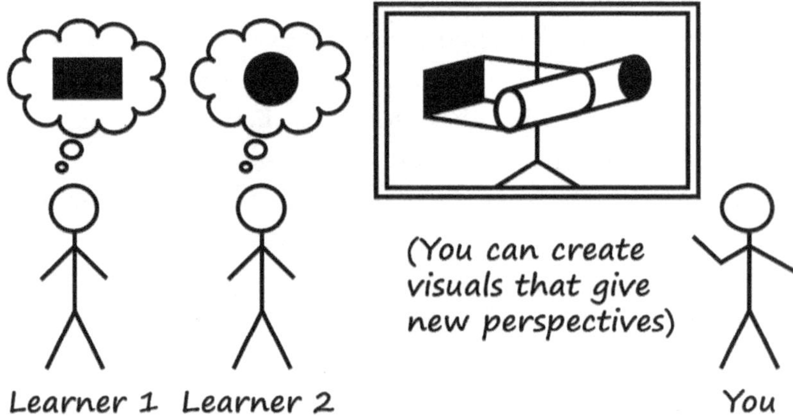

In addition to the C.R.A.P. model of visual design, consider visuals that help learners gain new perspectives. This is how you can impress your prospects and clients.

Visual design is important for learnin' materials because, ultimately, we need the learners to DO something with what they're observing. Whether it's a change in behavior or just awareness of concepts. Previously, we talked about WHAT good design looks like in Step #11 (C.R.A.P.). In this lesson, we want to look at three practical ways you can actually develop your visual design skills to wow your clients.

1. **Observe.** The first way to develop good design skills is to be observant. This holds true if you are at the farmer's market on Saturday morning with your family, upskilling on Coursera, or scrolling through Instagram or TikTok. You can find inspiration from each of these places to provide you a guide on what good design looks like. Which ads draw you in? What do all those graphic t's with skeletons on them that you like so much have in common in terms of composition?

2. **Practice.** Get an Instagram account. Start taking pictures. You'll start to see the world in frames. How can you use pictures to get a message across? Brainstorm a movie poster for your favorite film (We know it's *Die Hard* and that's okay even if you think it's a Christmas movie). As an ID, often you're taking storyboards from fellow IDs and bringing them to life in Adobe Premiere (video), Rise, and/ or Storyline. Or, you're writing the storyboards and THEN developing them yourself. In that process, great IDs are always looking for coherent, cohesive, and sometimes even fun ways to display and guide learners through information.

3. **Iterate.** One design doesn't fit all. Good design finds the sweet spot where the client, content, and end user come together. How do you achieve this? Get that feedback, bb! It may be difficult to hear you missed the mark or that revisions are necessary. Literally no one is perfect with design on the first try. Even the most experienced designers get feedback with every pass. Just google "10 Horrible First Logos of Major Brands."

Now that you have an understanding of the what, why, and how of good visual design the rest is up to you. Don't be afraid to ask friends and other freelies for their opinions. People love giving opinions, so you might as well take advantage of that!

STEP #15

DO I REALLY NEED TO GO TO AN INSTRUCTIONAL DESIGN BOOTCAMP OR ACADEMY TO BE A GOOD ID?

The instructional design bootcamp or academy seems to be the latest thing on LinkedIn. There are a number of L&D companies that are eLearning providers talking about providing these learning opportunities. These boot camps and academies can cost anywhere from a few hundred dollars to a few thousand dollars. That's a lot of plant babies. We had a friend of ours pick our brains about the topic (because honestly, we were too tired to write it all down ourselves after playing *Candy Land* while watching *Sing 2* for the trillionth time). Here is a summary and a few key takeaways from the conversation.

Bootcamps and academies help, but you don't "need" them.

Andrea: The whole "after three weeks in this boot camp you're gonna know everything" deal… whenever I've looked into these things, it still kind of feels a little fluffy. Yes, there may be "real projects" you do, but only so much can be simulated. There's a risk of overcomplicating or oversimplifying what you will REALLY be doing as an instructional designer.

Parker: I've been a hiring manager in the past. What I tend to look for are some hard skills, for sure, what we call "resume skills." And then there are some innate talents/intuitions that people have. Sometimes you really don't get to know those talents until you actually talk with them, or see them in action explaining a portfolio piece, or have them try out a small project.

We have people in our Slack community and some of them we have never worked with before. But it's a great opportunity to kind of see their writing style, how responsive they are, how they interact with others, what kind of questions they ask. And what is it like in the dialogue you have, you know, when you give feedback on things they share, what kind of response do you get in the feedback? Are they listening? Are they defensive? Those kinds of interactions override the importance of an academy, or boot camp, in my opinion. When someone is easy to work with and responsive, you can help them hone the "hard" skills they need through working on projects.

Andrea: *The boot camps and academies that are being promoted on LinkedIn that we are seeing on our feeds, it's much more of a top-down structure. Like, "I'm the expert. And I'm going to convey this information to you. This is the way to approach things based on my vast guru knowledge."*

What makes IDLance special and different from the boot camps and academies is that it's much more of a bottom up, where we're kind of like all in this together, we can rely on each other as a community of learning. We're learning by doing and making mistakes, the challenges are learning opportunities. It's a comfortable environment to ask questions and figure stuff out - everything from "Hey what do you think of this client situation?" to "How much do you save for taxes?" to "Can you give me feedback on my portfolio?"

Be curious.

Andrea: *I know not everybody has this sort of "I'm just gonna go for it" personality. But if you can into that mindset (with some humility, of course), you'd be surprised by what you can get involved in. I was able to weasel my way into an instructional technology specialist job at the Orange County library system in Orlando. Without ever having an instructional design job or a degree in the field!*

I just was self-taught and was curious. I had some great contacts along the way that answered my questions and provided me with readings and resources to help grow my knowledge. It paid off when I was hired for that job. I just kept reminding myself that whatever happened in the job, I'm sure I could figure it out and ask questions and, well, Google it (haha). What mattered is that I genuinely was excited by the work and could visualize myself doing it.

The job interview was intense, too. I had to take a very realistic case study and then fill out a worksheet on how I would apply the ADDIE model. I felt like, "Thank God I taught myself this stuff! Because I had no idea like six months before what that even was, lol." But when you know those basic terms and you can kind of talk the lingo and relate to people who are doing the job, that can get you "in." When it comes to freelancing, if you put yourself out there I feel like you can make those connections and get little gigs here and there which can lead to bigger ones.

Leverage your network & connections.

*Andrea: Having a network is critically important because I think it's a lot easier to get a first freelance gig from someone who has taken on too much work, or a freelancer whose business is growing, and they're like, oh sh*t! I need some help. That's the good way to go at first as opposed to going straight to an agency or trying to get a direct client. Once you have a few smaller gigs under your belt, you can go for the agencies, and talk about your experience freelancing in addition to any other salaried or other work you've done in the past that is even somewhat related. I used my Media Studies MA to my advantage when I started out. It's such a vague field so I really played up the courses I took that were relevant such as "Museums as Media" which was about how to use media to teach large groups of people to care and learn about a topic, and Media Theory which had a unit on media in education, and stuff like that.*

Essential ID Skill: Understanding of basic adult learning theory.

Parker: Okay, if you've been doing instructional design, brush up on general development theories like ADDIE or SAM. When you look at something like ADDIE, or SAM, it's common sense, but being able to reference them is helpful in certain situations.

Andrea: Just think about it. Let's take the ADDIE model for example. You've got a bunch of content. A big pile of random stuff from the client. Yeah, you have to analyze it (ANALYZE). Oh, and then you take what you found after analyzing and come up with the plan/order for the content that fits with the learning objective (DESIGN). Then, you have to actually make the course/materials/whatever (DEVELOP). Then, you have to give it to the people who need it and put it into action (IMPLEMENT). Then, you find out if it works or not (EVALUATE).

Don't overcomplicate it, like, yes, it's important to know the lingo and how to approach projects, but these models are often just explicitly stating the logical way to work through any problem anytime you're making anything. But it does matter to some people and clients and stuff that you know the terms for it because it shows familiarity with the field.

A good hard skill to have: Analogical reasoning.

Parker: Basically, what that means is a fancy term for making analogies to connect something that's new or novel to you to something that you already know. When I first started work with Andrea, on a project, I was looking for five writers. And Andrea was one of the five.

I divided up the labor and that's when I discovered her writing. Andrea was really good at making analogies and it could be anything from simple stuff like cooking to cultural references. And she also used humor because humor does add to learning. It can enhance learning and provide a sense of discovery in the material. She was using empathy. And empathy is a huge part of writing, being able to connect with the reader or the viewer, you know, the learner. And so all those elements are often missed when you're just super focused on learning all the dry industry techniques (which are helpful, don't get me wrong).

You can go to bootcamp, you can get to the academy, you can go to get a Master's in Ed Tech or Instructional Design, and miss out on all the importance of analogies, humor, and empathy in the learning process.

A good soft skill to have: Open and easy to talk to.

Andrea: I would say at least 50% of what's important when you're working as a freelancer is being able to facilitate information out of the brains of a wide array of personalities, and in a wide array of styles.

Whether that's the traditional type of "crusty" SME that people talk about, or another instructional designer who's working at the company full time. Or, maybe, you're getting information from a whole team at once.

Learning how to be open and easy to talk to and make people comfortable is extremely important. Your clients must feel like you have their back... without coming across like an arrogant expert who walks into the room like, "This is what we're going to do. I know what I'm doing, you're blessed to have me." And you don't want to be the opposite type of person that's like "Oh, just happy to be here! Whatever you guys think is best I'll do it." You gotta be somewhere in the middle.

You can't be wishy washy, but you also can't be like, "Oh, let me tell you how this is going to go... whether you like it or not." These are soft skills that everyone who isn't a jerk will admit they're still improving all the time.

*When we are evaluating who to work with in terms of subcontractors, that's something that we look at. How are they reacting to change? How are they reacting to the client who's a nice person, but maybe a bit gruff? How do they react to clients who are total a***holes? Think about how you'd deal with those situations, because you never know who you're really going to get when you start a project. When you're a freelancer, it's not like a salaried job where you can learn to navigate the team or certain people and build relationships over a super long-term. Freelancing needs you to create great relationships almost immediately. It's an art, not a science!*

Parker: *If you can compartmentalize your emotions and be able to just deal with tricky stuff in the moment with flexibility, you can get the information that you need. Especially when it comes to the actual "knowledge delivery" from your stakeholders and SMEs. Some people want to give you written stuff, some people need to have a call and want to just say stuff out loud while you feverishly take notes. Being able to adapt to those different ways and knowing when to guide the stakeholders and when to let them decide certain things is an important skill. These are a set of skills that aren't always explicitly talked about.*

Congratulations! You are two months into your journey! This set of steps looked at ways to sharpen and expand your instructional design freelancer toolbox. Make sure to revisit them as often as you need. Now keep on truckin' and as famous Communist and folk singer and somehow endearing yet deadbeat dad Woody Guthrie used to say: "Take it easy… but take it!"

5 MONTHS BEFORE YOU DITCH YOUR CUBICLE

CREATE SMALL STARTER PORTFOLIOS

When you're serious about going freelance, you need to show potential clients you know what you're talking about. A portfolio is one excellent way to show this to clients while also showing off your skills. If you're new to ID, then start small. You can make a few mini courses, maybe add in a few advanced Storyline interactions, and a job aid or two.

The best part about your portfolio is that everything you create for it is actually increasing your skill set. Aim to learn one new technique with each portfolio item you create. Think of your portfolio like the Triple Dipper appetizer at Chilis. Each item is different and showcases a unique and impressive flavor. (Then the question is, which of your portfolio items will be the shining star that is the Southwestern Egg Rolls???)

STEP #16

WHAT'S THE BEST WAY
TO DEMONSTRATE MY ID CHOPS?

A starter portfolio should be a showcase of what you can do, but it should also highlight what you *want* to do. Think about which part of the ID process you like the most and focus on that. Do you love analyzing data? Then include some needs analysis and show step-by-step how you figure out the best training solution to solve a problem. Do you prefer developing courses? Then make sure you include some amazing-looking eLearning interactivity.

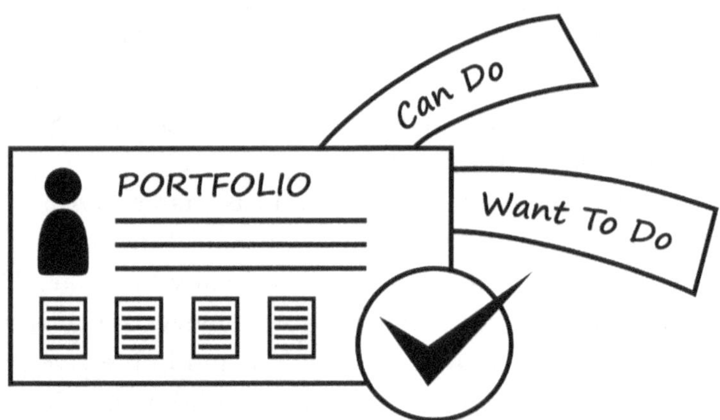

As a freelance ID, pursue your dreams. So, in your portfolio, remember to focus on what you WANT to do in addition to what you CAN do. What a great recipe to show who you are and what you're made of!

If you love it all, then there are a few items that you can include in your portfolio to show the world what you can do:

Show three different Storyline course samples of at least five "slides" each. Create at least three different course samples that include all the bells and whistles. They should showcase what you know, so put a lot of time and effort into this piece. Do a modified needs analysis, create learning objectives, and create a storyboard. Be like Will Smith in Men in Black and make it look good. Hmm, suddenly we're craving sugar water.

(Author's note: If you can correctly count all of the Vincent D'Onofrio references in this book and let Head Honcho Andrea know via email or postcard or other means, you shall receive a grand prize to be divulged later.)

If you're stumped on what your course should cover, try to think about a problem you had at your previous job. How would you solve it? If training would help, create a course on that topic. If you're still having trouble coming up with a topic, use something that you know a lot about and create a course on that. Do you love scuba diving in abandoned swimming pools? Do you knit socks from your cat's hair (if you do, please don't tell us about it)? Do you create vegetable platters depicting Biblical scenes? Whatever you love and know well, create a course teaching others how to do some part of that activity.

Now, if you've racked your brain and you still just cannot come up with a topic on which to create a course, check out the E-Learning Challenges on Articulate's E-Learning Heroes site. There are some great examples of eLearning on that site, which are sure to inspire you. Pick a challenge and give it your all. You can also find some fun topic ideas at godesignsomething.co. This site is great because it's just vague enough to resemble the information you'll get from a real client.

Demonstrate advanced interactions. Take your three Storyline courses of five slides each (or your Rise courses with Storyline blocks inside) and add some advanced interactions. You can google some templates and tips to see what's possible. Did you make a course sample on how to change a baby's diaper? See if you can do an interaction where you click on the baby and if you do the wrong thing first it cries and/or pees in your face. There's always a way to kick it up a notch!

Make it look nice, okay? Whether you love graphic design or not, your portfolio needs to be visually appealing. Unfortunately, hiring managers do judge books by their cover. If your course looks like it's straight out of the original Oregon Trail, they might make some snap judgments. (Though honestly, if it were up to us, we would consider awarding major style points for doing this.)

Think about visual assets that you might have created, such as slide decks, icons, handouts, or infographics. As we mentioned before, you might want to study up on basic graphic design principles, such as composition, color theory, and layout. Instructional designers do not have to be a jack of all trades, but it does help set you apart from the competition if your assets look amazing. Also, you can use Canva or Envato and similar sites to find some sweet templates and well-designed things to edit and make your own. That's what they're there for!

Add those job aids! Along with graphic design assets, you can include a couple of job aids to show that you're more than just an ID with a pretty eLearning course – you can create handouts, flowcharts, surveys, and more! Again, use what you created at your past job. It is easy enough to take something that you've already created and rework it for your portfolio. Make that handout look visually appealing, include useful information, and maybe even add some action steps for the learner to accomplish.

You're the total package – don't be afraid to show that package (your professional portfolio one) to anyone perusing your portfolio.

Stick to your dream field (academic, financial, cat wrangling, or whatever). A wise man (lol, Parker the Wise) once said, discover what you LOVE to do, and discover what you're REALLY GOOD at, and there you will find your niche.

We all have a dream job and field in mind – something that we would absolutely LOVE to do each day. Hopefully, instructional design is your dream job, but maybe you haven't gotten into your dream field just yet. Well, create some eLearning materials within your dream field! This will not only give you a taste of what you would be doing in your dream role, but it also highlights your interest in that field.

No matter what you include in your portfolio, make it your own! It should reflect your personality and work style. It could be fun and playful or serious and professional. Your portfolio is often the first-time clients will see you and your work, so make sure you put a lot of thought into your portfolio. Your first portfolio is a starter portfolio, but you should be continually updating and improving it. It does NOT have to be perfect and, like almost anything in this life of mortal peril, will never be.

Your portfolio will change as you grow professionally, but the first step is actually getting it out there so clients can see what you can do.

STEP #17

WHERE CAN I SHOWCASE MY WORK?

Okay, so you've got a portfolio – now where do you put it so clients can actually see it? If a tree falls in the forest from exhaustion after making the world's best instructionally designed showcase of work, and no hiring managers are around to look at it, will anyone ever give a sh*t?

One of the easiest ways to show off your portfolio is to use Articulate Rise, provided you have purchased an Articulate 360 license. You can easily create a portfolio that doubles as a way to show off your ability to make an eLearning course. As a potential client looks through your Rise portfolio, they get a sense of how Rise works and how creative you can be with the tool.

However, if you are really new to instructional design, odds are you are not exactly swimming in cash just yet. Don't worry – there are plenty of low-cost and free options out there for your portfolio. You can always upgrade, move to a new platform, and revamp.

Which would you rather have? Your portfolio out there for the whole world to see? Or having a portfolio that no one knows about? In the freelance world, you need to get your portfolio link out in your LinkedIn profile and your ongoing social media posts. Find where the "heavy traffic" is and let the world see what you've got to offer!

Let's talk about some of the options out there. This list is not exhaustive, simply because there are A LOT of options available, and we don't have all night (Law and Order: CI marathon is on) to dive into each one.

GoDaddy: If you think GoDaddy sounds like something left over from your Angelfire and GeoCities days, that's because they have been around since 1997. GoDaddy is one of the biggest names in website hosting and design. A lot of instructional designers start with a GoDaddy website (or a similar platform) and upgrade as they grow professionally. One of the best features of GoDaddy is the affordability of both the website builder and website hosting. You can get a yourname.com website for 99 cents a year – try and beat that, we dare you!

- Cons: GoDaddy can feel a little dated, and you don't have a ton of options for customization. The website builder tool is very basic, and it feels that way from the outside, too. Also, it is very unfortunate that once you choose a theme and start building, you will have to start over from scratch if you change your theme.

Wix: Wix is a very popular website building platform for instructional designers. It's unique in the website building realm because it provides blocks that you drag and drop wherever you want on your page. If you have spent some time playing around with Rise 360, you may notice some similarities here. Wix is a great website builder with some super easy to use templates!

- Cons: Wix is free as long as you don't mind a wixsite.com web address. Many new instructional designers use the free version of Wix, and that's perfectly fine. Again, instructional designers do not have to know how to do everything, so letting it go at website design is a valid choice. Once you get more established though, you may want to pay to drop the wix part of the website address and do something that's like www.yourname.com. But, baby steps!

WordPress: You probably already know what WordPress is and what it can do, but it's really the Holy Grail of website creation platforms. It is open-source and highly customizable, and you can basically do anything with it. You can get started for free and it's fairly easy to install and start using. There are tons of apps and plugins that you can use on your website, so it can be really fun to make your portfolio something special and different. If you're overwhelmed by that kind of thing, there are more templates on WordPress than chicken options at the Golden Corral (and they're less likely to give you food poisoning). Just like with Wix, you can get a free ".wordpress" site but it costs money to upgrade from that.

- Cons: WordPress has a huge learning curve and can be extremely difficult for those who have little to no website building experience. There are simply too many options for some people, and you need to know a bit of coding to really make WordPress your own. It can also become pretty expensive to use WordPress if you want something unique or more custom.

Google Sites: I'm sure you already know this, but the biggest advantage to Google is that it costs $free.99. Google is also very easy to use, and most people have experience with Google products these days. You've probably used Google as a professional, a student, or just in your personal life.

With Google, you don't need web hosting or extra website storage – it's just there, ready to house your amazing eLearning examples. It is also extremely easy to create a website and publish with Google. There are no special skills or knowledge needed, and you can work on that website from anywhere.

- Cons: Very limited in design and function, and you are limited to Google's layouts and available apps. Your website will also have a sites.google.com/site/ address, which is a bit long and doesn't exactly roll off the tongue. But hey, that's what hyperlinking words are for, right?

Rise 360: We've already mentioned that Rise 360 would be a handy platform for creating and storing your portfolio. Rise was created as a web-based eLearning authoring tool, so it allows you to create a portfolio that is very interactive. Instead of just telling a client what you can do, you can actually show them as they navigate through your portfolio.

Rise looks professional and is easy to use. You can create a portfolio very quickly and have it published and ready to send to potential clients in no time at all. The platform allows you to drag and drop various blocks to create a scrollable showcase separated by lessons.

- Cons: Rise has many options for adding content, but it is still somewhat limited compared to, say, Storyline 360. You can only do what Rise allows you to do, even though that includes quite a bit of interactivity. Rise also requires an expensive license, so that can be very limiting for those who are new to the field.

There are a lot of options out there for your portfolio depending on your website building knowledge and budget, but most importantly - just get that portfolio out there! Until you have an internet presence dedicated to showcasing your work and skills, you will not be known to potential clients. Create something, get it published, and get that first freelance gig. Go little rock star!

STEP #18

WHAT DO CLIENTS WANT TO SEE IN MY PORTFOLIO?

Once your portfolio is out there on the interweb, you will probably get a few potential clients and recruiters contacting you about jobs, gigs, and contract roles. That most likely means that they found your portfolio somewhere and they liked what they saw. But what should you have in your portfolio to really attract the attention of potential clients? What do clients want to see in your portfolio?

Ahh... now we are getting to the heart of the portfolio – you know, if portfolios had hearts, that is. Now we are really thinking about *why* we need a good portfolio and what a good portfolio looks like.

Let's try an analogy to figure this out. In Texas, barbecue is like, really, really popular. Lots of people travel to Texas to eat barbecue, and they might just head to Franklin barbecue in Austin, because it is famous not only for barbecue but also for really long lines.

If you went all the way to East 11th Street in Austin to get some famous barbecue and stood in line for 3 hours to get that barbecue, what would you order? What if you've never had a barbecue and so you tell the cashier to just give you anything at all because you just want to see what Texas barbecue is all about?

Well, first of all, if you did that at Franklin barbecue, they would probably get pretty annoyed at you, but let's go with this analogy anyway.

So, imagine that instead of making you a meal, the chef just starts throwing barbecue ingredients at you. It's not yet a barbecue, but you've never had a Texas barbecue before, so you don't know. They could hit you with brisket, some onions, some brown sugar, maybe some tomatoes, and a chunk of pecan wood. But what would that accomplish?

Nothing, because you don't yet know the *substance* of Texas barbecue.

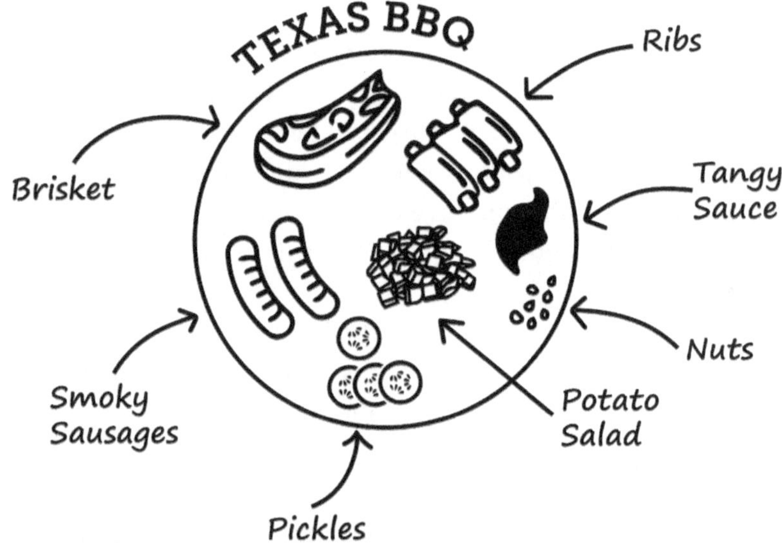

When you create a portfolio, think of the Texas barbecue analogy. It's not just the ingredients you have, but it's the meal you can prepare with the ingredients. So, your portfolio should be a really good "meal" you can offer your clients.

Your portfolio can be just like this experience. You might have a lot of little pieces of projects and stuff that you know how to do, but if you don't have any real substance, it's pointless to clients.

You can have some juicy interactions or really tender branching scenarios (sorry, that analogy made us hungry and weirdly aroused), but that doesn't really make you a good instructional designer.

You need to pay a lot of attention to the content that you are placing in your portfolio. Yes, you're always improving, always getting better at designing courses, but you really need to put your best stuff out there.

Right now your best stuff might be 15 slides explaining why it is bad to harass a coworker. That's okay. We all start somewhere but make that start as awesome as you possibly can. Don't just make it look awesome, focus on the content.

If you were ever a teacher, then you can easily guess what this means. Use your favorite learning theory and figure out the why and how for your project. Show the client that you've done the analysis and investigation and now you know exactly how to present the material to accomplish the learning objectives.

If you were not a teacher in the past, think about any projects that you've headed up or participated in. What were your goals for the project? How did you accomplish those goals? Most likely, you had to take a series of smaller steps to get to the big stuff. Think about that process and use it for your sample projects. Put more effort into the planning and the *why* for each project.

What else do clients want to see in your portfolio? How about yet another Texas barbecue analogy?

Texas has a huge Czech and German heritage, and settlers from those areas would come to Texas and open butcher shops years ago. The butcher shops would occasionally have leftover meat at the end of the day, and the owners would smoke the meat to preserve it. So barbecue is part of the Texas heritage, just like cows with oversized horns and old forts that don't have basements, but hundreds of people look for it every year anyway (thanks, Pee-wee).

But if you went to Texas around lunchtime and you didn't know anything about Texas barbecue heritage, you might miss out on an amazing experience and order Thai or clam chowder or something not Texan at all. Your portfolio is the same! Clients need to know the *context* of what you're including in your portfolio so they can truly appreciate it and experience all that you have to offer them.

As you create assets and samples for your portfolio, keep the design documents, storyboards, and text scripts that you create. All of these planning materials can be placed in your portfolio as well. A lot of instructional designers detail the entire process of creating a course, from the initial needs analysis or action map to the storyboard, script, and prototype.

You can create a page on your portfolio that details all of these steps, which would really show a potential client that you are able to see a project through from conception to finished product. A blog post on each of your projects would be a great way to convey this information to clients. It's like a little story about your projects.

This shows context. This shows what you had in mind as you sat down to create that project. Just like truly appreciating barbecue in Texas, the client needs to know the background to your projects to truly appreciate them.

Finally, keep in mind that name-dropping is actually a good thing for portfolios. If you have worked with some big names, include them in your portfolio (Note: Be careful about NDAs! Don't include the actual projects from those clients unless you have their written permission.). Have you created "How to Clean Up Dog Doo Doo the Right Way" for the dog walking company Wag!? Or maybe you made a Storyline simulation for accurately making mouth-watering Chipotle burritos? Either way, if you've worked for a big company, or even contracted with an agency to create something for a big-name company, mention it!

GET ACTIVE IN THE FREELANCE MARKETPLACE

Now that you've got your amazing starter portfolio created, you might be wondering what you should be doing with it. Well, aside from sending a link to potential clients and printing it out on 8x10 cardstock and throwing it into the Ouze of York while praying to the pagan gods to bring you work... you should be posting the link to your portfolio in all the places it makes sense. We mean online. Not a literal post in your town square.

STEP #19

WHICH FREELANCE PLATFORMS SHOULD I CHECK OUT?

There are a lot of platforms out there for freelancers, and some are amazing while others are meh. If you've already decided on your niche, keep that in mind as you look for platforms to check out. Some of the platforms will be better suited to your niche than others.

Since there are so many possible platforms out there for freelancers, we'll focus on the biggest ones for instructional designers and hopefully take out some of the guesswork for you. So let's get to it!

Upwork: Upwork is probably one of the biggest and most useful platforms for new freelance instructional designers. You can find clients and projects, learn to pitch ideas, and create proposals, communicate with potential clients, and get paid all through this one platform.

Upwork allows clients to post their projects, then freelancers submit proposals with a bid to complete the work. Clients can interview through the platform and choose who they want to hire. Upwork does charge 5-20% commission, so you should plan for that when you submit proposals.

Upwork is a very easy platform to use as a new freelance instructional designer, even if you have no experience pitching to clients or even very little experience creating eLearning. You can just jump right in, submit some portfolio samples, find clients, and start getting work. If a client ends up being flaky and tries not to pay you, Upwork has freelancer payment protection in place so you will still get paid. Follow the rules and your experience on Upwork can be easy and fun.

We will talk a bit more about Upwork and how to win bids in the next section.

Fiverr: Fiverr is different from other platforms because it is considered a marketplace for micro-tasks. So instead of offering to create an entire course, a freelancer might offer to create just a storyboard for a course, or only create 5 slides in Storyline. Fiverr allows freelancers to post tasks that they can do, then clients can hire them instead of clients posting their needs and freelancers bidding for the job.

The platform originally advertised that you could find talent for as little as $5, but now freelancers can set their rates at any price. It's very common for freelancers to set their prices in tiers from basic to standard to premium, each tier offering a bit more detail and more complex deliverables as the price increases.

We will also learn more about Fiverr in the next section.

Learnexus: This platform is another marketplace, but it specifically connects instructional designers and other freelancers to clients. Learnexus boasts that their freelancers go through a rigorous and thorough screening process to ensure that they are the best of the best. Don't let this deter you from creating a profile with them just because you're new to freelancing. The company will work with you to help get your profile approved and to give you the best shot at winning client bids.

Before you decide to work with Learnexus, make sure you are very comfortable in front of a camera. The company prefers that you create short videos to share your experience and passion with clients as well as to submit proposals. When you think about it, recording a video might actually be easier and less time consuming than writing a lengthy proposal!

You guessed it, we will discuss Learnexus some more in the next section.

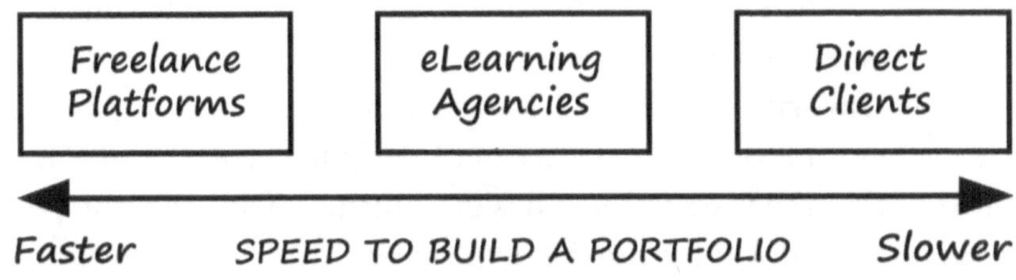

If you are just starting out as a freelance ID, start with the freelance platforms so you can quickly build samples for your portfolio. This starter portfolio will help you land gigs offered by eLearning agencies. In turn, your portfolio continues to grow with more samples you might be approved to show to your direct client prospects. Ultimately, you want to have a substantive portfolio that demonstrates your talents and experience - so that you can land gigs with direct clients.

LinkedIn: There is a whole section on making the most of your LinkedIn account coming up, so we won't spoil that chapter for you here. Just know that LinkedIn is one of the best ways to find gigs when you're freelancing. Make sure you are networking, posting relevant content, and searching for those who are hiring people like you.

You can also do a traditional job search on LinkedIn, but filter the search to only include contract roles or temporary and short-term roles. If your portfolio is optimized, you will also most likely get lots of messages from recruiters seeking to fill contract instructional design roles. Best practice is to at least respond to the recruiters, letting them know if you are or are not interested in such roles. Don't ghost the hand that feeds you! You never know when a recruiter might be trying to fill your dream role, so keep that connection open!

IDLance: Okay, this is one of our personal favorites (lolz). IDLance is not just for learning everything you could ever need or want to know about having a freelance instructional design business, it is also a community. Within this community, you can find gigs, network, learn from other freelancers, and share memes. It's like a big family without the creepy uncles or constant invites to play farm games or buy gross chocolate from your niblings on regular social media.

Your favorite "celebrity" instructional designer: Odds are, you follow one or two instructional designers with "celebrity" status within the instructional design industry. These are the people who either went from being teachers to six-figure instructional designers overnight or learned "accidentally" that they are instructional designers while working for some big corporation, and now they seemingly have "hit the big time!" No matter what their stories are, these people know their stuff.

Fortunately, these people also tend to share that knowledge with fellow instructional designers. Some have communities for their followers which include round table discussions, webinars, classes, and certifications. It can be pretty expensive to participate in all that these gurus have to offer (people gotta make a living!), but some of these industry experts also have free forums or Slack channels that you can join to network and find job postings.

As an added bonus, you can follow these celebrities on LinkedIn and learn a lot about the industry through their posts. Some of them even respond to your comments and questions, which is amazing. Celebrity instructional designers... hey, they're just like us!

Slack: Slack is a messaging platform that combines the look and feel of a web forum with the fun and convenience of instant messaging. Slack organizes themed chats into channels, which you can join and follow. There are tons of super helpful Slack Groups dedicated to instructional design and freelancing.

As we mentioned, well-known instructional designer communities often have their own Slack channels (*cough* IDLance *cough*). You can also find many Slack channels by Googling, looking through other communities that you already belong to, and by searching Reddit for the specific industry's Slack channel that you're interested in joining.

Once you've joined some channels, stay active by answering questions that are posted or asking your own questions. Gigs, tips, and tricks get posted a lot on Slack channels. Plus, you can make new industry friends by developing a long-distance direct messaging relationship! Please don't pull a Catfish on any of these groups. Though it might be kind of fun to see Nev and Max talk about IDLance on national tv…so…

eLearning Heroes Community Forums: eLearning Heroes is not just a great place to learn new Articulate skills and participate in challenges, they also have a forum where you can ask questions, learn more about instructional design and Articulate products, and even find jobs (jobs, jobs, everywhere)!

You can search the job boards and actually reply to the person who posted the job. You may or may not get the job, but at least you'll be networking and making new connections. Connections and networking are the main ingredients to a happy, healthy freelance career.

Trying out several freelance platforms is one of the best ways to get your feet wet in the freelance world. Try them all, get used to the look and feel of each one, and decide what works best for you and your business. Each platform has its own unique attributes and benefits, so embrace as many as you can. Best to do it at a bit of a run if you're nervous.

STEP #20

HOW DO I LAND GIGS IN UPWORK, FIVERR, OR LEARNEXUS?

Knowing about these platforms is all fine and great, but how do you actually land gigs on them? Some might say that landing gigs are an artform that you must learn to master, but really it just takes a lot of time and effort.

Like anything in life, how successful you are in your freelance career is almost always related directly to how much attention you give it. Like a little baby, it grows and thrives when you feed it and give it cuddles. When it starts to stink, change something, and see if that helps. But really, it just takes time. Before you know it, your homely little newborn baby will stop looking like a knee and turn into the cherubic, admirable little tot it was meant to be.

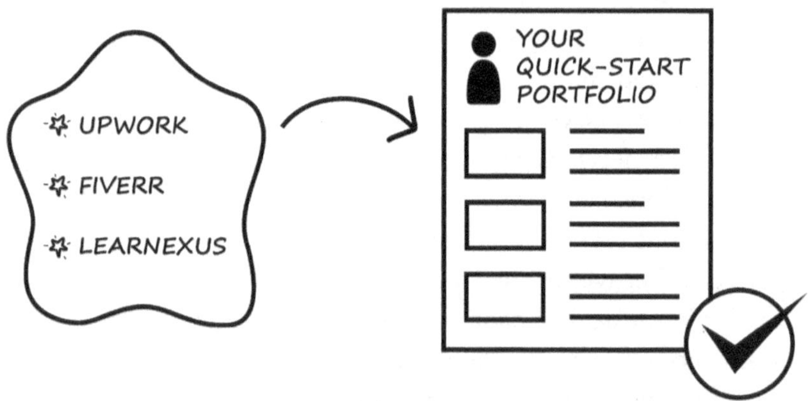

Are you just starting out with a portfolio? A quick way to get a portfolio started is to land small gigs with freelance platforms. The gigs are often short and quick. Nevertheless, these are important to build a quick-start portfolio so you can show to future prospects!

Let's talk a bit more about the three freelance marketplaces that are most relevant to instructional designers: Upwork, Fiverr, and Learnexus. We already gave you a basic overview of what these platforms offer, so let's focus now on how to actually land gigs.

More on Upwork: Upwork is a great way for new freelancers to find jobs, but just like sitting in a restaurant while the wait staff and your family sing "Happy Birthday" to you while you sit on a saddle or kiss a stuffed moose, it can be uncomfortable, and it can take some time.

You will be submitting proposals to potential clients – lots and lots of proposals. Sometimes you will submit 40 proposals in one day and you won't get even one interview. But sometimes you will submit just one and get the job.

It takes a lot of up-front effort to be successful on Upwork, but once you put in the time and effort you will start to develop your freelancer social profile. It means clients will seek out your experience. You'll eventually have clients looking for you, contacting you first, and requesting to interview you.

But how do you get to that point? There are a few steps you can take to make your proposals a bit more interesting to clients and make your work stand out. Remember, there will be dozens of other freelancers also bidding for the job.

1. **Optimize your profile.** Use keywords in your heading, profile description, and in your portfolio items that relate to your niche. This will make your profile stand out when clients search for specific items.

2. **Use Upwork's features to your advantage.** Utilize the portfolio feature to highlight some of the projects that you've previously completed and add testimonials from previous clients.

3. **Use keywords when you search for jobs.** Have a niche and use keywords that are specific to your niche when

you're looking for jobs. This will help you find jobs that you are highly qualified for, reduce some of the competition, and will make you more likely to win the bid. It's all about specificity!

4. **Use several profiles.** Upwork allows you to create a profile for multiple job searches. If you are multi-talented and would like to do instructional design and graphic design for instance, you can create separate profiles for each one and switch between the two to search for jobs.

In order to bid on any Upwork jobs you have to submit a proposal to the client. This can seem a little scary at first, maybe it sounds like cold calling clients or sending out mass emails. The truth is each proposal should be completely unique and specific to the company and role that you are bidding on.

How do you accomplish this? Try including the following when writing your proposals:

- Right away, tell the client what value you can bring to them for their specific project and tell them what you do best.
- Turn your experience and expertise into something that the client must have. Make your experience and knowledge relevant to them based on that project. What have you done previously that is similar to their project?
- Include links to your portfolio in your proposal.
- Mention the specific need the client is trying to fill with the job posting and tell the client how you would approach the role. This is a great way to show the client that you've really thought about the role while also highlighting your expertise.

Sure, you can Google "Upwork proposal hacks" or search for the same thing on TikTok. If you search this, you might find some interesting ideas, but they may not be the best ideas. The only true hack for Upwork is to just devote a lot of time to creating proposals and sending them to clients.

More on Fiverr: Fiverr is different from Upwork because instead of submitting proposals to clients, freelancers advertise their services and wait for clients to find them. Clients (called buyers on Fiverr) can browse through various categories to find freelancers (called sellers) that fit their specific needs. Buyers can look through the seller's profile and portfolio and then hire them to complete the task if they like what they see. It's a lil bit like Hinge or Bumble, but without the emotional expectations.

As mentioned previously, Fiverr is a platform for micro-tasks, so it is unlikely that you would be hired to complete an entire eLearning course. You are more likely to be hired to complete one of the steps in the course development process at a time, so you would adjust your pricing schedule accordingly.

To get started on Fiverr, simply sign up and start working on creating a profile that is optimized for the types of micro-tasks that you want to market to buyers. Place a few items in your Fiverr portfolio that reflect your ability to complete the micro-tasks that you have in mind.

Next, start adding "gigs," or micro-tasks. You will fill out an overview for each gig with the following information:

- **Gig title:** Describe the service you are offering. Use a catchy title that will make you stand out from other sellers.
- **Category:** Select a category and subcategory. You can post several gigs within various categories if necessary.
- **Service type:** What service are you offering to buyers? This is just another way to categorize your gig.
- **Gig metadata:** This is where you can show your buyer that you support various social media platforms, which is not always relevant to instructional design. You can leave this blank unless you are offering to create micro-courses on Instagram or something similar.
- **Search tags:** Choose keywords that will attract the right buyers to your gig. If you are offering to create with a specific tool, include it here.

Now, you are ready to price your gig. Fiverr uses package pricing, which means you offer a basic task and add on revisions or extras that allow a buyer to choose exactly what they want. Fiverr gives you a pricing template with three pricing options, you simply fill in the details on the template:

- In the "name your package" field, give each section a specific title that shows exactly what is offered with that option.
- Describe the services that you would offer in detail, explaining the difference between each level.
- Choose the delivery time for each level.
- Choose a pricing schedule for each level.
- You can add extra services if you wish, or keep this area blank.

The next steps are pretty self-explanatory. You will describe your gig in detail and let the buyer know what you need to get started once they hire you. You can add some photos of your previous work or stock images that relate to what you're selling. Now, make it official and hit publish!

To make your profile and gigs stand out, you should optimize your profile and gigs with keywords, just like any portfolio on any freelance platform. You know what you want to do, so mention those things in your portfolio so buyers will find you when they search for whatever your niche may be.

Utilize the portfolio section of your profile to highlight what you've done and what you can do for the buyer. As you complete gigs for clients, ask for testimonials to include on your profile as well.

When a buyer hires you, they are able to rate your services afterwards, which future buyers can see. Ask for five stars from every buyer. If they have a reason that they do not want to rate you that high, ask them what you can do to make their rating higher. Sometimes a buyer will tell you what can be done to improve the rating and it is an easy fix, other times you can use their feedback to improve the next gig.

Lather, rinse, and repeat. Eventually, clients will be coming to you regularly because you will have so many highly rated gigs and testimonials. Grab those crystals and pendulums and start manifesting now!

More about Learnexus: First of all, you should know that Learnexus is very different from other freelance platforms because they focus specifically on helping organizations connect with and hire learning and development professionals. Other platforms are very open-ended and able to provide clients with almost any type of freelancer, but Learnexus helps clients find L&D freelancers exclusively. So it's a no-brainer that it's certainly a platform that a freelance instructional designer such as yourself should check out. It was literally made for you!

Learnexus promises that their freelancers are among the top 3% of all candidates due to their rigorous screening process. If you decide to join the Learnexus platform and submit proposals for projects, keep in mind that joining and getting approved to work is a process. You will not be able to submit proposals right away, but it is definitely worth the wait.

One really nice benefit to working with Learnexus is that you can connect with their recruiters and staff on LinkedIn, and they are very helpful and willing to speak with you and answer questions. If you're having trouble getting your profile completed, they will work with you to get it approved and ready to go. You will also have a virtual interview with a Talent Engagement Manager, which is another opportunity to ask questions and get feedback on your profile before you are approved. Kind of like a profile concierge service! But, please, don't ask them on "special errands" in the middle of the night.

Not only is the profile approval process rigorous and lengthy, but you will also create videos explaining your background, experience, skills, and more. You will later submit video proposals for many of the jobs as well. Make sure to get camera-ready, because Learnexus recruiters encourage you to choose the video proposal option when it is available. As we said before, sometimes recording a video to express yourself and communicate your capabilities is a bit less daunting and time-consuming than writing a cover letter.

The main idea to keep in mind as you create your profile on Learnexus is that your profile should be 100% complete before you submit it for approval. You will need to add at least one work sample from a previous project, and you should record a 1–2-minute introduction video. If you really take the time to create a great profile, you will be approved faster and with less stress. Then you can start submitting proposals to clients.

The proposal process on Learnexus is a bit different from other platforms. On the project description page, you will usually see a video where a recruiter explains what the client is looking for, what skills you should have to apply, and what will be required of the freelancer if they are chosen for an interview.

According to the Learnexus website, best practices when submitting a proposal include recording video answers if the option is given to you. Not sure if we mentioned this but they *REALLY LOVE* video responses, so just go for it. Maybe your smiling face will win the client over, or maybe they will see your Slytherin banner and Venus fly trap plant in the background and feel compelled to hire a fellow Potterhead. Who knows? Just try and see!

As for pricing your bids, keep in mind the job posting will have an estimate of what the client is willing to pay and the general amount you should expect for that project. Think about those numbers and determine if you would really want to work on the project for that amount of money. Each job has different requirements and workload, so do some analysis about what you'd be willing to take on. If you want to get some gigs under your belt, it's ok to work for "cheaper" than normal. Just remember what we said back up in the section about setting your rates.

There are no magic hacks to help you get chosen for Learnexus projects, but it does help to make sure your profile is complete and eye-catching. Make your video responses lively and full of personality - but not obnoxious. Please don't choose video recording day to wear your favorite Family Guy t-shirt - as we have learned in our own work/life (*cough*marriage*cough*), it's a very polarizing show. Provide samples of past projects you're proud of and show that you are an awesome instructional designer. Ok, that's it for now.

STEP #21

WHEN SHOULD I USE
THESE FREELANCE PLATFORMS?

Take a deep breath, 'cause we just covered a whole lot of platforms and a smorgasbord of techniques for selling your skills to clients. Your brain may be full-up by now. Go take a walk or look at your fish tank or something. If you don't have a fish tank, use this moment to visualize how you might decorate one if you did. SpongeBob theme? Pirates? Mermaids? So many options.

Feeling better?

You might be wondering if you should continue to use every one of these platforms every day for the rest of your life, or if there are specific times that you should focus on each one. The answer is so incredibly simple – *it depends.*

Think about what you are trying to accomplish at this particular moment in your life. Are you just focusing on finding full-time mid-length contracts? Maybe you should spend your time on platforms that allow you to network and make professional connections. Put a lot of time into creating proposals and bidding on contract roles. Think Learnexus, LinkedIn, and Slack.

If you just want to find some smaller side gigs to supplement your full-time job, or just to help you gain experience in instructional design, then look towards Fiverr or Upwork.

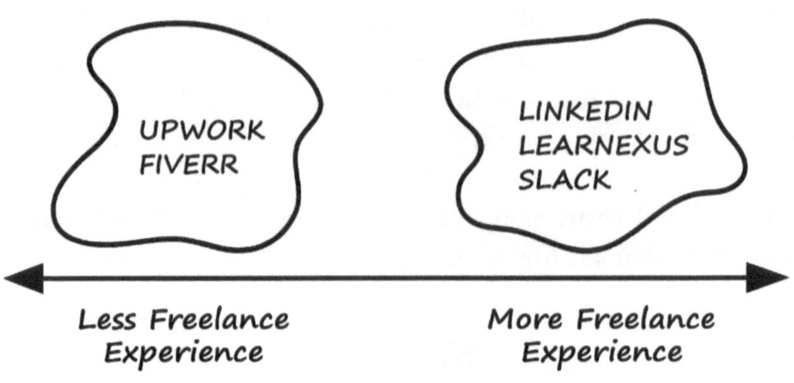

Which freelance platform you choose could depend on your freelance experience level. If you are just starting out, try landing gigs with Upwork or Fiverr. As you gain more experience and build a portfolio, spend more time on other platforms like LinkedIn, Learnexus, and Slack.

If you're not necessarily looking for gigs or contracts at the moment, then this is a great time to focus on improving your skills and learning more. This is when forums and industry experts' communities could be where you spend your free time.

WELL, OBVIOUSLY, IDLance is perfect for all these situations, so always, always spend every waking minute (yep, even when on the loo) on the IDLance website, blog, Slack channel, Instagram, LinkedIn, or YouTube. We are everywhere, so there is no excuse not to follow us like any family dog when you're carrying around a slice of pepperoni pizza. If you're a good boy/girl, we might even throw you a slice.

4 MONTHS BEFORE YOU DITCH YOUR CUBICLE

ASSESS YOUR PROGRESS

Alright, so it's been 3 months since you started on this freelance journey of yours. A quarter of a year (or maybe you're reading this book all in one sitting. Does that count as time travel? Someone call Doc!).

Anyway, can you believe it? Stop and take a moment to remember all those feelings you had at the beginning. The fear! The excitement! The terror! The motivation! The anxious toots! You've made a BIG LIFE DECISION and you're just a part of the way there.

This is the month where you will take a good, hard look at the progress you've made, make some necessary adjustments, and continue on your path to escaping your 9-5... FOR GOOD. Or, for as long as you want. No worries either way. (Actually, like most, we're worrying both ways PLUS a secret third way. We just care about you, okay? WE WANT YOU TO SUCCEED!)

STEP #22

HOW AM I DOING WITH MY FINANCES SO FAR?

First up, we're going to have to revisit the math. (Hey, stop hissing and put that crucifix down!) But if you don't run the numbers *regularly*, you will never have a true pulse on your freelance business. Seriously – you'll have to get used to doing this often. As a freelancer, your finances will require consistent review and refining. The more you get used to it at the beginning of your journey, the more comfortable you'll be by the time you're counting up those monthly millions like CEO, entrepreneur, born in 1964, Jeffrey, Jeffrey Bezos…or Scrooge McDuck.

Back in the beginning (three whole months ago!), you came up with some numbers related to both your income and expenses.

Income: First, you landed on your hourly rate. Whether you just knew what you wanted to make hourly, or you decided how much you wanted to make annually and used that to determine your hourly rate, at the end, you had a number. And based on this number, you estimated your first trimester of freelance income. (Gestate that freelance bb, baby!)

In fact, you asked yourself the question: "How much cash monies can I *really* make in my first few months as an ID freelancer?" The answer back then was "*It depends*." But NOW, you can actually answer that question!

So, "how much cash monies did you really make in your first few months as an ID freelancer?" And how does that number compare to what you estimated back then? (This part almost feels like a "Choose Your Own Adventure" novel, but choose one of the below…

- **I blew my expectations away harder than the nose of a grandma with a sinus infection!** This is GREAT news! You must have really hit the ground running and snagged some lucrative contracts. But wait! Before you start changing all your projections for the rest of the year, remember that freelancing can fluctuate. Keep a close eye on what contracts are coming to an end and what you have in the pipeline. What's starting and what's ending as you enter the next quarter?

- **I just hit my target RIGHT NOW!** Well, friendo, you did a great job projecting your income! You knew your hourly rate, how many hours you wanted to work, and you snagged the contracts that put you right there. Great job! Now…how ya gonna keep up the momentum? Just like the life of a stage actor, a freelancer is only as good as his last performance!

- **I didn't quite get there.** This happens even to the most seasoned of freelancers. Identify the obstacles that prevented you from hitting that projection. Did you take on a client at too low of a rate? Did you work less hours? Could you not find clients or land contracts in the first place? As you head into the second quarter, look at what you can do to bring yourself closer to your estimated income. Is there anyone you can chat with who may be able to help?

Regardless of which option fits your situation, as you move forward into the next quarter of your freelance business, you need to re-evaluate your progress and determine what your next quarter (and the next and the next) will look like.

Go back to the income goals you set for yourself and ask yourself some hard questions:

- Do these goals still make sense?
- Am I on track?
- What needs to change?

Now is the time to do that! Remember, goals don't have to be set in stone. Circumstances change and your income goals can change with you. Maybe you realized you can command a higher hourly rate. Maybe you realized that you need to change how many hours per week or how many projects at once you can manage. No matter what, it's all good! This journey isn't linear. Things will shift all the time.

So take a moment, review the goals you set, and make those changes. Write down your new income goals: what will you bring in next quarter, and what does that mean for the rest of the year? If you want, get yourself a brand new fresh-paged notebook to commemorate the occasion. You deserve it!

Pro Tip: The knock off Moleskin notebooks are just as good and way cheaper. Especially when every cent counts in the beginning of life as a freelie! You know what else is cool? Decomposition notebooks. Sustainable, too. Can you tell we love notebooks?

Expenses: Bringing in money is certainly the goal here, but almost more important than knowing how much money you brought *in* is knowing how much money went *out*. And is the first number bigger than the second? (Hope so...at least eventually!)

To be a successful full-time freelancer, your income will need to cover all your expenses (including taxes and savings – you can't forget that part!). And while you may still have your full-time job as you're navigating the freelance world, one day, that safety net won't always be there (if you make the FULL leap someday).

Note: We know this part isn't fun. Especially when you could be working on that cool freelance contract and making money with this time. Or, frankly, just kicking back and enjoying that iced Mayan mocha latte you know you've been dreaming about since chapter one while putting together that Harry Potter Lego set you've been saving. But we can't underscore enough the importance of regular financial check-ins.

So, let's take a look!

You're going to need to repeat the steps from earlier:

1. Log into your online banking
2. Check your credit card statement
3. Grab that income number we just talked about
4. Create your visual

So what's your number? And how does it compare to what you estimated back in month one? (We could do another "Choose Your Own Adventure" here…)

Remember, if you're still working your full-time job, you don't need to fully cover your expenses (YET). But you want to see progress. Or at least a path forward (with a plan)! If you've been surviving just fine on your salaried income, maybe put away most if not all of your side-gigging moolah to have on hand when you DO make that leap.

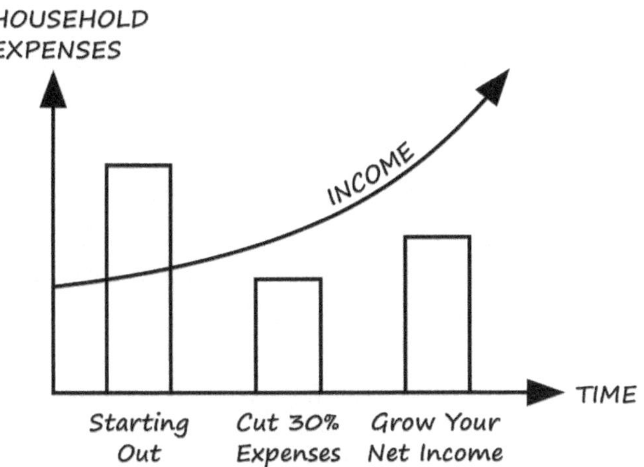

If you were to suddenly leave your full-time job, you may find that your household expenses far exceed your income from a new freelance biz. This is why you need to find a way to cut at least 30% of your household expenses immediately. As you grow your freelance income, you will also grow your net income after expenses. Nice, huh?! At which time, you can choose to increase your household expenses (a little) to suit your quality of life!

This is where the relationship of your income to expenses is so important, and if there's a gap, you'll want to revisit lowering your expenses.

Do you remember that whole conversation in month one about how you can reduce your expenses by at least 30%? Or did you block it out? No hard feelings.

In all seriousness, reducing your expenses will make it so much easier to build your freelance business sooner. (Think about it… the less you need to spend, the more you can save, and the sooner you can ditch your 9-5. Which then means you have more time to build your freelance business and make even MORE money!)

So, while ultimately reducing expenses isn't AS important as making sure your income can cover them, it's definitely a good practice to frequently look at where your money is and trim it down like that Bob Ross chia pet you have.

If you tried to reduce your expenses, keep reading. (If you didn't, you can skip down to the last paragraph of this section). Do a gut check.

How did it go? You made an estimate of your expenses and decided to try to reduce them by 30%. Did you get there (or close)?

30% is absolutely a huge reduction, so if you didn't hit that number, that's totally ok. Now's the time to identify where you were able to cut back (and celebrate that!) and what areas you still have room for reduction. Don't forget the handy list we gave you:

1. What's on TV?
2. Learn to make that cup of coffee
3. Refinance your mortgage
4. Insurance stuff
5. Hire help
6. Sell your new car for a lovely pre-owned gem
7. Use coupons

8. Shop smart
9. Conserve energy
10. Consolidate your debt

This is not an exhaustive list by any means, but it's a great place to start (and revisit!). As you flip back to reread all the details about each of these, take note of the ones you maybe haven't tried yet, and set a goal to tackle at least one or two of them in the coming weeks.

Remember, your ultimate goal is to be a freelance instructional designer. To get there, you'll have to do the less fun things, like analyzing your finances. But you can do it! And ya kinda have to if you want to kick that 9-5 to the curb.

STEP #23

HOW AM I DOING WITH MY ID SKILLS, PORTFOLIOS, AND GIGS?

Now that your finances are in the rear-view mirror (at least for now), we can look at something a little more fun! How is your progress going on all things instructional design?

Let's start with your skillz! Assessing your skills can sometimes be challenging. Because when you're starting out, you don't always know what you don't know. So it can be hard to identify areas you'd like to improve. But back in month one, you took a short (oh, who are we kidding – that thing definitely took you some time to fill out) self-assessment, and you reflected on your results.

Remember the first question? *Based on my self-evaluation, my top three skills are...*

Think about those top three skills. REALLLLLY think about them. Think about where you were with them then. And think about where you are with them now. How have you been able to develop those skills over the last three months? Have you deepened your knowledge? Do any of these skills come more easily? More comfortably? And even more importantly, can you articulate the jobs or tasks you've done that have provided you that growth? (The answers to these questions can give you insights to note in interviews and cover letters!). OR, have your top three skills totally changed? Hey, stranger things have happened! Like the time a bug flew into Andrea's ear in a Chili's bathroom, and she didn't know what to do so she asked the teenage server as if somehow being a server gave her all-knowing power and authority to fix the situation. Know what worked? Going out of the restaurant into the dark. The bug flew out towards the majestically bright parking lot lights.

As you continue on this journey, and are continuously learning and improving, don't forget your strongest skills. There is always room for growth there, and just because they are (right now) your strongest skills, doesn't mean you should let them plateau.

This is the perfect segue into another important topic we just mentioned briefly: Are those STILL your top three skills? There's no right or wrong answer here, but just like your finances require consistent check-ins, so does your professional skill development. Acknowledging where you've grown and where you haven't will only make you a stronger instructional designer. And person.

Now, let's circle back to a question you answered all those months ago: *"Based on my self-evaluation, I want to learn more about the following skill(s)..."*

So... did you?

No, furreal furreal... did you?

We get it – learning new skills on top of transitioning your career, getting contracts, and working is HARD. Are there really enough hours in the day? But what will set you apart as an instructional designer is the skills you have. Clients are often looking for specific skills and abilities, so the more that you can speak to (and competently demonstrate), the more marketable you become and the wider the pool of gigs you have access to. Which leads to more contracts, more experience, and more income!

If you have been able to develop the skills you listed, now's the time to set a goal to further refine them. Ask yourself:

- What does mastery look like, and where are you?
- How can you get there?
- What nuances to the skill are you missing?
- Are there specific pieces you need to improve to feel more confident?
- What time frame can you set for mastery?

If you weren't able to develop these skills (or you only learned about one or two of them), commit to them now. Set up actionable goals that will help you continue to build your sweet ID skills. (Remember, building a thriving, long-lasting freelance biz requires you to spend time on things that don't make you money right away. But, learning and developing new skills will absolutely make you mad money later, yo).

	I'm about ready to ditch my cubicle!	I'm doing okay!	I still need to do more work!
ID SKILLS	O	O	O
PORTFOLIO	O	O	O
GIGS	O	O	O

How are you doing so far in your quest to ditch your cubicle? Rate your progress for: 1) Building ID skills, 2) Developing a Portfolio, and 3) Finding Gigs. This will be important to assess before you reach Step #25.

Now that you've given yourself the old once over on skillz assessment, let's determine how you're doing with developing, refining, and spicing up your portfolio. We're going to let you in on a helpful secret first. You should always consider your portfolio "a work in progress." You heard us right. For the entirety of your natural time on this planet Earth, your portfolio should exist in a near constant state of flux– an incomplete compendium of your life's work that is never to be perfected. Like Sisyphus himself, you will spend all your days rolling a proverbial portfolio boulder up that hill over and over and over again.

Isn't that reassuring!? For a minute there you were feeling some anxiety about your portfolio, weren't ya? Hey, that's what we're here for! You're welcome!

Seriously though, we're going to go over some criteria to assess your 'folio against, but don't sweat it too much. There really is no such thing as a portfolio that's "done." Things change! Your style may change, the skills you want to showcase may change, heck your entire eLearning ethos could change. Some of us were wearing bright red, ankle-length denim skirts with a front slit back in middle school. The point is, people change and so do portfolios.

First of all, does your portfolio represent YOU? Your portfolio should reflect who you are not only as an instructional designer, but also as a person. Don't try to make your portfolio fit into some weird abstract idea of what a "professional" portfolio *should* be. There is no blueprint for how your portfolio should look, and odds are, if you try to conform to that 'idea of a portfolio,' it'll just look kinda weird and forced, in an *American Psycho* sort of way. You can use branding to put glimpses of your shining personality in there. Or if you're a goth (very cool btw), try inserting an animated .gif of a bat saying, "I'm BATTY for ID!" See, easy!

Are you demonstrating a variety of different skills? No one is saying you need to be the Martha Stewart of ID or anything, but you should try to show off as many traditional and non-traditional design principles and multimedia elements as you can. Ya know, we're talkin' about the "good stuff" like scenario branches, motion graphics, videos, case studies, screencast tutorials, and VR/AR/XR, oh my! But don't go nuts! Every course doesn't have to contain the whole kit n' kaboodle of design principles. Not only would this be exhausting, but most hiring managers will only look at the first few screens of each sample. Make the first 5-7 screens count in each of your samples, and you can cover all your bases that way!

Is your portfolio visually appealing and well-organized? This one is pretty self-explanatory. No one is going to be impressed if your 'folio is looking straight out of Internet Explorer in the year 1996. Alright, we might be a little impressed just because '96 ruled pretty hard. Here's a hot tip–check your portfolio regularly to make sure the tech is working properly and displaying the way you originally intended it to. Don't ask us why, but computers are bedeviled machines that often bungle things up for no reason at all! Just be sure everything has an attractive visual design and is easy to navigate. You got this one.

Are you remembering to show off your beautiful work on the Internet? You can have the most beautiful portfolio in the entire world, but if no one's checking it out then your efforts will be all for naught. And that would be very, very sad, bud. This is not the time to be humble, promote yourself! At the very least, you should be sharing samples on LinkedIn. That's where a lot of hiring managers are going to be hanging around, sniffing out new talent like you (ew, gross). From there, you can expand your horizons to Facebook, conferences, or that weird, secret "Garfield the Cat" forum you're a member of. That guy sure hates Monday's, doesn't he?! Not you, freelie! Mondays are acceptable now.

Lastly, are you impressed by your own portfolio? We sure spend a lot of time in this life wondering what everyone else thinks about us. That's why we think it's a good idea to stop and ask YOURSELF what you think of your portfolio. Are you impressed? Summon your inner Buffalo Bill and give yourself an honest but generous self- assessment of your work thus far. If you're struggling with this exercise, ask a friend who you trust for feedback. We bet you're doing a great job though!

Ok, you've assessed your wealth of sick skillz and your jaw-droppingly gorgeous portfolio, now it's time to determine how the gig search is going. This one is a bit trickier to assess as there are more elements that are "out of your control" than there are when it comes to skill building and portfolio development. But we can still define some measures of progress! But first, we're going to drop a fun fact on you– "gig" is spelled the same forwards as it is backwards. We'll give you a minute to pick the bits of your brain up off the floor because surely, we've just blown your mind.

Are you keeping a positive attitude? Alright, we know this is an intrinsically annoying suggestion to which the only appropriate response is, "Are YOU keeping a positive attitude?!?!??!" But really, you'd be surprised how far an optimistic outlook can take you during the job search. It'll boost your productivity, help potential clients feel comfortable around you, aid decision-making, and act as a motivator in expanding your job search. It might even help you build up some resiliency when a potential gig falls through. You can use that positive demeanor to see opportunities all around you! Ok, we'll shut up now.

How many hours are you spending on the search? Are you treating your gig search like a job in and of itself or are you telling people, "I looked all day," when in reality you did a combined total of 40 minutes between old reruns of Bridezilla. On a side note, that show used to be SO good! Right? As we were saying, do your best to prioritize your time and limit distractions in the home. If that sounds impossible to you, find a quiet place like your local library where there is absolutely no chance of watching TV. (Hot tip: technically you can watch TV at the library with a pair of headphones and a streaming service on your Bridezilla machine...ERRR, we mean, laptop.) Searching for gigs should become a part of your daily routine. It can't hurt to keep a daily log of your progress either!

How many potential clients have you reached out to or interviewed with? Listen bud, there's a difference between "searching" and "acting." It's easy to compile a running list of potential gigs but sooner or later you gotta jump on those opportunities. We know it can be super intimidating, especially if you don't have much experience, but think of this as an opportunity for growth. If your number is pretty low, expand your network or increase your time spent schmoozing on LinkedIn. Despite what you may think, there are tons of people and hiring managers out there who would love to see your work and chat with ya. Try setting a goal for yourself, like "I'll meet with x number of potential clients in x amount of time." If you need to start out slow, that's ok! As long as you're focusing your efforts on growth, you're doing great!

Are you following up with potential clients? You got an interview? That's incredible! But, are you following up with the potential client afterwards? Any lame person can send an informal email – try to go for the gold here! Take time to make the extra effort of making a call to the hiring manager or sending a handwritten note. We don't really recommend an Edible Arrangement as that's kind of a BIG statement and also, ew, yucky! Plus, technically any arrangement CAN be an edible arrangement if you try hard enough. There's that positive attitude again! Wow, it really expands the mind and the palate!

Lastly, are you celebrating your wins? While landing a gig is always the end goal, it's not the ONLY goal! We want you to take time to reward yourself along the way because this ain't easy. It can be hard to put yourself out there in any context, let alone as a brand-new freelancer. You got an interview? Buy yourself some fresh jammies. Made some new connections on LinkedIn? Go on a solo date to the movies and gobble down a tray of extra sloppy nachos. Small wins usually lead to a big win, so don't forget to treasure these moments!

STEP #24

HOW AM I DOING WITH MY PARTICIPATION IN ID COMMUNITIES?

Global ID communities can be an awesome place to meet and network with fellow instructional designers. And like we said before – it helps you realize you're not alone! (Because as much as we love our remote freelance life, sometimes it's nice to talk to someone other than the pet snuggling under your desk. And while what our pets can teach us *is* super valuable and has been proven to lengthen our lifespan, you'll likely gain more professional insights from other instructional designers. Dogs don't pay the billz.).

But just being a part of the community isn't enough. To really get the full benefits (the relationships, the skill building, the opportunities, the lolz) that come from being a part of a community, you have to be *active* in it.

When you wrote your goals, were any of them related to building your instructional designer network? Regardless of whether or not you set that goal, ask yourself: "*What professional connections have I made in the last three months?*"

That's it. The whole goal of participating in ID communities is to develop strong, professional connections that become your network. Your ID people. Truly, the importance of building a network cannot be overstated. If you haven't taken steps to build yours, move that up to priority #1! Not only will it help you become a better instructional designer, but it will help you stay focused on your goal of becoming a freelance ID. So where should you go?

Earlier, we did a deeper dive into the IDLance community. You heard what we do there, got a sneak peek into some of our most popular Slack channels, and you even met some active members of the community. While we hope that you've joined us already, we also know that prioritizing this in the midst of everything else you're doing isn't easy (or even something you really think about).

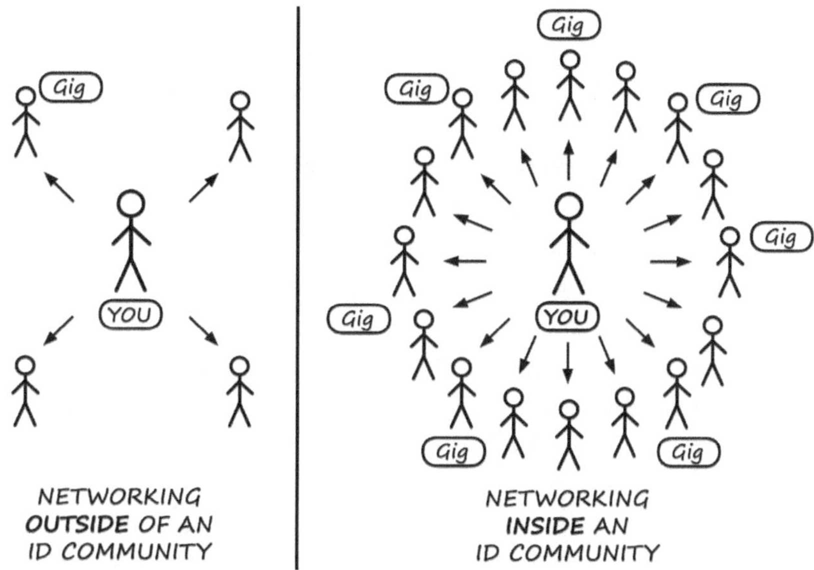

Which scenario would you rather have? On the left, you have a network outside of an ID community. You might find a gig with someone there. On the right, however, you have a network in one or more ID communities. That means a greater chance of finding a gig with someone. So, join several ID communities and keep networking!

So let's do another lil pluggy-plug. Joining a community like IDLance can provide so many glorious opportunities for you:

- **Networking:** Members pose questions that you may just know the answer to. And when you provide your insight… BAM! You've made a connection with someone else in the community. Inviting that person for a (probably virtual) coffee chat deepens that connection, and now you are starting to build relationships. Go you! *performs outdated cabbage patch dance move*

- **Skill building:** Members often share new skills or tech tools. Some will undoubtedly be familiar to you, but can't you always benefit from someone else's insights? Others will be so far out of this world to you that you'll need the primer version to start. But now you know it exists and with a lil effort, it's in your instructional design bag of tricks. The best is when you see someone using a tool that you "think you know" in a totally new way and your soul leaves your body… without the ayahuasca.

- **Referrals:** Going back to that whole networking and relationship building thing… It's no secret that one big reason we all do it is because there are so many opportunities out there and having personal connections with other instructional designers increases our chances of hearing about (and landing!) awesome gigs. But, we can't stress enough the importance of being genuine – building relationships just for the sake of landing gigs won't get you far.

So… what are you waiting for?!? We are ready and waiting with freshly bathed open arms to welcome you into our community!

STEP #25

IS FREELANCING STILL MY THING?

OK…so, how are you feeling? Are you hyperventilating or are you sipping a martini thinking, "I got this"? We've gone through a LOT this month, and you've had to really reflect on your progress so far.

We've touched on different goals that you should be setting right now: financial, skill building, and networking (at the very least). But this is the time to reflect on the rest of the goals you may have set for yourself and assess your progress on those.

Way back when at the beginning of this journey (are you starting to detect a pattern here?), we talked about setting specific mini goals. So what were yours?

Even though the time frame you set may not have passed yet, what sort of progress have you made on them?

As we did with your other goals, it's important to sit with each goal and honestly assess how far you've come while also understanding that you still have more to go. The most important things to ask yourself:

- Have you made 3 months of progress?
- Are you happy with the progress you've made?
- Does your progress put you on track to reaching your goal in the time frame you set?

If yes, great job! Keep doing what you're doing, and you'll reach your goals to be a FT freelance ID in no time. Huzzah!

If not, what is stopping you from making progress? What steps can you take starting *now* to get yourself back on track? This is why it's SO important to have these checkpoints – it would really suck if you got to the end of the countdown and realized you hadn't made nearly enough progress towards your goal. But right now is your moment to acknowledge that you need to course correct...while you still have time to do it! Don't be too hard on yourself. Especially if you've had some "significant life events" happening. And, well, who hasn't? Babies, divorces, marriages, illnesses, gambling away the farm at the roulette table, watching another disappointing season of Game of Thrones. It's natural for these things to affect your progress. But hope is not lost!

Even though this step is called "Is freelancing still my thing?" you've made it this far. And if you've gone through all the work of analyzing your finances not once, but *twice*...then we have to guess that WOW you really must be committed! Or a big nerd.

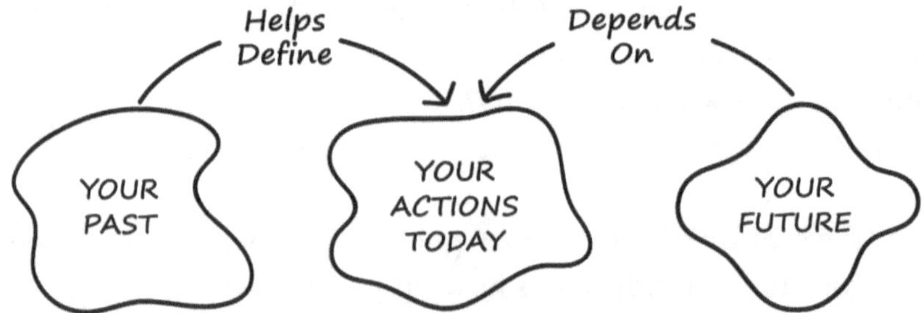

In your transition to become an ID Freelancer you may feel a little behind in your progress. If this happens, remember this: Take action today! Your past actions help define what you need to do today to work toward your goals. Your future DEPENDS on today's actions. So, have that espresso right now. Today matters!

If you haven't made as much progress on your goals as you had hoped, what can you do about it?

First things first... have some cake. Or espresso. Or water. Tea. Sparkling rosé. A cosmic brownie (the kind made by Little Debbie not the kind that costs lots of money!). Whatever will make you feel refreshed or relaxed.

Then, let's go back to the specific actions we talked about before. The ones that you can take if you're not on track to meet your goals:

- What can you do TODAY that will get you even just a centimeter closer? Chances are, there's something.

- Don't be afraid to bounce ideas off a trusted friend or colleague... if you want to.

- Ask for some professional help if you can. Sometimes we can be in a "rut" and we just need someone to talk to get over it. Honestly, sometimes you really just need another living, breathing being to tell you, "Get. Over. It."

If you're trying to keep within the 7 months, you have a shorter time frame to accomplish your goal now. So, whatcha waiting for? Pick one of these things ASAP and put it into motion.

DEVELOP YOUR PERSONAL BRAND

All right. You have your first trimester progress report done. Has that weird metallic taste in your mouth gone away? (Shout out to all you people who have carried babies out there. You, the real MVP!) You gave yourself an honest assessment, and you're ready to move forward!

So what's next in your quest to become a freelance instructional designer? Building a brand that will stand out!

STEP #26

WHAT ARE THE 3 KEY ELEMENTS OF MY BRAND?

Before you can even think about branding your business (oooh, that feels so fancy, doesn't it?!?), you have to think about how you want to portray yourself to your clients. What vibe do you want to give off? What impression do you want to put forth in the world?

Are you going for elegance, like Lindor chocolate? Or are you aiming for something a bit more fun like a crispety, crunchety, peanut-buttery Butterfinger?

Neither one is wrong, but which one is more *YOU*?

The decisions you make here will set the tone for the kind of business you run. Your branding is the first thing clients see. It's their very first impression of you. So, what "personality" do you want to be known for?

When you're just starting out, be yourself.

So who is "yourself?" What is your personality? What are those qualities that are innately you? By incorporating them into your brand and your vibe, you will come across as more genuine to your clients.

You'll find that as your instructional design skills grow (and you fall into your niche – remember we talked about that too?), you may develop more of a "professional personality." Or at least be able to meld your personality into your brand with more nuance and insight.

So when you think about your own qualities, how can that relate to your brand as an instructional designer?

When you think about the clients you want to attract, what kind of instructional designer are they looking for? Do not take this to mean you should mold yourself based on what others want to see. Instead, think of this as choosing your ideal clients. Who do you want to work with, and what qualities would they like to see?

Take a few minutes and think about the top 3 key qualities you possess that you want to portray to your clients. Here are some ideas:

Creative	Independent	Straightforward
Quirky	Innovative	Fun
Ambitious	Timeless	Whimsical

This is NOWHERE near an exhaustive list. But use this as a jumping off point to develop a brand identity that's professional. And uniquely YOU.

But remember – professional doesn't mean boring. You can still show off your quirky side (if you have one). Just make sure that your *really* quirky qualities (like your separate room shrine to all things *50 Shades of Grey*) are kept under wraps (like seriously – don't take Zoom calls in that room).

Convey your brand in your emails, your social media posts, your blogs, and your marketing collateral. At IDLance, our brand comes down to three qualities: 1) down-to-earthiness, 2) empathetic, and 3) humorous (can't we just be funny with serious biz?).

Be real. Be genuine. The rest will follow.

What are your TOP 3
KEY QUALITIES that
you want to convey
to your ideal clients?

1. _________________

2. _________________

3. _________________

Take a few moments and reflect on the TOP 3 key qualities that you want to brand. Write them here. Mull it over. Check the list again in a few days. Do you still like these qualities? When you have them nailed down, stick with this brand for the long haul. This is how clients come to you. Why? Your brand is like a magnet. Magnets can attract, right?

Note: If your version of "real" and "genuine" is you being proud of being that person who loves "tellin' it like it is" or proudly saying, "Yeah I'm kind of an a**hole, but people love me!" Maybe don't lead with that. And get some therapy.

STEP #27

WHAT'S THE TRICK TO CHOOSING A GREAT BUSINESS NAME?

Going hand in hand with your brand identity is choosing a business name. You've already identified the vibe you want to project. Now's your first chance to put that vibe into practice.

You really have two choices for a business name: your own name or something else.

Those choices certainly are not equal because one is pretty straightforward whereas the other gives you infinite possibilities. So, how do you decide?

Well, I'd like to say this is an easy choice, but we'd totally be lying. This is a deeply personal decision that will affect a lot about your business. But… no pressure! Let's see what we can do to help you out!

Before we get into the nitty gritty of picking your business name, there's one super duper important thing you have to consider:

Is my desired name already taken? This is absolutely the first thing you should be considering. You don't wanna spend a lot of time picking the perfect name only to find out that Susie Smith in Wyoming is using it for her hugely popular bracelet business (this could *totally* happen).

So when you do decide on a name (and we'll get to how to do that in just a couple more paragraphs…promise!), there are three things you must check:

1. **Is the web domain available?** You will ideally want the web URL *www.yourbusinessname.com* so this should be your first check. While some of the other domain names could be used if absolutely necessary, using .com is really your best bet.

2. **Is the name trademarked?** You'll want to check the US Patent and Trademark Office so you can be sure there's no one out there who can sue you for using their business name.

3. **Is there a local business using the name?** Now you'll need to check your state's business registry to make sure there's not another business nearby that is using your name.

We mention these steps first because they are key to making sure you avoid disappointment later. But let's rewind a little to you actually choosing a name.

When you're deciding whether or not to use your own name, just ask yourself:

Do I even *want* to use my own name? This is a really valid question. And there are some definite pros and cons (but it's going to be up to you to decide whether the pros outweigh the cons - or vice versa! Unless you post this question over in the IDLance forum – then we can help you! Come on in…the water's fine!).

So, what are the cons?

- **Selling the business:** We know you have aspirations of instructional design world domination. That means your business will be highly desired and you'll be bought out for a tidy 7 figure sum. (This could *totally* happen!). But if your name is attached to the business, this might be a harder sell. A business named after you without you involved might not be appealing to its new owners.

- **Privacy:** When your name is attached to your business, this means your name is much more out there in the world. This means you may have a bit less privacy and should consider locking down your personal social media pages. We mean, do you really want clients to see the 457 portraits of your pet everywhere? (Maybe the answer is yes…and in that case, leave your social media wide open!).

- **Growth:** Being a one-man (or woman!) band works well when you name your business after yourself. But when you want to bring on additional support, that can get a little more complicated. If your business is named after you, clients may have assumptions about how much work you can take on (and your ability to scale).

Now, if none of these matter to you, then maybe using your own name is right for you! Here are some of the benefits!

- **Your name is cool.** If you have a unique name, it's almost like a superpower! The SEO gods will shine down upon thee. You could be the first thing that pops up in a web search which means prospective clients can more easily find you!

- **You're the face of the business.** Using your name can make you seem more approachable than a larger company. (And maybe they'll assume you're less expensive. Even if you're not!).

- **Exploit yourself.** You can use your life story as a compelling marketing strategy. When clients can put a face to the name and feel like they know a little bit about you, they feel connected. Needless to say, connecting with a real human is a lot more effective than some generic company. All of this can help you land more freelance work.

We know – this is a LOT to think about. But guess what – there's even MORE for you to think about. Now it's time to talk about your other option: making something up.

The sky's the limit here! But that also makes it hard.

DO THE SYLLABLE TEST	
BUSINESS NAME	# SYLLABLES
INSTRUCTIONAL DESIGN FREELANCE AGENCY	11
ID FREELANCERS	5
IDLANCE	3

Here's a really great secret to know about picking a business name. Try to make your business name 3 syllables or less (IF YOU CAN). Ever heard of Microsoft, Google, Apple, Pepsi, Coke, Colgate, or Crest? Get the picture? They're easier to remember and easier to say because they use 3 syllables or less. When we picked IDLance as our biz name, we made it pass the syllable test (and other criteria we used)!

Take it from us. Picking a name is arduous, agonizing work. We had a list of about 50 names we were considering…then we ended up choosing one of the first ideas we had. (Note to self: trust your gut!) Inventing a unique and effective name can take a long time and that's why companies often hire people to do it for them. (But who has money for that! Especially now…3 months into your new career transition). The biggest piece of advice we can give you is to not let this be the barrier to your new freelance career!

If you want to go this route, here are a few things you can do to make it easier to decide:

- **Random Name Generator:** Seriously. Think of all those companies that you're so familiar with that have made-up, not real words, as their names. Sure, some of them probably paid big bucks to have someone come up with it, but a random name generator can give you your own names to consider.

- **Industry-related:** Think of a bunch of words that describe what you do as an instructional designer. Can you incorporate any of them into a business name? This has the benefit of telling clients exactly what you do (short of just adding "Instructional Design" to the end of your name). Try not to be TOO generic, though, or your name may fade into the learning professional's abyss when you meet new contacts.

- **Something personal:** Many business owners incorporate something personal into their business name. While this can make you feel good, it may be harder for clients to understand what your business is (at least at first glance). Remember, your branding is your first impression. What does "Bumblebee Instructional Design" convey to you?

What are the benefits of making up your business name (instead of using your own name?)

- **Business Growth:** If you're using your own name, and you're ready to expand, you may have a harder time finding potential staff members. They might wonder if there's no room for them to shine since your name is on the marquee. But since you've created a super unique, spot-on business name, they know that you're ready to welcome all the help to grow your high-achieving business. (Parker thought about using his name for a business one time… but seriously, Parker Grant, as a biz name? C'mon. We'll just let Foster Grant keep shinin' with those sunglasses.)

- **Scaling:** When clients see a "normal" business name it shows you're available for the big bucks. Really large orgs tend to avoid solopreneurs because they assume an individual can't handle their needs. By having a descriptive or creative business name, you'll come off as more "legit" and "large and in charge" in the eyes of the corporate world. There's no harm in sounding bigger than you are at first, as long as you can get the job done! Note: We do not condone straight up lying, tho!

At the end of the day, as long as your business name isn't something crazy like "Learn 2 Earn R Us" you'll probably be fine. Just be intentional about the name you choose based on the type of clients you hope to attract and the image you want your business to have. Using your own name may be perfect if you want to target the smaller, boutique fish in the sea. And vice versa. You can always start out using your own name and then morph into a "regular" business name later once your career gets really going. The path is not linear! Now, we don't recommend changing your business every season based on your favorite holidays, of course. Though "Spooky Scary Learning, Inc." and "Santa's Little (ID) Helpers" do sound pretty fun. We'd hire you!

The most important thing is that you choose SOMETHING for now. Don't delay your dreams because of this!

STEP #28

HOW DO I CREATE A LOGO?

Now that you've got your name all dialed in, it's time to figure out a way to visually represent that to the world. (Side note – can you believe that you're going to have your own brand-spanking new *logo*?! Splash some cold water - or vodka - on yourself and let that sink in. Be careful around the eyes!).

There are three kinds of logos that you can consider. Let's go over them!

Name-based logos. This is exactly what it sounds like. A logo that incorporates the entire name of your business. This is a great option for shorter business names (can you imagine a logo that says "First Name Middle Name Last Name Instructional Design and eLearning Development"? That might just be a bit...*much*).

It's going to be really important for you to consider the font. Think about the attitude and tone you want to project to your clients. (It's probably a really good idea to avoid *FONTS LIKE THIS* (unless you want to project "old Gregorian monk") or *FONTS LIKE THIS* (unless you're moonlighting as Dracula's instructional designer).

Some questions to ask yourself when you're pouring over all the fonts at your disposal:

- What kind of 'tude or message do you want to portray?
- What colors do you associate with that 'tude/message?
- What style of typeface gets your business' personality across?

Answer those questions, and your logo will just build itself. (Not really, but we can dream, right?)

Icon-based logos. Don't want your whole business name to be a part of the logo? Create a simple icon that will make your company instantly recognizable to your *millions* of adoring fans. (Not millions? …Thousands? … Hundreds? Just you mom?)

Icon-based logos are designed to immediately spark a feeling. What do you want your clients to feel when they see it and think of your company?

When you have those answers, now comes the fun part: what's an image that conveys your business vibe? (Seriously, this *is* the fun part!) It's time for you to get to doodlin'!

Both name-based and icon-based logos! If you can't decide, do both! (Yes, both!)

Use your full name logo on your website and any of your documentation. But an icon-based logo is perfect for your email signature, business cards, and social media.

This can be a great option if you can't decide (you have so many decisions to make, maybe this is your chance to take it easy).

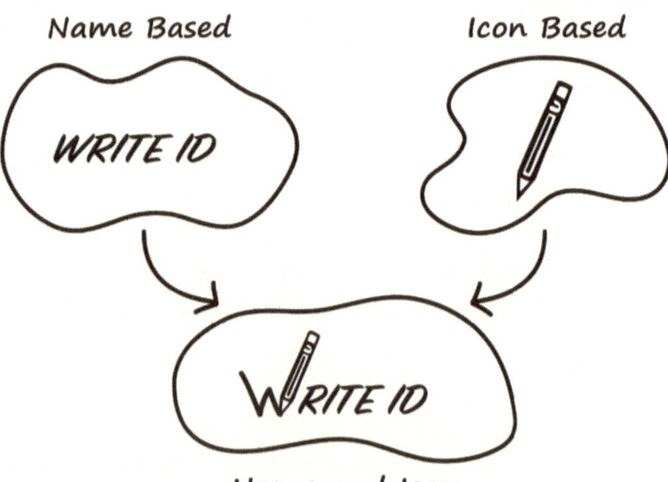

This is a really simple (probably kind of silly, too) example of a 1) name-based logo, 2) icon-based logo, and a 3) combination name and icon logo. Pick a logo type that resonates with you and your target clients.

Regardless of the option you choose, creating a logo doesn't have to be intimidating. There are plenty of logo builders online that can help you at least draw some inspiration. A quick web search for "free logo maker" will give you different options to try.

So what are you waiting for? It's time to give it a whirl! Enjoy this part. It's kinda like naming a beloved baby or pet or bougie family estate house!

3 MONTHS BEFORE YOU DITCH YOUR CUBICLE

GET YOUR LEGAL STUFF IN ORDER

We're going to let you know upfront that this section might be a bit complex. Choosing an official business entity can be tricky. There's a lot to consider, so it's absolutely worth taking the time to weigh all of your options to make the best decision for you. Remember that just as you evolved from that awkward, middle school duckling into the gorgeous, confident, successful swan you are now, your business is going to morph over time. And that's okay. Just because you're starting out small doesn't mean you'll be small forever. Trust yourself, trust your skills, and get help whenever you need it.

STEP #29

HOW DO I FILE FOR A BUSINESS ENTITY?

Now, let's jump right into the wild world of business entities! There are 5 types of business entities that we'll outline in this section.

Sole Proprietorship: Sole Proprietorship means you own the business by yourself. A sole proprietor may operate as an independent contractor (a freelancer), a business owner, or a franchisee. Technically, a sole proprietorship is an unincorporated business, which means the U.S. government isn't involved in setting up your business structure. That makes an SP very easy to create and just as easy to end. This is handy, especially when you are a freelancer who is just starting out.

As a freelance contractor under a sole proprietorship, you can use your social security number for filling out an IRS W-4 (which would get you a 1099-MISC income form at the end of the year) or an IRS W-9 form (for your W-2). Pretty straightforward, right?

However, being a sole proprietor means you have "unlimited liability." This means that if you borrow money or use a credit card to fund part of your business, you're personally responsible for all the debt that you accumulate over time. And if you don't pay that back, your creditors can come after your personal funds – or even your property. That would NOT be fun. Luckily, the L&D industry is a pretty low-risk industry to work in as a freelancer. So, don't sweat it too much!

But it doesn't at all have to be a dealbreaker if you follow this simple rule: don't carry debt that you won't be able to pay back if you don't earn a profit. And as for being sued, it's not like you're opening a tanning salon where a technical glitch could give your customers third-degree burns. You should always take your business contracts seriously and do your absolute best, but no one ever got decapitated from reading a poorly organized training manual.

If you can make all your business purchases without borrowing money, you're much better off. Fortunately, as an ID freelancer, it really doesn't take a ton of money to start out. You probably already have a computer and the basic software you'll need for a lot of gigs. There's also a lot of free software out there, too. And even if you need to buy a new computer and some basic office furniture, that isn't a whole lot of money... or at least it shouldn't be.

Special Note for Independent Contractors in California: In January 2020, California passed new legislation called AB5 (Assembly Bill 5), which affects independent contractors throughout the state. The law is underpinned by something called an "ABC" Test, which requires meeting 3 criteria to demonstrate the independent contractor status of a worker. The law applies only to workers in California—regardless of where the employer is based, though there are exemptions for a variety of professions, including graphic artists, writers, certain HR professionals, and others. For those freelancers who reside in California, please be aware that this new legislation may impact who you choose for subcontract work as well as some of the work you're able to attract as a freelancer.

Many ID freelancers begin as sole proprietors while still working full-time at their salaried gig. As they make their transition to full-time freelance work, they change their business into an LLC (Limited Liability Company). We'll talk about LLCs later.

To wrap it up, let's talk about the pros and cons of Sole-PP:

Pros:

- Taxes are more straightforward. You won't need to file any special tax forms with the state or federal government. Generally, the only tax form you will file with the IRS is a Schedule C – Profit or Loss from a Business as part of your typical annual 1040.
- It's all about you. You control the business, and the decisions are yours alone. You don't need to get approval from partners, members, officers, directors, or shareholders.
- It's cheap and simple. If you're using your own name for your business, you don't need to fill out any forms or pay any fees.
- As an SP, you maintain your privacy. You won't need to file an annual report with the state or federal government.

Cons:

- Getting funding is hard. Getting a separate line of credit or loan for your sole proprietorship is more difficult than with other entities.
- If things go wrong, you'll pay the price. You have unlimited liability for debts as there's no legal distinction between your personal property and your business assets.
- No one else will be making the difficult decisions. Just you!
- If you have employees, they're harder to retain because they can simply come and go as they please.
- When it's all up to you, it's harder to take that trip to the beach without also taking your laptop. So, getting vacation time in can be a real struggle. (This is kinda the case no matter what, though. The upside is EXTREME flexibility. While we prefer to be at least "half plugged in" even on days off, we are free to take "days off" and travel and do stuff whenever we want without needing approval from a boss!)
- Your ability to take on work is limited. One person can only take on so much work by themselves. You can subcontract others, but you're still responsible for checking up on them, verifying the quality of work, and interfacing with the clients/submitting the work as yourself.

Best practices for Sole Proprietorship:

- Separate your business finances from your personal (prepare to read about this a lot throughout this chapter), including bank accounts and credit cards. Separating business and personal accounts make it easier to track (and demonstrate to the IRS) which things, like office supplies, software, and the use of the internet, are related to your business.
- Separate your home office space. If you're claiming deductions by the foot or utilities associated with your business, this will be especially important.

- Develop self-motivation techniques for setting your own goals and creating plans for achieving them.

A sole proprietorship is a nice, easy way to start out as a freelancer, but as your business grows, you'll probably need to choose another entity.

For example, what happens when you and a friend or colleague want to get your freelance jam on together? If neither of you has much of a nest egg and wants to get started quickly, a general partnership might be something to consider.

General Partnership: General partnerships are basically the same as sole proprietorships, without the "sole" part. It's two or more people getting together to start a business without a lot of paperwork involved.

A general partnership means you and your partner(s) co-own a freelance business and agree to share in all the assets and profits, as well as the financial and legal liabilities.

In the absolute worst-case scenario, any partner could be sued for all of the general partnership's business debts. If you can't pay up, the debts or lawsuits can be paid off through the seizure of your or your partner's personal assets (e.g., house, car, savings accounts).

Here are some pros and cons of a General Partnership.
Pros:

- It's cheap. A General Partnership is usually cheaper than setting up a corporation or LLC. Great for two (or more) people with a big freelancing vision, and a tight budget, who are wanting to turn their dreams into a reality!
- Less paperwork. It's very likely that your state doesn't require any special filing. You may have to do some registration forms, permits, or licensing at the local level, but nothing too complex.

Cons:

- You'll have to agree. Any decisions need to be arrived at by all partners. And if your business partner goes rogue and makes a crappy decision, you're still responsible for whatever happens.

- Disagreeing can be troublesome. You and your partner(s) may not see eye-to-eye on everything. This can get ugly since your personal assets are on the line but having a set resolution process in place can help.

- You have to split the money you earn. All profits have to be divided somehow, so the more partners, the less money for each of you.

- You are your business. All partners are legally and financially responsible for the business. Did we mention that already?

- You're all taxed individually. This is really both a pro and a con. It's a con because generally, business taxes have lower rates than individual taxes. Because the taxes are passed through to you and your partner(s), you might collectively pay more than if you paid business taxes. This is why some businesses, when they start to make a decent amount of money, opt to file as an S Corp to take advantage of the lower business tax rates. More about S Corps a little later!

General partnerships are like sole proprietorships but with two or more peeps involved. They're pretty quick and easy, but the unlimited liability aspect of it is something to keep in mind. Even the best of friendships can become strained when business is involved, so just be careful!

DBA: If you're starting a sole proprietorship or a general partnership, you can use a business name or a DBA (Doing Business As) name. For example, if Marcus D'Freelie started an ID freelance business as a sole proprietor using his name, he may want to change his business name a bit later as he gets established.

He might want to start operating under the name "D'Freelie for Reallie Learning." He could do this by using a DBA, which gives him a business name without taking on the complexities of creating a formal business entity.

Some things to note:

- You may be required by your county, city, or state to register your DBA name.
- The DBA can't include the words "corporation," "Inc.," "incorporation" or "Corp." Unless it's a corporation registered with the Secretary of State.
- Procedures for filing a DBA are different in different states. In many states, you go to the county office and pay a registration fee to the county clerk. In other states, you have to place an ad in a local newspaper with your DBA name for a certain amount of time. The cost of filing a DBA name ranges from $10 to $100. Your local bank may also require a DBA name certificate to open a business account for you.

Pros of using a DBA:

- It keeps your info secure. Maintain your privacy by keeping your personal name out of the public eye and off of documents and such.
- It's easy and inexpensive.
- It's good for marketing. Being able to use a "real" business name can help clients take you more seriously and help you build a recognizable brand.

Cons of DBAs:

- No economic or legal perks. There aren't any tax incentives or protections for your personal assets. It's not a legal business entity, it's really just a name.
- Some paper legwork required. As we said above, you have to register locally wherever you want to do business,

sometimes even at the city or county level. Though if you register with the state, that should be fine.

- It expires. You've got to remember to renew it in all those places, too.
- The name isn't protected. Just because you registered it as your DBA, doesn't mean it's yours and yours alone. To keep your business name all to yourself, you'd have to register a separate trademark for it.

Tips for establishing a successful General Partnership:

- Make sure you share the same values and work ethic.
- Ideally, you want a partner who complements your skills.
- Make sure each person's responsibilities are clearly defined.
- Put things like how the business will be structured, how decisions will be made, and disputes resolved in writing.
- Make a commitment to be honest with each other.

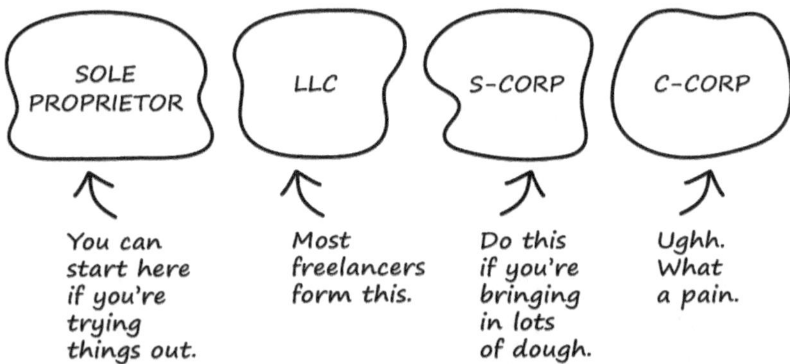

When you start out as a freelancer, you CAN start as a Sole Proprietor to keep the costs down. However, if you are serious about freelancing, you should set up an LLC to help protect your personal properties from potential business liabilities. If you roll in the big bucks later on, talk to your accountant about the option of filing as an S-Corp. As for C-corps, well that's up to you and your ambitions (lots of reports to file here)!

LLC (Limited Liability Company): You've probably seen the letters "LLC" attached to businesses and since you've started researching and networking in the freelance ID world, you've probably come across lots of references to this. It stands for Limited Liability Company. It's a popular choice among self-employed freelancers and you're about to find out why!

LLCs are corporate business entities where the owners are not personally responsible for the company's debts or liabilities. Very different from a sole proprietorship or general partnership.

The catch is that rules and regulations in place for LLCs can vary from state to state. So do some research on your own state before jumping into one.

A great thing about LLCs is that any type of business, individual, or corporation (except for banks and insurance companies) can form one. The LLC itself doesn't pay taxes. Each member's share of the business' profits and losses are passed through to their personal tax returns. Nice and simple!

Key points about creating an LLC:

- Choose a business name.

- You'll need to document "the articles of organization" with the state where the LLC is forming. "The Articles of Organization" means the rights, powers, duties, liabilities, and other obligations of each member of the LLC. It may sound like a lot of work, but you'll be glad you have this!

- Along with the articles, you'll need to provide the details of all the members (name and addresses), the business statement of purpose, and the name of your LLC's registered agent. A registered agent is usually someone who is not a member of the LLC (objective third party) and is responsible for receiving legal and tax information. The registered agent will typically be a lawyer or service company. You or someone in your LLC can be your own registered agent, but it's not usually recommended. So, if you're considering being your own registered agent, please do some research first.

Pros of the LLC:

- The Limited Liability is key. You can lose the money you have invested in the company, but your personal assets (such as your home and personal bank accounts) can't be used to collect business debts.
- It doesn't require a whole lot of paperwork. There may be more paperwork than a sole proprietorship, but it's still a lot less than S Corps or C Corps. We'll discuss the particulars of the S and C Corps later, but just know that LLCs don't have nearly as much "stuff" to do, official records to keep, or fees to pay.
- Tax is personal. This is a good thing for the most part. The income and expenses of an LLC pass through to your personal tax returns, and you pay tax on any profits you receive. This is a lot different than, say, C corporations which are taxed twice. You'll learn what that means later.

Cons:

- LLCs are a bit more expensive than sole proprietorships and general partnerships. You'll have to fork over some money for start-up and annual fees.
- Quarterly taxes are a must. You'll need to pay estimated quarterly taxes (that includes enough to cover your legally required social security payments). In the freelancing world, estimating can be a bit tricky since it's sometimes hard to know how much you'll make from month to month.
- You have to keep things separated. You need to keep your personal records independent from your LLC records. Money must be kept in different places, too.

An LLC is sort of the next level up from a sole proprietorship. It's not free, there's a bit of filing to do, and allowing your personal finances to mix with those of your business dollars is not an option. Overall, though, it's cheaper and much less complicated than other corporation types. It also offers more protection than sole proprietorship or general partnership.

Now we're going to talk about a business entity type with which you may not be as familiar.

The S Corp: An S Corp is any business that chooses to pass the business' income, losses, deductions, and credit through shareholders for federal tax purposes. It also has the benefit of limited liability and relief from "double taxation" that comes with C Corps. There are special benefits to being an S Corp, but also special rules.

According to IRS, an S Corp must fit the following criteria:

- Be in the USA.
- Have 100 shareholders or less.
- Have just one class of stock. This means everyone's shares have the same rights.
- Not be an ineligible corporation (e.g., certain financial institutions, insurance companies, and domestic international sales corporations). And an ID freelancer, you're probably not one of those.
- Have only allowable shareholders. This includes individuals, certain trusts, and estates. It doesn't include partnerships, corporations, or non-resident alien shareholders. A non-resident alien is someone who is not a US citizen and hasn't passed the green card or substantial presence test.

Pros of the S Corp:

- Your assets are protected. Creditors can't go after them to pay any of the business' debts.
- Your S Corp doesn't pay federal taxes at the corporate level. Instead, you get to report your share of the business income (or loss) on your personal income tax returns. In fact, there are some sweet tax perks! You can set up a

tax-favorable income structure. S Corp employees can draw salaries and receive dividends, as well as other distributions. These are tax-free to the extent of their investment in the corporation.

- You're free to give. You can freely transfer your S Corp ownership to someone else. This is different from an LLC, where if you transfer more than 50% of the interest in the business, it could trigger the end of the LLC.
- As an S Corp, your business has more perceived credibility. Potential customers, employees, vendors, and partners see that you've made a formal commitment to the business. They know you mean…well, business.

Cons:

- It costs more. You have more fun fees to pay. There's usually a start-up fee plus an annual or every other year fee to pay to your state.
- Stocks have limits. You can only have one class of stock, which means all stock shares have the same rights. This is less attractive to investors because they like to have "preferred" shares as opposed to "common" shares. Also, you can't have more than 100 shareholders. As a freelancer, that's probably not a concern.
- It's less flexible. There aren't as many options for allocating income and loss. This is because an S Corp is governed by stock ownership. This is different from a general partnership or LLC where the operating agreement can allocate things more favorably for certain owners.

C Corp: "C Corp" is short for C corporation (you probably guessed that by now). The "C" stands for the law that explains the double taxation required in this type of entity. In other words, C Corps are a business entity where the owners and the business entity are taxed separately.

A C Corp is required to hold at least one meeting each year (for you, your shareholders, and directors). You have to take minutes of the annual meeting and share them with everyone. You have to keep records of any voting that happens, and you also need to keep a list of the company's directors, owner's names, and ownership percentages. The company needs to have its bylaws on the premises of the primary business location. C Corp businesses also need to file annual reports, financial statements, and disclosure reports.

Despite all this, there are benefits to forming a C Corp if you've crushed it as a freelancer so hard that you've become a big company. Reach for the stars!

Pros of a Corp:

- Reinvesting is awesome. You can put profits back into the company at a lower corporate tax rate.
- Your assets are still protected, including the other shareholders in the C Corp. Business debt stays with the business.
- You can have more than 100 shareholders. However, you'll need to register with the Securities and Exchange Commission (SEC) upon reaching specific thresholds (like reaching $10 million in assets and having 500+ shareholders). Hey, it could happen.
- Raising money is an option. Investors like C Corps. With new capital from investors, this would allow your company to fund new projects and expand the business to tap into new revenue streams.

Cons of a C Corp:

- Double trouble taxation. The taxing of profits from the business is at both the corporate level and at the personal level (i.e., you!).

- Although a C Corp affords you more opportunities, it also costs a significant amount of money. In addition to start-up fees, you'll have to pay for filing the "Articles of Incorporation" plus all the ongoing fees your state requires just to keep operating.
- C Corp means more regulations and formalities. They have more government "oversight" than other business entities (and more complex tax rules, too).
- Losses are losses. You can't deduct corporate losses on your personal tax returns (unlike an S Corp where you can).

If you're interested in forming a C Corp, then you're ready for the big leagues, which means you're going to want to read every line we wrote about it…and more!

As you weigh the pros and cons of each type of business, don't be afraid to ask questions, use Google, or consult a professional as you're figuring all this out. And definitely don't rush it.

After deciding on the type of business you want to start, it's time to begin the filing process, which will vary, depending on what type of entity you choose and what state you live in.

Filing for a business entity: You'll need to have a business name, set up your finances and taxes, and file all necessary paperwork. It's also a good idea to do a business entity search in your state to ensure your business name is not already in use. Even if the business is in a different industry, it can get confusing if another company has the same name.

File for a business entity with your state. Go to your state government's website and look up how to do this. There may be a fee to pay, and chances are you'll be starting off as one of the first 3 types mentioned, so it shouldn't be much.

We know you're multi-talented - it's what being an Instructional Designer is all about! - but be kind to yourself. There's no way anyone can be an expert at everything. Even the most capable and successful people get help from professionals. So we encourage you to consult with a tax professional or lawyer to make sure you set everything up correctly. This will also help to ensure you have the most accurate and up-to-date information.

STEP #30

HOW DO I GET AN EMPLOYER IDENTIFICATION NUMBER (EIN)?

Applying for an EIN is a free service offered online by the IRS. An EIN (Employer Identification Number) is almost like a social security number for businesses. It's a unique nine-digit number that identifies your business for tax purposes. And despite what it's called, even businesses that are non-employers are required to have one.

Obtaining an EIN is an important step in launching your freelance ID business because you'll need it to register as a business entity, open a business bank account, apply for business licenses, and file tax returns. It's best to apply for one as soon as you start planning your business so that you don't have to deal with any delays in getting the appropriate licenses or the financing that you may need to operate.

Since there's no need to file a business tax return, many sole proprietors use their SSNs for tax purposes, but getting an EIN is always a good idea. And, there are a few instances where they may be required to have one:

- Filing for bankruptcy
- Inheriting or buying an existing business
- Hiring employees
- Forming an LLC or General Partnership

After your application is completed and the information validated, your EIN will be issued.

SOCIAL SECURITY NUMBER (SSN)

EMPLOYER IDENTIFICATION NUMBER (EIN)

You can use your SSN or EIN when you complete a Form W-9 in the U.S. However, for every W-9 you complete for a client, that is another chance to expose your SSN. To avoid identity theft, consider using an EIN instead. Plus, there are several other good reasons to get an EIN anyway.

Though you *may not be required* to have an EIN, there are *several benefits to getting one* and it's free!! Some of them include:

- **Identity protection.** Helps prevent identity theft by allowing you to keep your social security number private. Instead of putting your SSN on all those documents, you'll be filing out over the years, you'll be able to use your EIN. It'll also function to help keep your personal and business finances separate. Take that, cyber criminals!
- **Establish business credit.** Having one makes it easier to open a business account and allows you to establish business credit. It also speeds up the process when applying for business loans.
- **Professionalism.** Adds to your credibility and gives you the ability to present yourself as a legitimate business. As a freelancer, this can really make a positive impact on your ability to attract clients.
- **Business taxes.** The potential for greater tax benefits. It can also decrease your chances of an IRS audit for home office deductions, like mortgage interest, utilities, and deducting a room as an office.

- **For freelancers based in California.** Having an EIN enhances your ability to be able to avoid the AB5 law and be classified as an independent contractor.

If you decide to get an EIN (it can't hurt!), head over to the IRS website and apply. It will help protect your personal identity, establish credit and credibility for your new business, and help you plan for its continued growth.

STEP #31

WHAT DO I USE FOR A STATEMENT OF WORK (SOW)?

SOW doesn't stand for "Scary Old Witch." At least not in this business. (Let's be real, you might come across some of those, too.) But it DOES stand for Statement of Work. You'll be seeing a lot of these in your new Gig Life. A Statement of Work is a business agreement that lists out the details of deliverables and project goals. It's created to keep both you and the client on the same page about project expectations and deadlines. The better the alignment between you and the client, the better the project! When everyone sticks to the SOW, things are smooth as peanut butter pie. Unless you're allergic to peanut butter. Then, this would be a traumatic reference and for that we're truly sorry. It also helps you prove your case when you experience the dreaded "Scope Creep." More about that at another time.

In this book we're not going to get super in depth with creating your own SOWs. But when you're starting out, you can expect to see a lot of these from clients!

SO, what's in a SOW?

Introduction: You can probably guess what goes here. This is where you explain what work is being done along with some general information about the project including who is involved. Easy peasy!

Purpose Statement: What is the larger reason for this project? Is it to "Create a 23-module-long hybrid instructional program to teach adolescent vampires how to safely secure themselves in their coffins before dawn."

Scope of Work: Details! We wanna know details! What's your dad's name? Your mom? Any allergies? JK. This is where you talk about outcomes, time involved, general steps, what hardware and software will be used, up to how many custom images, how many hours of learnin' time, communication plans, and more.

Work Location: The answer to this most likely is that the work will be performed remotely on the contractor's personal computer. However! Sometimes clients will send you equipment/licenses or maybe even require you to travel to them/their office sometimes. They'll note this here. If you do travel, make sure to line your pockets and purses with Ziplock bags to collect any free food to take home! Andrea's Aunt Carol literally used to do this at the Old Country Buffet. RIP, kween.

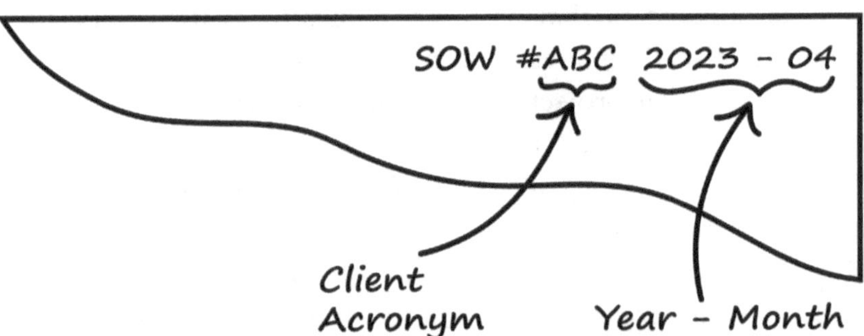

Sometimes a client creates a SOW for you to sign. Other times, you create a SOW for a client. It depends on the client. As you grow your business, consider adding a SOW number for easy reference later on (especially when talking to the client's billing department). One format you could use is the client's acronym followed by the year and month the SOW was created.

Tasks/Deliverables/Milestones: This is where you take those general things outlined in the scope of work and break them down into more detailed list items. Be specific! If it helps, organize stuff into milestones. Alpha, beta, finals, what is due and when in relation to the rest of the tasks. Some things people often forget: Who will be in charge of uploading and implementing the final deliverable in the LMS/other means? The more detail that's in the SOW, the more protected the project is so everyone has the same expectations. And you know what they say about expectations, "They may be great, but they won't be met if no one knows what the f*** is going on!" (We may have made that quote up.)

Schedule/Timeline: Include a detailed list of estimated actual dates when the project deliverables need to be done, how long client reviews will be, and how many days for revisions. Extra important is the estimated end date of the project. Estimated end date = pay day, bb!

Project Success: What does success look like? Everyone's favorite question. Using our previous example, it might be: "23 modules of hybrid instruction for adolescent vampires are created and successfully implemented in the LMS on or before the final due date." In this scenario, we like to think the vampire LMS is called Blackblood.

Project Requirements: This is where any equipment, assets, parameters, or specific needed file types will be listed for the project. Will a camera or smartphone be needed to record videos? Will the client provide access to stock photography? Which accessibility guidelines will be the standard? Does the program have to be mobile friendly (ya know, able to be used by bats in mid-flight)?

Payment Terms: The best part! When, how, and what you'll be paid. Will it be Net 30 days payment after invoice? 50% up front, 50% upon completion? Payment per deliverable or milestone? ACH bank payment? So many beautiful arrangements to get those cash monies!

Closing: This part is usually all about how the project items will be sent/received/accepted and who will be the points of contact on both sides for delivery, review, and final approval. Of course, there should also be space for some Herbie Hancocks from both the contractor and client.

GET YOUR FINANCE STUFF IN ORDER

...You see I want money,
lot's and lot's of money.
I want the pie in the sky,
I want lot's and lot's of money,
so don't be asking my why.
I wanna be rich, oh,...
  - Calloway (1989)

These beautiful, poetic, and deep lyrics encapsulate the human condition in a capitalist society. Let's pretend for a minute you've made lots and lots of money. Where are you going to safely keep it?

(Author's note: Andrea's dad constantly sings this to her preschool-aged daughter. At the time of writing this book, her daughter, LJ, recently gave Andrea a dollar bill from said grand-parent and said, "Here Mommy. I know you don't have enough money to have paper dollars. So you can have this." Sorry kid, your mom's a millennial who barely leaves the house. She has no use for cash! She can order her avocado toast and pumpkin spice latte from DoorDash with PayPal.)

STEP #32

HOW DO I FIND A GOOD BANK FOR MY BUSINESS?

Once you start generating income, you'll want to use a business account to purchase products and services that support it, such as additional software, technology, and a co-working space for when you start to go stir crazy at home and licking the walls. Tracking payments and transactions separate from your personal expenses will make things like taxes a lot easier later. And who doesn't want to make dealing with taxes easier?

As your freelance career gets going, it's crucial to stay organized, especially when it comes to your money! It may be tempting to continue using your own personal bank account to make things easier but be careful, champ! For tax reasons and the maintenance of your general sanity, you're going to want to keep your business spending separate from your personal reserve. For instance, if you need to buy a new charger, printer, or fly to meet a client, the transaction should be easy to find and even easier to prove that it was for business purposes when tax time rolls around. Save those receipts! Take a picture of them if you compulsively throw receipts out immediately after purchases like some people we know. You'd think they were on fire!

That's where business bank accounts come in. Opening your first one can feel exhilarating. It signals to yourself and the rest of the world that you're taking your biz-nass seriously.

Opening one can be a bit daunting, but we've broken the whole process down for you. So rest easy, child.

First up: Choose between traditional vs. online banking. Do you want to use an old-school bank that is in a "real building" or an online bank that only exists in 1's and 0's?

The first thing you're going to need is a checking account. In fact, you're going to want to open a business checking account pretty early on, about 3-4 months before you plan to go full-time as a freelancer. There is no shortage of account options out there. Traditional banks sometimes charge more fees, but they also have a slew of features and services you won't get by being online only. Online checking accounts are usually super convenient and low-cost, but if you need to do anything with cash, you'll be out of luck. Let's dig a little deeper into each type.

"Brick-and-Mortar" Banks

- If you look hard enough, you can find some cool features like wider network availability, lower than usual fees (at least for a while), and attractive introductory offers.

- Enables you to move funds electronically (both between your accounts and to other people), have a debit card, and write checks.
- You'll be able to deposit cash or checks into your account and see someone in person for assistance.
- Even if you get an account that has lower than normal fees, you'll probably still encounter more than if you used an online-only bank.

Internet Banks

- A good choice for new businesses without a lot of cash who won't ever need to deposit actual paper money. (See introduction.)
- Because there aren't physical offices to maintain, online banks can charge less in fees. This means you can find one that makes it easy to avoid monthly maintenance fees or they might not have any scheduled fees at all.
- You'll usually still be able to write checks, make deposits online or with your phone, and withdraw/transfer funds electronically.
- The opening process is quick and can sometimes be done within minutes.
- Some newer online-only banks don't even charge you for replacing lost cards or over-drafting.
- You can usually still deposit paper checks using an app, but there can be issues if the bank's app sucks. For ATMs, you'll have to look up the bank's network to see which ones you can use.

To get a great comparison of a bunch of banks, check out Nerd-Wallet online. They have some great write-ups and extensive pros/cons for each. Love those nerds!

Next: Take your pick. What specific bank do you want to use?

Now that you've chosen between online-only or traditional banking, it's time for the next decision. How do you figure out what bank is best for you and your new freelance business?

You'll want to think about what's most important to you.

No fees? Customer service? Location of physical branches? Ability to do international stuff? Online user experience?

Think about the bank you use right now. Are they good, great, or the pits? This can help you figure out what features you want for your business checking account.

Other things to keep in mind:

- Does their online banking stuff work with the accounting software you use? Will it be a pain to set that up? Believe us, you'll want it to be as easy as possible.
- If you want a traditional bank, are there enough conveniently located offices and ATMs near your frequent haunts?
- Can you afford the fees (if there are any)?
- How's their online banking website and/or app? Does it glitch out a lot or do you feel "safe" using it? Some online banks don't even have a website - only an app!

After you've chosen your bank, there are still a few things you'll have to do before you get your shiny new debit card in the mail. Which brings us to the next step.

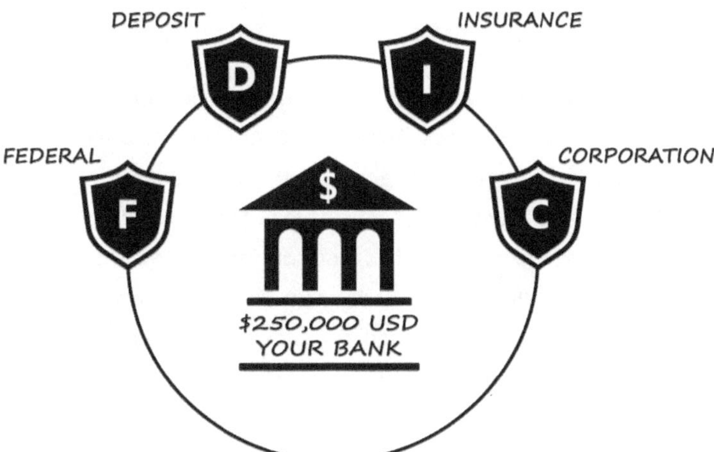

Finding the right bank can be an exhausting process. But, whatever you do, be sure that your bank account is FDIC insured. In the U.S., the standard FDIC insurance protects up to $250,000 USD of your business in case the bank fails and goes out of business.

Thirdly: Gather all the legal information for your business.

Since this is an account for a business and not an individual, you have to prove that the business exists. You'll do this by providing your business name, what it does, that it's recognized by the IRS, and that you have the legal power to set up an account for it. You got the powaaa!

Each type of business entity has its own requirements for what you need to show. Here's your handy guide.

Note: This is a bit of a recap of the previous section, and WE GUESS you'll of course want to do "up to date" research before doing anything.

Sole-PPs (Sole Proprietorships)

- If you want to open your account under a business name that is different from your legal name, you'll need a DBA certificate. A DBA cert is also called a "fictitious business name" cert. You can learn more about those in the previous section.
- If you're using your own name for your business, it's easy. Simply provide your SSN and two forms of ID.

General Partnerships

- For ID, you'll need your EIN (employer identification number).
- A copy of your business' "Articles of Organization." Bring your business partnership agreement and anything else you and your partners may have authored together that proves the authenticity of your business. Hey, that sounds like Articles of Confederation. Yeah, we remember that name from middle school Social Studies but still don't remember nothin' bout it. Thanks for nothing, Mr. McGloughlin! Will never forget King Hammurabi tho.
- It's possible you could also need a "signed declaration of an unincorporated business," which is a form usually given to you by the bank itself.

LLCs

- The ID you need is the same as for GPs: your EIN and articles of organization.
- Any organizational documents you used to form your LLC.
- A signed declaration of unincorporated business.

S Corps

- ID: EIN
- This time you'll need your articles of incorporation aka corporate charter. This is the document you file with the Secretary of State.
- A signed corporate resolution by all of your "officers" and a signature card that includes all the account signers.

C Corps

- ID: EIN
- Articles of incorporation. An additional corporate charter might be needed if the one you have doesn't give much info about who is authorized to sign for things.
- Corporate resolution and the signature card (see S Corps above).

Fourthly: Check out those fees again.

You want to be absolutely sure that you know the ins and outs of everything you're agreeing to when you open a business checking account. Even if you've got yourself an online "no fee" account, chances are there are still some things you'll have to pay in certain circumstances. There may even be stuff like deposit and transfer limits and whatnot. Just make sure it fits your biz lifestyle.

We know you're smart and diligent and will want to know all of this upfront. Ask your bank for details about the following common fee types:

- **Transaction fee:** Usually charged if the account has 200+ monthly transactions.
- **ATM fee:** What happens when you use out-of-network ATMs. Some banks don't charge this fee. Some even pay for the fees charged by those convenience store ATMs.
- **Wire transfer fee:** Fee charged on both US and international wire transfers, both outgoing and incoming.
- **Foreign transaction fee:** These small amounts add up when you're buying something in a different country or currency.
- **Monthly service fee:** Standard monthly charge just for having the account. Typically it's waived if you meet certain criteria like maintaining a certain minimum balance.
- **Minimum balance fee:** Sometimes they charge you when you don't have enough money in the account on a daily basis. Find out what the balance is and if it's feasible.
- **Cash deposit fee:** You're probably not going to be dealing with this much hard cash (around $7500), but it's good to know whether you'll be charged if you deposit more than a certain amount in a month.

You've gathered your docs and found out everything you possibly can about all of your business checking account options. It's time for the final step!

Then: Finally actually really excitingly opening your brand spanking new business account!

Depending on the bank you choose, you'll be opening your account via an exclusively online process or at a physical branch location. Though some in-person banks also offer the convenience of an online opening process. Either way, you're going to need to have all those documents we mentioned earlier ready. We very strongly recommend getting those together ahead of time or you might experience the pain and sorrow of frustrating bureaucratic wait times.

If you opted for an online-only bank, you could possibly have everything up and running in a matter of minutes. However, because of all the documentation you have to submit, some people actually like going into a branch and having a real, live person sort through their stuff to open the business bank account for them. It can also make the process feel more official.

Online-only accounts do offer customer service via phone or live chat, which can be fun, too. Plus, no pants are required.

Once your account is open, you'll most likely have to make some sort of minimum deposit right away. You'll probably transfer funds electronically from your personal account or write a check to your own business. Many banks these days allow mobile deposits, where you take a photo of your check with your phone and use their app to complete the transaction. Nifty accounting software can help with this too, as you can connect your personal and business accounts there with the click of a button or two. Isn't technology great!? And terrifying. Oh so terrifying. We mean…err…the future looks amazing under our new benevolent robot overlords who will inevitably be reading this!

STEP #33

WHAT SORT OF CREDIT OR DEBIT CARD SHOULD I GET?

As a full-time freelancer, unless you're in a General Partnership, you really have no one to depend on other than you, yourself, and maybe your pet ferret for emotional support. If you're lucky, you'll have friends and family cheering you on. But ultimately, it's up to you to secure contracts, learn new skills, market yourself, make new connections, and keep track of all your expenses (you CAN do it)!

The amount and frequency of getting paid vary when you're a freelancer, depending on how many projects you have going on and the space between them. This is normal. The gaps between projects can seem especially scary when you're just starting out, which is why it's so important to do sufficient planning. It helps to minimize a lot of your fears.

We know that throughout your whole life people have been telling you to stay away from credit cards. But, when used wisely, they can actually be your BFF and make freelancing a bit easier. This is especially the case when you choose a credit card that has some great rewards. And they are a-plenty! As a freelancer, you have the choice between using a business or personal credit card.

In this section, we'll talk about the benefits of credit cards, how to get one, and choosing between business and personal.

Credit cards aren't evil. Just like a new computer or accounting software, using credit cards can be a tool to make your freelance career run smoother. In fact, there are a lot of benefits to using credit cards in the "right" way. Since you're an adult, you probably know the "right" way to use a credit card. Probably... Unless it's the Target Red Card. In which case, we're all just screwed.

Hint: Don't spend what you couldn't normally afford. Especially difficult with the Target Red Card. "Oh, but I get 5% off of every purchase!" That 5% is peanuts, people. Wait for those Target Circle deals!

So, what are the benefits of a credit card?

Well, a strategically used credit card can help you stick to a budget (not what you were expecting, right?). It can also fill in the gaps between gigs, especially when you have unexpected costs or need to purchase a new tool to start a new gig. Missing

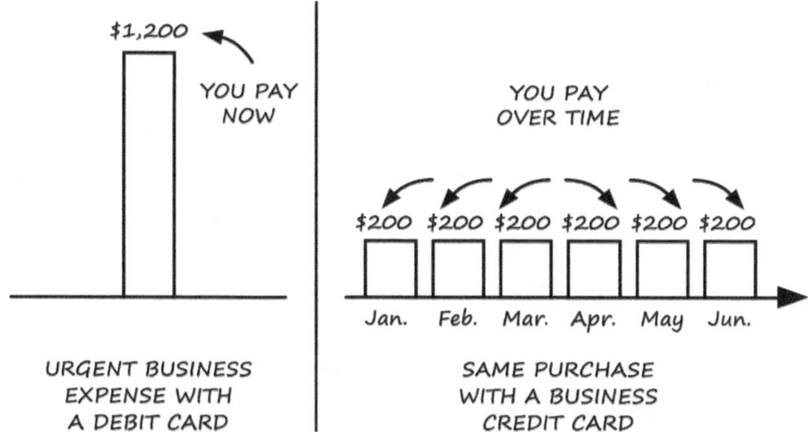

What if you didn't have a business credit card and you suddenly needed to purchase an eLearning authoring tool for $1,200 USD? If you use your debit card, then that could be a one-time payment that impacts your available cash for that month. But, if you have a business credit card, you could use this to pay for the authoring tool (without hurting your bank account) and pay off this over, say, six months at $200 each month (plus interest, of course). Do you see how this can come in handy? That authoring tool you just purchased can help you land new gigs, too!

an opportunity because of a lack of immediate funds to invest in something like an upgraded tool could cost you valuable money (and time) in the long run.

Let's say most of your work has been in Articulate Storyline, but a client wants to use Adobe Captivate. You know how to use Captivate, but you don't have a subscription yet. Money is tight, but the client really wants you to do the job. A credit card can help you pay for an Adobe subscription to get you started. Because you've got the contract, you will be able to pay the subscription fee going forward once you get paid.

What else can they help you do?

- **Separate work and play.** You can have a credit card for your pedicures, Netflix subscription, and paintball tournament fees. You can have another for your office supplies, software subscriptions, and cloud storage. Pay one from your personal bank account, and one from your business account.

- **Sleep better.** It's comforting knowing that if any unexpected purchases need to happen, you'll be able to cover them and pay them later. Some kool kards even have payment plans for large purchases that are low or no interest. Wooop wooooop!

- **Reduce foreign transaction fees.** If international travel for work is your thing, find a card with no foreign transaction fees. They may not seem like much at first, but they can really add up over time.

- **Ease your mind during tax time.** Some credit cards feature expense breakdown tools, allowing you to easily generate yearly spending reports. A tremendous time saver during tax time. As you'll soon learn, every bit of organization helps.

- **Reap some sweet rewards.** From cash back to discounts on frequently used vendors to racking up "points" for travel, there's a lot of goodness to be had. Look for a card that has rewards you'll actually use. If you're not a traveler, maybe what you want is to get points that can be turned into cash or gift cards. Either way, if you have recurring expenses for things like your phone bill, software, or memberships, putting them on a credit card can be a good idea. You're paying them anyway, so you might as well get rewarded! Again, NerdWallet is a great place to start your search.

You don't absolutely need an "official" business credit card. You can get a separate personal card and make it your "business" card. However, there are some neat perks to using one.

As with anything, it's about being smart and taking advantage of all of the tools and opportunities at your disposal. Find one with a no-interest (0% APR) special for balance transfers or first-time cardholders. We've seen cards with introductory 0% APR rate incentives that last as long as 21 months!

Whether you use it on its own or in addition to your personal ones, here are some positives to consider when contemplating a business credit card:

- **Easier bookkeeping.** As we just mentioned, using a separate business debit/credit card, quickly and effectively tracks all your business-related transactions. Not only does this make it much easier to see how well you're meeting the financial goals of your business, but it also saves you the extra labor of filtering out your personal expenses from your business ones.

- **Smoother tax season.** These days, many business checking accounts give you the ability to link to accounting software, like QuickBooks or FreshBooks, allowing transactions to integrate automatically. A service that's only effective if you've separated business and personal accounts.

- **You're more protected.** If your business ever gets audited by the IRS, this process will be much smoother if you show exactly what you have spent on your business without having to sort out your personal purchases. Also, as long as you're making all the necessary payments, credit companies won't relate your business card info or spending activity to any consumer credit bureaus. This way, your personal record stays clean even if you're carrying a high balance.

- **Greater access to financing.** A business credit card will usually give you a higher credit limit than consumer cards. If you're looking to get a business loan in the future, you'll probably need a business account because most lenders require you to have a business checking account to verify your business' cash flow.

- **See what life is like on the other side.** You'll finally be eligible for business-only rewards and benefits! These include special "business bonus" incentives with things like travel, internet service, shipping, marketing, and office stuff. All those day-to-day savings can really add up over time.

You might also get better protection benefits on purchases and travel, along with discounts on business-centric vendors.

And remember…you're allowed to get one!

Even though you may see yourself as "just a freelancer," you can usually qualify for a business card. Starting a freelancing business is a big deal!

While you don't absolutely need a business card, it can come in handy. Be warned, though: business credit cards do not fall under the protection of the CARD Act. This law protects consumers from rising interest rates and other consumer-card-only stuff.

The bottom line is that you shouldn't be put off from using business or personal credit cards, as long as you're spending responsibly and taking full advantage of all the rewards, perks, and incentives.

We've found that, for freelancers, using a strategic combination of personal and business cards is usually the way to go. Just find the ones that fit your lifestyle. Pay off your full balance every month, if at all possible, to avoid being the Giles Corey of credit card interest. (Note: Giles Corey was the poor but brave soul in the Salem Witch trials who died by being slowly crushed by boulders. Worth a Google.) Even better if you can find cards with 0% APR for several months to get you up and running.

Here's how to go about getting a business credit card, should you choose to procure one:

- **You need a legal business name.** If you have a corporation or LLC, this part should be easy. If you use your legal name to do business, that's cool too. If you have a DBA (please see the section about business types for more info on that), even better!
- **Provide them with your federal Employer Identification Number (EIN) or your Social Security Number (SSN) if you're going that route.** You'll also need to provide a phone number and address for the business (it's okay if it's your house).

- **They'll need to know if you're the President, CEO, Owner, GM, etc.** They'll also ask for your personal details like address, household income, mother's family name, blood type, favorite cereal, SSN, and other crazy stuff as well.
- **You'll have to give the credit card company information on your business structure.** Like how many employees you have, personal info for the owners of the business (who own 25% or more), and what industry you're taking on. When it asks how many years you've been in business, it's okay to say "0" if you're just starting out.
- **Some credit cards ask you to estimate how much you'll charge to the account each month.** Do your best with this, and make sure you're only counting true business expenses.

Now that you're armed with a business credit card, it's time to pat yourself on the back! This may seem silly, but it's actually a huge accomplishment. You have a credit card for your BUSINESS. YOU have a BUSINESS.

STEP #34

WHERE DO I FIND A GOOD ACCOUNTANT?

Your relationship with your accountant may end up being one of the most meaningful, enlightening, and lucrative relationships you have in your whole life. You could have the most high-end accounting software in the world, but it's often the bit of human TLC that helps you make the most sense of it all. Their expertise can help guide your financial decisions as your business grows and they can also provide insight and advice to help you save for retirement (which we'll get into in an upcoming section), which can be challenging for sole proprietors if they don't know their options.

This section is about how to find the right accountant for you - who to find, where to look, and what to ask.

Who is best for me? Before we can talk about finding the money person of your dreams, let's take a second to cut through the many kinds of accountants and get you who you really need. As an individual starting a business, there are just two genres of tax professionals you should be looking at:

- **Enrolled Agents:** When you are speaking to an enrolled agent, you'll know that either they used to work for the IRS for five years or passed a special IRS test to gain this title. EAs are our tax-focused friends. It's possible that their whole life revolves around doing people's individual tax returns. Because of their limited focus, they can be cheaper than CPAs, which we'll talk about next.

- **CPAs:** CPA stands for "Certified Public Accountant." These smart money-pros have gone through special training and passed state-level exams to gain their title. They often serve as trusty consultants to help businesses analyze their financial situations and reach their monetary goals. If you find a good one, they're like a paid financial guide. CPAs are helpful for business planning in general, but they're not all tax experts. So if you want to use one for your individual taxes, make sure you choose one that has the experience you need.

Next up –

Where do I find them? When you're in the freelance biz, you're responsible for your own taxes. Which can feel a bit overwhelming, especially if you're used to your employer taking care of all that.

Here are some tips on how to find yourself a pro:

- **Explore databases.** You can find a CPA using a national directory such as CPA Directory or CPA Finder. Read the customer reviews and check their professional details before adding them to your shortlist of top candidates.

- **Go for experience.** Try and find an accountant that has direct experience dealing with your specific industry. They'll be able to steer you away from common tax traps and find deductions you never could have found on your own. Magical!

- **Phone a friend.** Ask your freelance friends what they do for their taxes. If they work with someone they really like, ask them to give you a referral. If you're a lone wolf, don't be afraid to check out review sites (like Yelp) or professional organizations for their suggestions and ratings.

- **Call up your neighborhood's Chamber of Commerce.** Or check out the National Association of Enrolled Agents and the American Institute of Certified Public Accountants.

- **You want to find a match that fits your situation.** Certain accountants are only trying to work for those with larger incomes. When you're screening potential candidates, be honest about your income situation and new freelancer status. You will find many that are happy to help while weeding out the no-nos.

- **Check their credentials.** When it comes to trusting your financial life with someone, you can never be too careful. Stalk your short list of potential accountants at the IRS Office of Enrollment and/or the Better Business Bureau. This isn't paranoia, it's smart business! Don't take the info on their website for granted. One time we were about to hire someone, and their website said they were rated "A+" at the BBB. So we went to the BBB directly to verify this. Turns out they just took a screencap of another business' A+ rating and put it on their site. Smooth. They actually had an "F" for pretending to be an A+. True story.

- **See if you click.** Make sure to have a real, live phone or video conversations with your top accountant choices. If you can meet in person, even better! You're going to have to talk to this person a lot, so it should feel comfortable for you. When you meet, bring your past tax info with you so they can get a sense of who you are, too, and decide if they'll be a good fit for your situation. Don't forget to ask how much they charge! You may find your accounting soulmate just to realize they cost way more than you can afford. Unlike what JLo says, their love does indeed cost a thing…or two…or three…or two-fifty…

After you've narrowed down your list of possibilities, it's time to get to know them and find out if they're a good fit.

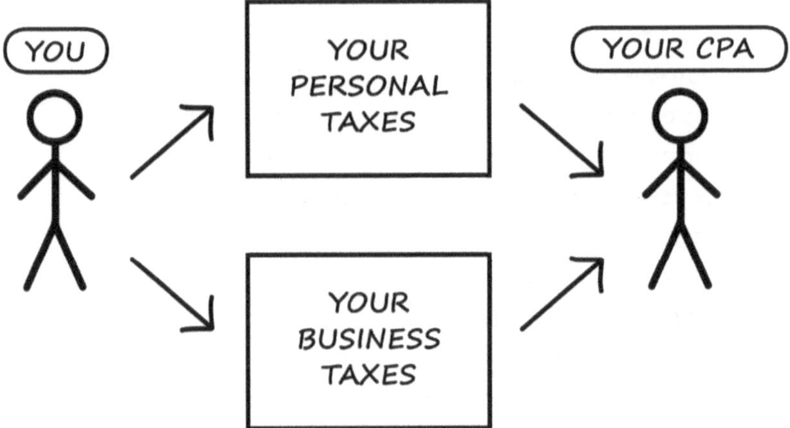

When you pick a CPA, try to use the same person to handle your personal taxes AND your business taxes. The key advantage here is that your CPA will be able to build electronic tax records for both your personal taxes and businesses taxes, year after year. In turn, you can make better financial decisions because your CPA has instant visibility to the "big picture" of your home and business finances.

What questions should I ask? The money you spend on a professional now could save you beaucoup bucks in the long run. Don't be afraid to ask them as many questions as you need to feel comfortable.

Are they the financial peanut butter to your freelance jelly? Here are some things to consider and questions to ask your top accountant suitors to know if they're a true match:

- **Are they into you?** When you interview a CPA or EA candidate, does he or she show interest in what you do for a living? Do they ask you questions about your business? Do they answer your questions thoroughly? Do they ask questions to make sure you understand the terminology? If not, it's time to say: NEXT.

- **Will they do your 1099s?** When business is booming, you'll need to subcontract out work to other ID freelancers. This means you'll need to submit 1099s to the IRS for anyone you paid $600 or more. Will your accountant handle the 1099s? Or are you expected to complete them yourself? If you can swing the fee of about $10 per 1099, it's convenient to have your accountant take care of them and send them out every January.

- **What about the 1096?** A 1096 is an Annual Summary and Transmittal of U.S. Information Returns (very important). It needs to be mailed to the IRS by January 31st every year. Will they do this for you and mail you a copy? We hope so. January can be a busy time of year for a freelance ID because clients usually have fresh, well-stocked budgets. It's a good time to secure new business while working on current projects.

- **Will they stay the quarterly course?** If you have an LLC, one of the best things your accountant can do is serve as an accountability partner to help you pay your quarterly estimated taxes. A good one will give you a friendly nudge via phone or email to keep you on top of your game.

- **What's their style?** How will the accountant prepare the tax return info for you? Will they put everything neatly into a 2-pocket folder? Or will it all be in the cloud? Will they hold your hand, if necessary, giving it a lil squeeze of support as they show you step-by-step instructions that say what to mail, by what date, and to what address?

- **Are they flexible?** There will be tax years when you owe money. It's just a miserable fact of life. The last thing you may want to do in those years is pay your accountant at the same time! A flexible accountant can be a great boon for a freelancer.
- **Do they have specific experience with business taxes, not just personal taxes?** Do they know all the ways to deduct expenses? Tax software is really convenient, but great accountants are like walking and talking deduction encyclopedias.
- **Is their advice on point?** Knowledgeable accountants will be able to tell you all about the tax implications of different business entities. Ask your front-running candidates the same questions and compare their answers. Chances are the cream will rise to the top!

Even if you use QuickBooks or FreshBooks or are just really good with numbers, you'll undoubtedly still need some experienced support to stay on the right side of the law. Accountants can help you avoid growing too fast in the wrong way. As your income increases, so does your tax liability, and working with an accountant can help you avoid a loathsome underpayment surprise at tax time. They can help take a big-picture view of your business and help you better plan for retirement.

Speaking of retirement…

STEP #35

SHOULD I SET UP A RETIREMENT FUND?

Just because you're working for yourself instead of an employer, there's no need to feel like you're somehow jeopardizing your retirement. There are planning tools you can take advantage of, and the sooner you start saving for retirement the better. But unlike being an employee, where employer-sponsored 401(k) plans allow you to be on autopilot, saving for your retirement fund as a freelancer does mean you'll have to take initiative.

Running a freelance ID business, there's a lot for you to keep up with - all of your taxes as well as health/dental insurance costs and business operating expenses like ID tech, website hosting, professional development, and sometimes competing goals such as paying down debt or saving for your child's college fund. So it can definitely feel challenging taking on the task of putting additional money aside and determining what type of retirement vehicles.

But first things first. Before you start saving for retirement, it's a good idea to make sure you have at least six months of living expenses and three months of business expenses put aside first. To be super safe, having twelve months of expenses in an emergency fund is ideal.

After that, you want to determine what percentage you want to contribute to your retirement savings. Do you want to travel to every aquarium in the country? Would you like to MAKE SURE you have enough saved so you can live in the forthcoming Harry Styles-themed 55+ community? The saving for retirement goals and process will be unique to who you are, where you are in life, and your personal needs - so we won't get into that here. However, there are plenty of good tools available to assist you with making this determination. And if you want more personal support, a good financial advisor will be able to guide you in establishing retirement goals that are best for you. (Author's note: At the time of this writing, Parker is approaching his *ahem* 60's in a few years... and that "retirement" alert is sounding off its alarm. So pay attention to your savings because time flies faster than you think!)

The amount you plan to save each year will help determine the best account for you, so once you have solidified your retirement goals and savings plan, you'll need to set up one or more retirement accounts where your savings can live and grow.

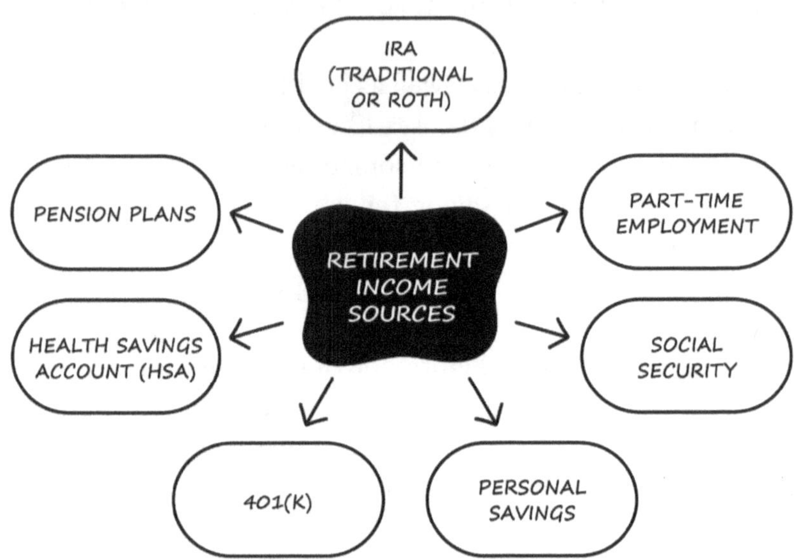

As a freelancer, it is important to know how you plan to obtain income in your retirement years. You could always consider freelancing as a part-time source of income. However, do look into other options like 401(k) plans, social security, personal savings, HSAs, and pension plans that you may have from a prior employer. The more sources, the better!

Here are a few retirement options that may work for you:

Traditional or Roth IRA: A debate as old as time. (Just like the one about whether or not Beauty and the Beast is about Stockholm Syndrome or not.)

This is one option that may be ideal if you want to roll the 401(k) from your old job into an IRA. A Roth IRA is also worth considering if you want to put aside additional money after you've contributed to other retirement vehicles and meet the income ceilings. Both are also excellent options if you earn a modest income.

At the time of this book's publishing, you can contribute a maximum of $6,000 a year to an IRA. Or if you're age 50 and over and need to play catch up, you can contribute an additional $1,000 annually.

We encourage you to do additional research to determine what's right for you, however, here is a basic summary of the two types of IRAs.

Traditional Taxes	Roth Taxes
Contributions grow tax-deferred	Contributions grow tax-free
Tax deductible	Not tax-deductible

Traditional Contributions	Roth Contributions
Pre- or after-tax dollars	After-tax dollars
Contribution eligibility: Anyone with earned income	Contribution eligibility: Those with earned income below a certain level

Traditional Withdrawals	Roth Withdrawals
Penalty-free but taxed as current income after age 59½	Penalty- and tax-free after 5 years and age 59½
Mandatory distributions after age 72	No mandatory distribution age

An IRA is probably the easiest way to start saving for retirement. There are no special filing requirements, and you can open one online brokerage in just a few minutes. It's almost TOO easy to give your money away to an institution that holds it hostage until you're far past child-bearing age...

SEP IRA (Simplified Employee Pension Plan Individual Retirement Account): This one sounds like a sorority. Gag me with a spoon! But it's actually a cool account. This is a tax-deferred retirement plan for anyone who is self-employed, owns a business, employs others, or earns freelance income. It's a great solution if you've maxed out contributions to a Roth or traditional IRA and you're looking for another place to save retirement funds. Very similar to a Traditional IRA, with two key differences: more generous limits on annual contributions and the fact that only business owners or sole proprietors can make contributions under the plan.

There is no Roth version of a SEP IRA, contributions are also tax deductible and you're not required to pay taxes on the money until you withdraw funds in retirement. Although with this type of plan, contribution limits change from year to year.

At the time of publishing this, you can contribute up to 25 percent of net income (after expenses), or $61,000.

Key considerations of the SEP IRA include:

- Contributions for retirement are tax-deductible as a self-employed person.
- Contribute the lesser of 25 percent of your income or $61,000 for 2022.
- Easy to open with an account provider.
- No Roth option, which means you can't opt to pay taxes on contributions now and take distributions tax-free in retirement.
- Must contribute an equal percentage of compensation for any employees.

A SEP IRA doesn't require much paperwork and you can choose from a variety of different investments to handle your SEP IRA based on your retirement age and your tolerance risk.

The Solo 401(k): A Solo 401(k) isn't a pair of sneakers made by Kanye West. It's an individual 401(k) designed for a business owner with no employees (except for spouses) and gives you all the benefits of an employer-sponsored 401(k) plan – the tax break for savings, the tax-deferred or tax-free growth and a generous annual maximum contribution – even if you're a small business. You also get to set up your plan at the broker of your choice instead of being bound by restrictive rules on the types of investments you can make in a typical 401(k) plan.

The total solo 401(k) contribution limit is up to $61,000 in 2022. There is a catch-up contribution of an extra $6,500 for those 50 or older.

Key considerations of the Solo 401(k) include:

- No age or income restrictions, but must be a business owner with no employees (spouses excepted).
- Traditional 401(k): Contributions are made pre-tax, reducing taxable income for the year. Roth 401(k): Contributions are made with after-tax dollars.
- Traditional 401(k): Qualified distributions are taxed as income. Roth 401(k): Qualified distributions are tax-free.
- EIN is needed to open an account.

HSA (Health Savings Account): Your health is nothing to sneeze at. And it can make you rich! Not only are HSAs a great way of paying for out-of-pocket medical costs, but they can also be used as an investment vehicle as well. You can use this savings account for outside investments like stocks, bonds, ETFs (Exchange-Traded funds), and mutual funds. Not only can this money be used for medical care, but it can also be used to fund your retirement. That's because, at age 65, you're allowed to withdraw money from your HSA for any reason, not just for medical expenses.

One major benefit to these kinds of savings accounts, especially as you consider the medical expenses you might incur as you age, is that unlike 401(k)s or IRAs, the money you withdraw for medical expenses is tax-free. Another factor that makes an HSA worth considering is that you're not required to withdraw funds once you get to a certain age like you with a 401(k) or IRA. As long as you use the money in your HSA account to pay for medical expenses, you do not pay any federal taxes. That's why it's at the top of the list of tax-efficient investment options for your retirement. The downside is that once you're eligible for Medicare, you're no longer allowed to contribute.

As of the publishing of this book, contribution limits are $3,650 for individuals and $7,300 for family coverage.

There are other benefits to an HSA account, but we'll get into that later on.

Retirement planning can be a real challenge, but there is no shortage of information and resources to help you, including a variety of online communities that can also be valuable.

Realizing your full-time freelancer dream is a major achievement. But it's important to understand that being in control of your income goes hand in hand with being in control of your own retirement planning. So, make sure you have a clear financial plan that works for you and your future.

STEP #36

HOW DO I PAY QUARTERLY ESTIMATED TAXES?

What are quarterly taxes? Quarterly taxes are estimated tax payments that most sole proprietors and business owners are required to make to the IRS throughout the year.

If you've worked a traditional job most of your life, you've probably become accustomed to taxes being automatically deducted from your income. However, now that you're a full-fledged freelancer, you are responsible for figuring out what all of your tax obligations are and when you need to pay what you owe. Not only that, instead of dealing with taxes once a year in April, you'll likely have to pay quarterly taxes four times a year. Oh right, you probably knew quarterly meant 4. Sorry, we didn't mean to mansplain numbers to you! You brilliant, beautiful, prescient dolphin wizard, you!

But paying this often doesn't have to be a bad thing. Taking care of your taxes quarterly, instead of in one (often unpleasant) lump sum, can give you a better sense of control with much less room for "oh sh*t!" surprise once a year. You get to pay your tax bill gradually over the course of the year instead of all at once RIGHT AFTER the holidays. (Damn it's like they planned that on purpose!) It also means you'll probably keep a better eye on your cash flow since you'll be calculating how much you owe based on your income a bit more frequently.

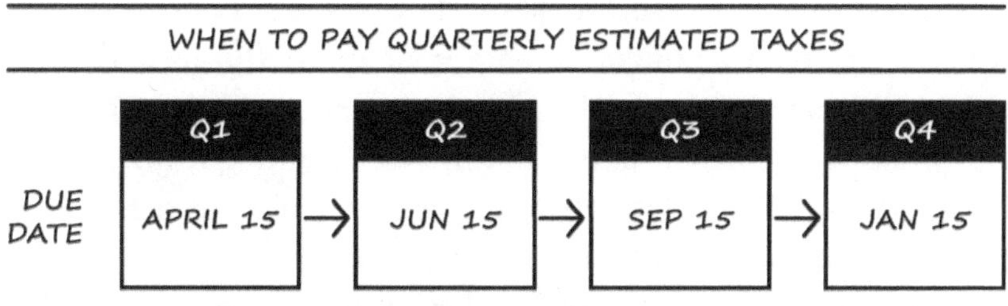

In the US, there are four dates to remember for paying your federal estimated taxes (and for some states, state estimated taxes!). Q1 - April 15th, Q2 - June 15th, Q3 - September 15th, and Q4 - January 15th. Pro tip: Add a calendar reminder so that you don't forget to pay.

To stay on top of your taxes and put your best foot forward, it's important to follow the best practices listed below right from the start.

Let's go over some best practices for managing your taxes as a freelancer.

Know the basics. There are two parts to the quarterly taxes you're required to pay: self-employment tax (15.3% as of the publishing of this book - are you sick of us saying that yet?), which includes your portion of the Social Security and Medicare taxes you would usually pay, as well as the portion typically covered by your employer; and income tax. You should also be familiar with freelance tax forms, like the 1099-MISC form, which you'll receive when you earn at least $600 from a client.

Understand your tax requirements and how to estimate what you owe. If you expect to owe $1,000 or more, you're required to pay estimated taxes quarterly, which are payments based on your estimated income for the current year. In the freelance world, where it's hard to know how much you'll make from month to month, this can be hard to estimate. There's no need to get bogged in the weeds of exact percentages. Most people use their previous year's taxes as a guide. These tax payments are based on estimated income, so you don't need to get it exactly right. As a general "rule of thumb" though, we recommend freelancers set aside 25-30% of their freelance income for quarterly taxes. It's safer to slightly overestimate than to underestimate your quarterly tax payments because if you overpay, you'll get the extra money back as a refund after filing your annual return. If you owe, you might be required to pay an underpayment penalty. There are bank accounts there that automatically set aside a percentage (that you choose) of whatever you bring into a separate "bucket" just for taxes. Google Lili freelance account! One of the Head Honchos highly recommends.

Know your business structure. Are you operating as a sole proprietor, an LLC, or an S Corp? This will determine not only how much you owe, but how you file as well. When running your own business as a freelancer, paying your quarterly taxes is a must, and getting it wrong when it comes to your tax requirements can be extremely costly. So, like the black forest gateau topped with candy cabins and realistically smoking chimneys you'll make in the final week's Showstopper bake in Great British Baking Show season you'll be participating in the future... you'll want to make sure you get it right.

Hire a tax professional. In addition to all of the reasons for working with a tax professional that we discussed earlier, it's important to keep in mind that the IRS is constantly making updates to its tax laws. And if you live in a state that collects income tax, you will also need to deal with state tax payments as well. For each tax year, you not only need to be aware of all of your tax obligations, but you also want to take advantage of all the tax deductions and benefits available to you. Given that you're probably super busy lining up your next contract, negotiating your pay rate, and keeping up with all the latest and greatest in the field of ID, adding the additional responsibility of "freelancer tax expert" might be a bit much to add to your plate. Plus, you wouldn't want to take the joy of accomplishment away from your friendly neighborhood tax geek. That would just be cruel!

Report all of your business income. You're responsible for reporting all your income, even if you didn't receive a 1099 for it. Sometimes clients make mistakes, so you want to cross-check your own accounting documents against the figures on the 1099 form. You don't want to get stuck paying taxes on income you didn't earn or receive.

Don't try to deduct everything. You don't want to risk an audit by trying to write off expenses that aren't legitimate. The expenses you deduct should be ordinary and necessary to run your business. We won't even make a joke about this because Fraud Is Not Funny! (Dear IRS: If you are reading this, see how serious we are! We're on your side! Please, nothing to see here, no need to worry about us... no, sir and/or madame...).

Pay your tax bill on time. One of the best things your accountant can do is serve as an accountability partner to help you pay on time. Because if you don't, you may be hit with penalties, which can include both a cumulative monthly percentage and a monthly interest charge. There's a penalty for each month you delay, so always want to pay your bill by the deadline. A good accountant will give you a friendly nudge or swift kick to the kidney via phone or email to keep you on top of your game.

Don't expect a tax refund. There are typically only a couple of instances when a freelancer would receive a refund: either they overpaid their quarterly estimated taxes, or they made such little money for the year that they are entitled to an earned income credit (EIC), which is refundable.

Keeping up with quarterly taxes doesn't have to be stressful, as long as you're able to stay organized and keep up with your bookkeeping. The easiest way to pay your quarterly taxes is online via the IRS' "Direct Pay" portal or by using the Electronic Federal Tax Payment System (EFTPS). You can also send a check or money order. Always keep a record of the date and amount that you paid (though, if necessary, it is possible to request a transcript from the IRS).

Though we've mentioned it before, it bears repeating - we strongly recommend hiring an accountant to handle tax preparation. An accountant can help you avoid making costly mistakes and identify opportunities to optimize tax savings. Look at you, you tax-paying, freelancing, wondrous unicorn of a business owner!

COME UP WITH A HEALTH INSURANCE PLAN

Working when you're sick SUCKS. And you DEFINITELY can't put your sweet cash to good use if you're holed up in bed. There are only so many terrible movies to rent on Amazon Prime before you start questioning your sanity as much as your ability to walk down the stairs to get a delicious bag of chocolate covered pretzels (we are taking any and all paid sponsorships for all chocolate covered pretzel brands out there).

STEP #37

HOW DO I FIND HEALTH INSURANCE
AS A FREELANCER?

One of the things that can be scary about starting your own freelancing business is not being able to get health insurance through an employer. It's often one of the biggest barriers to taking that big leap into the full-time freelancing world. Although health insurance options might be a bit complicated to navigate as a freelancer, good options do exist for you. With many of them, the cost is impacted by your unique situation, so you really want to take the time to research the different options available for freelancers so you can make an informed decision. Keep in mind that some of this information can even vary depending on the state you live in!

Here is a list of the most popular options for freelancers:

Your spouse's policy: Adding yourself to your spouse or partner's healthcare policy is the easiest way for you to secure health insurance. So, if you're married (or even sometimes domestic partnerships count!), you definitely want to consider this option. Just be aware that in some cases, you may have to pay your part of the premium to be added to their policy.

While this option is easy, you want to make sure you get all of the details about getting added. It's also a really good idea to cost compare with other options available to you, because you may find a better, more affordable alternative self-insuring through another method. We wish we could say it's easy to figure out, but just like influential poet and unsettling person Charles Bukowski once said:

Sometimes it's hard to know
what to
do

Affordable Care Act: The Affordable Care Act, also called the ACA or Obamacare, can be a really good option, especially if you need coverage for your family. The health insurance marketplace created by the ACA allows you to secure health insurance even if you're at high risk for a major disease or have a pre-existing condition. All the plans listed on the exchange meet certain basic government-mandated requirements. The marketplace makes it easy to compare the costs and suitability of the different health plans. Just be aware that your monthly premium may vary depending on where you live and how much your household income is (there are subsidies!).

To get a health plan through the ACA, you need to get a plan during the Open Enrollment period. But if you experience a major life event (like the birth of a child, a divorce, or quitting your job to become a freelancer), you can qualify for Special Enrollment.

If you're eligible for a subsidy, you'll want to buy health insurance through the marketplace so the government will cover part of your premium. To find out if you're eligible, visit Healthcare.gov. You can also change your income at any time, which can change the amount of your subsidy. Let's say at the beginning of the year you think you're going to earn about 40k. If halfway through the year you think you'll be earning about 90k, you'll want to update that info. If you earn "too much" compared to what you told them, you may have to pay back whatever subsidy you used when it's #taxtime.

COBRA: COBRA, aka Consolidated Omnibus Budget Reconciliation Act, which allows you to keep your employer-sponsored health insurance plan after leaving your job, is an option to consider if you haven't yet left your job (or have done so very recently). It can be quite expensive and is only offered up to 18 months after you separate from your job, but it can fill in the gap while you search for a long-term option. TBH, there are usually better options than this.

Freelancer's Union: The Freelancers Union provides health insurance plans specifically for freelancers. It can also provide you with dental coverage, life insurance, and disability insurance. You can learn more by visiting freelancersunion.org.

Also, check out your local Chamber of Commerce. Some of them may also offer group health insurance for freelancers and self-employed individuals.

Business Healthcare: If you're established as a legal, registered Instructional Design business, you may be able to ob-

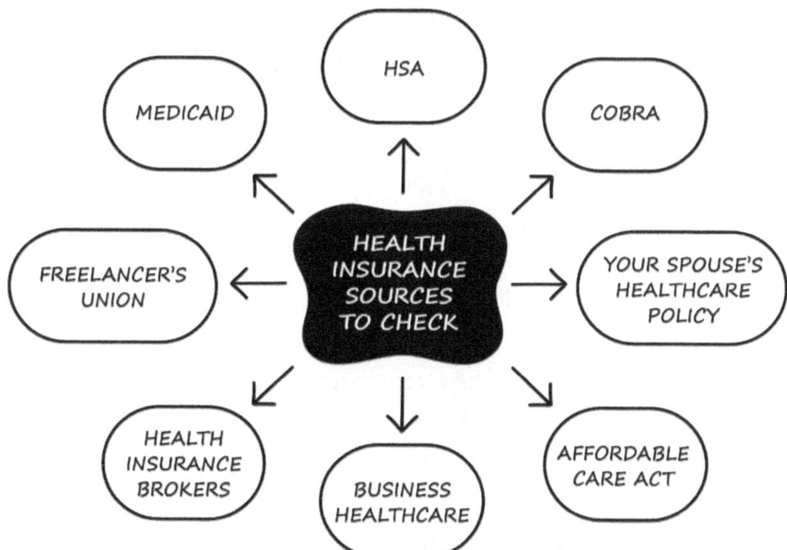

Become a student to learn about the health insurance market. Start by looking up these resources: Affordable Care Act, your spouse's healthcare policy, COBRA, Medicaid, small business healthcare options, Freelancer's Union, HSAs. Bonus tip: Talk to a health insurance broker to get many of your questions answered.

tain freelancer health insurance at lower rates for your family, and any employees you may have, by applying for it through your business. You want to check out the federal Small Business Health Options Program and find out what options your state may have.

Medicaid: For Medicaid eligibility, your income must be below a certain level. You may assume that you make too much to qualify, but the income level varies depending on the state you live in and the number of people in your family. Depending on these factors, you may be eligible for expanded Medicaid options with less stringent income requirements. Check with your state to see what's available.

Also, there are religious organizations, like The Alliance of Healthcare Sharing Ministries, which offer low-cost healthcare via pool-your-money programs. The program works by charging a modest monthly premium based on your ability to pay, with those in need getting their bills paid out of the pool.

HSAs (Health Savings Accounts): While this isn't a health plan, it's definitely something you want to consider when choosing which health plan works best for you. You're likely to have some out-of-pocket expenses regardless of what health plan you have (don't get us started on this). An HSA (Health Savings Account) is a really good way to help pay for medical expenses that aren't covered by your health plan. HSAs allow you to make pretax contributions, thereby reducing your taxable income. You can use the money in your HSA for any qualified medical expenses (excluding your premiums), including copays, deductibles, prescription drugs, and dental expenses.

One caveat though, is that some plans don't allow you to open an HSA. You will need to have a high-deductible health plan (HDHP) in order to use an HSA, so make sure you keep that in mind when you're shopping around for the health insurance options that work best for you.

Health Insurance Brokers: One thing we recommend is contacting a local insurance broker. Unlike an insurance agent, who represents a single insurance company, and is limited to only that carrier's options when recommending plans, a broker represents you, the customer. For example, in one instance, one of our family members was expecting to have some surgery done and we knew it was going to cost X amount. We have to re-enroll every fall, and so my broker suggested we change to a new type of plan with a higher deductible and lower monthly payment. This allowed us to put away the savings from having a lower payment and allocate it for the surgery. This saved us money because while changing to the new plan lowered our monthly health insurance payments significantly, there wasn't much difference in the surgery's out-of-pocket expense with either plan. This is just one illustration of how working with a broker can really be helpful to you.

Also, while healthcare marketplaces are great places to comparison shop for health plans, it can be a real challenge navigating the sea of options and variables. Brokers can assist you by offering guidance about public programs, premium tax credits, and other government-based cost-saving options. They can also direct you to ACA-compliant off-exchange plans as well.

Health insurance broker services are typically free because their fees are built into the cost of health insurance in general. However, there may be a cost if you want additional services.

When it comes to choosing the right broker, trust is a top priority. You want someone who makes an effort to understand your unique situation so that they can offer options based on your specific needs. They should also communicate their expertise about health plans in language that you can understand and proactively explain a plan's downsides. One of the best ways to find a good broker is to seek out referrals from trusted friends, family members, and fellow freelancers.

Having to pay monthly premiums, it's easy to see health insurance as a liability. A better way to look at it though, is as an asset since it protects you from having to pay much larger medical expenses when you need care down the road.

That being said, there may be some medical things that are just plain cheaper to pay for out of pocket than going through insurance. Again, don't get us started on that. All we're saying is...do your research!

STEP #38

HOW DO I KEEP HEALTH INSURANCE AFFORDABLE?

When you're self-employed, you're responsible for not only your living expenses but all business expenses as well. So it's important to take advantage of every opportunity to save money.

Especially when it comes to health insurance. Because when you think about it, keeping health insurance affordable can have as much impact on your finances as filing your taxes properly.

Your health insurance premiums as a freelancer depend on factors unique to your situation, such as your income level, family members needing coverage, your age, where you live, and the size of your deductible. While the cost of health insurance can be significant, there are a few ways you can save money on this necessary expense. We've already mentioned using the ACA's health care marketplace to compare different health insurance options in your particular area but read on to learn about a few more.

Deduct Your Premiums: As a full-time freelancer, your health, dental, and qualifying long-term care insurance premiums can be considered tax-deductible business expenses as you meet certain basic conditions, such as not having employer-sponsored health coverage. Currently, you're allowed to claim 100% of your eligible health insurance premiums as an income deduction. This allows you to use your insurance premiums to lower your tax debt. This is a valuable tax break, which can help you pay at least a portion of premium costs.

Subsidies: Depending on your income and family size, you may be able to get help meeting the cost of health insurance coverage. When you fill out a Health Insurance Marketplace application, you can find out if you qualify for premium tax credits and other savings. If you're eligible to receive free or low-cost coverage through the Medicaid and CHIP programs in your state, you'll be able to find that out as well. There are quite a few variables involved in determining who qualifies, so it's a good idea to check your eligibility level no matter what your income is.

Catastrophic Plan Option: Plans on the Healthcare Marketplace exchange fall into one of five categories: catastrophic, bronze, silver, gold, and platinum.

In addition to people under 30, catastrophic plans are also available to people who qualify for a hardship exemption that

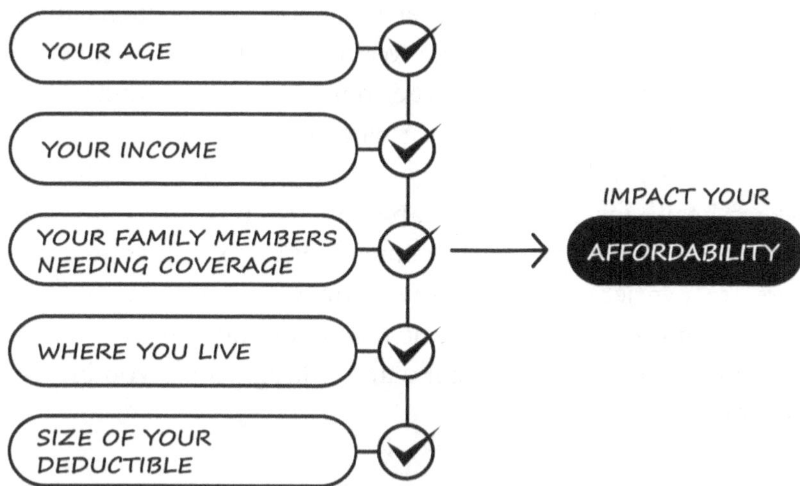

Knowing how to make your health insurance more affordable starts with these factors: your age, your projected freelance income, which family members need coverage, where you live, and what deductible limit you are willing to accept.

prevents them from being able to afford health coverage. These plans have the lowest monthly premiums and the highest deductibles, requiring you to pay 50% of your medical expenses. If you're pretty healthy and don't expect to use health insurance on a regular basis, that might be an option worth considering. The downside though, is that with those plans, you're not eligible for federal subsidies. So a bronze plan (with 60% coverage) might still be more affordable if you're eligible for a subsidy.

Cost Sharing: As a self-employed freelancer, you may be eligible for an additional subsidy for some health plans on top of the one available to them for all Marketplace coverage. This kind of subsidy is called a "cost-sharing reduction" and is designed to reduce the portion of a health insurance claim you're required to pay. One caveat though, is that unlike the subsidies mentioned above, which can be applied to any of the "medal" category plans within the exchange, cost-sharing subsidies are only available with silver plans.

For those who qualify, silver plans with the cost-sharing reduction offer costs comparable to bronze plans. So, if silver category coverage is what you need, but your budget limits you to bronze, cost-sharing could put it within your means.

As a self-employed freelancer, it may be more of a challenge to keep health insurance affordable, but it is possible. It just takes a bit of planning and yearly maneuvering. As you've just read, there are a variety of ways to save money on this expense. Luckily, you can learn about all of the resources and benefits that may be available to you by Googling and asking people you know in your same state.

STEP #39

HOW CAN A HEALTH SAVINGS ACCOUNT (HSA) HELP ME?

Now that you're running your own business as a freelancer, it's more important than ever to consider ALL of your options when it comes to your finances. As we mentioned earlier, having an HSA (Health Savings Account) is an excellent way to help you take care of your medical costs and plan for retirement.

But there are additional ways that having an HSA can help you.

As a self-employed freelancer, an HSA account can also help you:

- **Reduce your taxable income.** This is one of the most effective ways of reducing your tax bill. The more tools you have to help you to achieve this, the better.
- **Efficiently manage health care expenses.** Feel more comfortable carrying a high deductible plan, knowing the money you're saving on premiums is going towards building a reliable savings.

- **Fortify your retirement.** Having an additional tax-sheltered investment account helps diversify your portfolio.
- **Strengthen your emergency funds.** Although the purpose of an HSA is to pay for medical expenses. It is your money. Though you'll have to pay a 20% tax, if necessary, you can withdraw the money for something that isn't related to medical expenses.
- **Benefit from a triple tax advantage investment.** With contributions that reduce your taxable income, tax-free investment growth, and tax-free withdrawals (as long as they're for medical expenses), HSAs allow you to take advantage of one of the most tax-efficient investment options available.
- **Manage your responsibilities more efficiently.** Take care of two important things at once: both your physical and financial well-being. Anything that can help us multitask is a great thing!

As we stated earlier in the book, the limits are $3,650 for individuals and $7,300 for family coverage. And if you're 55 or older, you may be able to make an additional contribution of up to $1,000 per year.

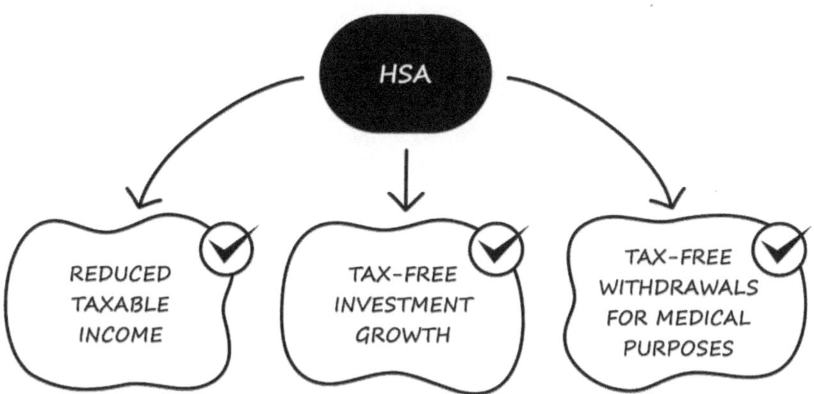

As a freelancer, having an HSA account will allow you to take advantage of a reduced taxable income and tax-free options for investments and withdrawals for medical expenses.

Even if you have other investment accounts, like a 401(k) or IRA, we strongly encourage you to consider taking advantage of the benefits that having an HSA can provide. The tax advantages offer you a great way to save money by reducing your taxable income, take care of your health-related needs, and be better prepared for your retirement years.

The popularity of HSAs continues to increase and as such, there's a growing number of options available. You can open an account through many financial institutions, and we encourage you to shop around for the HSA administrator that works best for you.

P.S. You probably noticed this section wasn't full of award-winning quips. That's because health insurance and retirement is serious business. In your search for the best plans for you, you'll encounter enough funny business, so we figured we'd get straight to the point.

Now, back to your regularly scheduled silliness.

2 MONTHS BEFORE YOU DITCH YOUR CUBICLE

BUILD THE OFFICE SPACE OF YOUR DREAMS

You're gonna be spending a lot of time in your house. Like, a lot. Sure, you'll go to the coffee shop sometimes or maybe even get fancy at a coworking space (both things we'll also talk about). But sometimes, life and work (especially meetings!) will keep you at home.

So make it C O Z Y!

Comfort and good vibez will help you succeed

Organization and convenience will help you lead

Zachariah the patron saint of home offices overseas

You every time you leave your office to pee (Stay hydrated out there, friends!)

STEP #40

WHAT KIND OF COMPUTER AND PERIPHERALS DO I NEED?

The computer you'll be using as a freelance Instructional Designer will be the foundation of your new business. Unless you plan on doing all of your designing and correspondence with an elaborate system of scrolls, stones, and impressively trained tarsiers. When you're starting out, your computer is likely to be your most expensive purchase. You may want to work with a computer you already have and make some upgrades to suit your needs as a freelancer. Or, you may want to invest in a brand-new machine. (Either way, tax deduction!) If you do decide on a new computer, it's important to really think it through, keeping in mind your needs over the long haul. You'll want to get a machine (or two!) that can handle the work you need to do and how you want to do it.

The question is, will it be a laptop or desktop?

A laptop is handy when you want to take your work on the go. But, having a desktop computer with dual monitors is a great option to have at home. Desktops can usually store more files, process at a higher speed, and allow for more USB options (for a webcam, microphone, monitor, and printer).

However, you can also make a docking station for your laptop to hook up to the monitors and external hard drives if a laptop has enough processing power for you.

So, let's help you figure out getting the perfect top: LAP OR DESK?

Here are three things to ask yourself…

What stuff do I want to do? By now you probably have an idea of the types of projects you'll be working on. Will you be storyboarding in PowerPoint? Creating simulations in Articulate? Making voice-over videos? Shooting and editing a YouTube talk show in 4K for all your adoring ID fans? The types of projects you'll be doing will help you decide what kind of computer you need.

In a perfect world, you'd have a "work computer" and a "personal computer." But realistically, at least for now, you'll probably be using the same computer to work as you use to stream Netflix and check Facebook and design Daniel Radcliffe fan art. Just do your best not to clog up your computer with TOO

MUCH random stuff, otherwise, it may not function optimally when your clients are depending on you at the eleventh hour.

How mobile do you want to be? In a pretty most perfectest world, every freelancer would have one decent desktop for their home office and one laptop for traveling the world. The desktop would be our computer powerhouse for intense Articulate use and video editing, with services like Dropbox to help us access all our files, wherever we choose to work on our laptop. And we make sure that both the desktop and laptop sync to "offline" folders in Dropbox. This way it's all automatic and we don't even have to think about syncing from one computer to another.

But, the world we live in isn't pretty or the most perfectest. And, we know not everyone has the budget to make the two-computer dream happen… at least not right now. Desktops are actually cheaper than a lot of laptops these days. But we know all too well the appeal of working from anywhere in your house, a local coffee shop, or even from the patio of your Airbnb during your travels.

You could get a decently powerful laptop (probably a "gaming laptop") with an external hard drive and an external monitor (or even a cheap, small tv) to use via HDMI cable, and get a desktop later. Totally up to you! All that matters is being able to get your work done with as little technical SNAFUs as possible. Don't stress, you don't have to make the decision just yet. Finish reading this chapter and take a walk around the block before you whip out your credit card!

Are you an apple or a window? When it comes to the operating system of your computer, the debate about whether Mac or Windows is better seems never ending. So, we're not going to take up too much real estate here adding to that debate. Both have their benefits and drawbacks. Windows offers the kind of flexibility and configurability that allows for a wide range of uses and out-of-the-box, integrated capabilities, and features. On the other hand, some people find Macs more user-friendly, aesthetically pleasing, and less prone to malware.

Bottom line, if you're looking to develop a lot with Articulate Storyline, a PC is going to be more compatible. The program is native to Windows, which means it was made for it. However, you CAN use Articulate on a Mac, but you'll need to use something called Parallels®. It's a way for you to use Windows on your Mac. We've used both and it just depends on what experience you want...and your budget, of course! The important thing is to keep an open mind when choosing the computer that'll work best for you in the long run.

We've summed up some important pros and cons below:

Windows - Pros

- Works easily with Articulate software
- Windows computers cost less for the same performance specs, particularly in laptops
- System compatibility with your business clients, most of which are Windows users
- Ability to upgrade and customize hardware to specific needs

Windows - Cons

- More prone to malware

Mac - Pros

- Integrating workflow from other Apple devices, such as the iPad and iPhone is super easy
- Works with Apple Motion and Final Cut Pro (PCs do not)

Mac - Cons

- Limited options for customization and upgrades (though memory and the storage drive can be upgraded)

- Using Articulate Storyline software requires the use of Parallels®, virtual environment software that creates a Windows interface (Rise is fine, though!)
- Higher cost

Are you a digital nomad? Some freelancers like to work from a "gaming" laptop - something that is portable for travel but can also be propped up on a laptop stand to elevate its monitor to eye level! When at home, a second monitor can be connected to the laptop to create a dual-monitor setup (which increases your productivity). When traveling, just bring your laptop and leave the other monitor home (how convenient)! Be sure to connect a separate keyboard and mouse to your laptop for ergonomic purposes.

There are some other considerations besides picking apples or windows. Next, we'll cover some of the physical components and the factors to watch for.

CPU (Central Processing Unit): This is the "brain" or central command of your computer. It's responsible for managing all of the computing tasks and allows for all of the different components of your computer to work together. Consequently, the type of processor you choose will have a direct impact on how well your computer performs. The faster your processor, the quicker and more agile it will feel. With a high-speed processor, not only will you be able to run more apps simultaneously, you'll be able to run apps more quickly as well.

Two factors you want to consider when choosing your CPU are the clock speed (gigahertz - cute name for a dog!) and the number of cores. A higher clock speed typically means faster performance. And the higher number of cores means the more your machine can handle at once. A high number of cores are especially important when it comes to video production software like Adobe Premiere, Adobe After Effects, and 3D rendering software. A computer with a good processing speed will allow you to be as productive as possible. So, it's worth it to invest in the most powerful processor your budget allows. It's very important that you're able to listen to that new Lucy Worsley documentary on YouTube while chatting about 90 Day Fiancé on Discord and silently livestreaming the yearly owl nesting at your favorite national park at the same time. Or something like that.

RAM (Random Access Memory): This functions as your computer's short-term memory. A good amount of RAM will allow you to return to a tab or app, right where you left off, without lag or glitches. You'll need to be able to work comfortably with a variety of apps (e.g., Adobe Illustrator, Articulate Storyline, Camtasia, Canva). Sufficient RAM allows you to be able to do this while also making it easier to edit large video files. So, you'll want to give strong consideration to how much RAM your computer has based on what kind of work you see yourself doing.

Storage capacity: Instructional designers work with lots of different files, many of them especially large. You want to make sure you have enough storage capacity for them. You can purchase a system that's configured for the amount of storage you need. Or, you may choose to buy an external or cloud-based storage and house your files there. Either way, try and think ahead of time about what you're gonna do to keep all your "things" safe. It's not being a nerd. It's called being a smarty pants with mad file management skillz!

Whether you choose Mac or Windows, it's really the performance specs of your computer that are most important. You've had a brief overview of the major components that you need to consider - CPU, RAM, and Storage Capacity. Now, let's talk about the stats and specs you'll need in your laptop and/or desktop to complete the things most IDs do.

Computer specs: Since computer spec stuff gets outdated quickly, we recommend a few sites for you to check out whenever it's time to purchase. The rule of thumb is, the more intense your task, the more intense your computer needs to be. If you're not going to be editing tons of video, making huge Storyline projects, storing huge media files, or always working in Photoshop, you can get away with an "average" computer. But if you are going to do those things, we recommend getting specs that are more "top of the line." The time you'll save from waiting for things to process and load is well worth it!

Best Buy has buying guides that can walk you through all your choices from laptop to desktop, mac or PC, and what specs you will need. Also check out the website DigitalTrends - they have a great resource that will help you, too!

Places like Best Buy ALSO have interest-free purchase programs and a price match guarantee. Take advantage of them! November is a great time to buy tech - remember Black Friday and Cyber Monday! There's really no excuse to ever pay full price if you're planning ahead!

If a new computer isn't in your budget, check stores for refurbished (aka pre-loved) ones and do some googling to see what your options are. They're usually just as functional as new ones and come with a guarantee if you do have any issues.

And don't forget to use your business account to make the purchase. If you have one, it's also an acceptable time to use that charge card. It's a great reward point collecting opportunity, especially if you're currently enjoying an intro-APR special.

Even if you don't have a business account yet, make sure to save all your receipts for when tax time rolls around. And it will roll around...quicker than you think! Take photos of those receipts and save them in a safe place. Sleep with them in your pillow if you have to!

Peripherals: This is just a fancy word for computer accessories. Being an ID usually also means being a multi-talented multi-tasker. Throughout your career, you may find opportunities to design, write, use various platforms, edit videos, record voiceovers, or do other really cool tech-y stuff.

The variety of skills you'll be using and honing means you'll probably need some extra stuff to go with your computer.

Here are some accessories you'll want to consider...

- **Webcam:** Most laptops and some desktops have a webcam built in, and it's probably fine for meetings. For video conferences and casual use it will get you through, but if you plan on recording video podcasts or doing some more serious webcam video tasks, you'll want to upgrade.
- **Microphone:** The internal mic on your computer is just fine for casual video chatting. But the time may come when you'll want to record some narration for an eLearning module. A good microphone will range between $100-200. And you'll probably want a headset mic for privacy, clarity, and to finally look like a fancy pilot.
- **Pop filters:** These are a must-have if you're recording narration. They take away that lip-smack sound that really undermines a professional sound. Remember, good audio in means good audio out! If you've never tried to edit out those kinds of sounds from a track, you've never known true DEFCON-5 frustration.
- **Audio interface:** It's what you plug your mics into to connect them to the computer. It makes your computer better at doing audio functions. You won't need one of these unless you're trying to work intensely with audio.
- **Keyboard:** If you've got a laptop, you're probably still going to want another external keyboard. This way you can put

your laptop on a stand to raise it to the perfect ergonomic height. Ergonomics are really important for your long-term health and happiness, so we'll go more into that later.

- **Mouse:** Trackpads are handy when you're on the go, but when you're doing some visual design or Storyboarding, or even attempting to highlight chunks of text in Microsoft Word…they can get old. Save yourself some serious frustration and get yourself a Bluetooth or wireless mouse for your heavier workdays. (LOL that sort of sounded like a Tampax commercial).

- **Printer:** Even if the majority of your work is eLearning, you're probably going to wish you could print some stuff out for meetings with your clients or accountant or to do those fun iron-on printable fabric designs with your new business logo! These days you can find them at sales for around $50 or less.

Let's talk screens. Whether you're working from a laptop or desktop, we recommend setting yourself up with a double monitor. The first time you pull up a YouTube instructional video (or British documentary on spoiled posh private school kids) on one screen and follow along with your task on Articulate on the other, you'll see why. It's also great for when you're storyboarding or compiling info. You can have all your source docs on one screen and your project on the other. It makes clicking and tab switching so much faster and smoother. You'll be saving lots of time, which ultimately results in making more money. And who can argue with that? Plus it makes your office look like the control center in the movie *Apollo 13* and who doesn't WANT that?

We recommend investing in a couple of 22–24-inch monitors or one very large monitor right from the start if you can make it happen.

Portable monitors are also an option. While the largest ones currently only go up to about 17 inches, these screens are slim and lightweight, giving you a convenient way to add more screen real estate wherever you're working—the coffee shop, office, or anywhere at home. Many of them have the ability to draw power from your laptop, so you'll want to charge your laptop while using it. If you have a MacBook and an iPad, you can actually use your iPad as a second screen. Once we figured that out for coffee shops, it was a game changer!

That was a lot of info. Now go forth, purchase, and set up that tech, bro!

STEP #41

WHAT DO I ABSOLUTELY NEED TO BUY UPFRONT FOR MY HOME OFFICE SPACE TO WORK FOR ME?

Being a full-fledged freelancer, it's important to make sure your workspace is fully outfitted with the right home office equipment, creature comforts, and accessories. The right home office essentials increase your productivity and work ethic, improve efficiency, and boost your confidence. Plus buying and/or making stuff is just plain fun! A home office space that works for you will make working at home more enjoyable and make you feel more professional. Plus, when you give tours of your space, you can be like, "Oh this? This is my HOME office tee hee tee hee tee hee!" (If possible, wear a monocle when delivering that line.)

So, let's get started with your personal workspace by helping you set yourself up for success!

Desk: Fundamental to a good workstation is the right kind of desk because it's the place where the vast majority of your work will be produced. Your desk should comfortably hold your computer along with plenty of extra workspace for your adult coloring book habit. Research touting the benefits of a standing desk has made it one of the most popular styles these days. Some of these benefits include reduced risk of weight gain, lower blood sugar levels, lower risk of heart disease, and lower risk of "surprise" desk naps. That being said, standing for long periods of time can be harmful as well. So, most experts advise you to put more focus on movement and changing positions throughout your workday if you're physically able to.

There are fixed-height desks that stay at your standing height and flexible desks that go up and down so you can sit or stand while you're working. Whether you buy a sitting or standing desk, there are benefits, drawbacks, and best practices for both, so please do some research before making your purchase. If your budget is tight, there are places to buy used office furniture, either online (via Facebook Marketplace for example) or at local discount office furniture outlets. You might also try constructing the world's "ouchiest" desk out of those Lego bricks you picked up at a garage sale.

Office chair: Even if you have a standing desk, you'll want a comfortable chair. That's where your butt lives after all! And whether you plan to have a sitting desk, or split your time sitting and standing, you'll need to have a chair that supports your back and encourages productivity. While they're more expensive than other kinds of office chairs, it's worth it to invest in a good ergonomic chair. We'll go more into ergonomics later, but in a nutshell, these types of chairs are specifically designed to ease lower back pain, support your spine, alleviate neck and shoulder pains, and promote circulation. Major bonus points if it's on wheels so you can roll about your office space with wild abandon and glee. If you're doing a fair amount of sitting, you want to be in a chair that's doing all of these things. Avoid that tech neck! Unfortunately, you cannot collect workers' compensation from yourself as a freelancer. However, you can keep a tube of M&M minis in your desk drawer to hit any time you're feeling physical pain.

Multi-port hub: Get your mind out of the gutter. If you're going to be doing any work on your laptop, chances are it doesn't have enough ports. A multi-port hub not only expands the number and kind of ports available, it also allows you to transform your laptop into a full-blown workstation with one plug. Simply plug it into your computer and use a multitude of other USB devices all from a single port. It's a REAL treat! It's also useful for moving a lot of data between USB devices. What might you be using "multiple ports" for? Wireless mouse dongle, keyboard, microphone, external storage, light up corgi phone charger... plenty of things! We also recommend pairing your port with a salty dry cheese, like Parmesan or Pecorino. Molto bene!

Wi-Fi: Yeah, sorry to break it to you but you'll need Al Gore's internet superhighway to do your work. Most likely, you probably already have it at your house. In case you don't (blink twice if you need help), now is definitely the time. Wi-Fi enables you to work from any nook and cranny of your home and even outside! Even if you do have it, consider getting an upgrade if it isn't fast enough for you to work AND stream *Love After Lockup* at the same time. Call your company and see if they're offering any deals for upgrading your Internet. You don't want to find yourself in situations where it seems you're late showing up for an important meeting with a client just because it takes too long to join the Zoom call. Sometimes it's even worse when you CAN join the call, but your audio keeps... cutting... during... times... when... say... important... things.

Supplies: Treat yourself to your favorite office supplies. Obviously, there's a wide range of items to choose from. But here's a list of some of the basics you may need:

- Printer paper
- Pens
- Highlighters
- Notebook/legal pad

- Nice-feeling markers for stress-doodling
- Post-it notes
- Binders
- Lisa Frank Folders
- Stapler
- Staples
- Staple remover
- Scissors
- Paperclips
- Document tray/holder
- Different types of "good job!" and "great work!" stickers

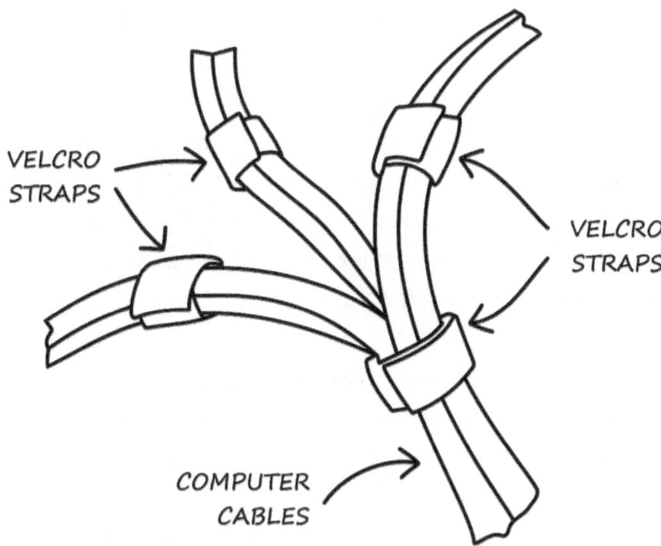

Here's a pro tip: Use Velcro straps to organize all of your tech cables. Without them, the wires can get in your way (hands, legs, and feet). The cables can even be tripping hazards!

Storage/Office organization: Documents, papers, and notes can get overwhelming if they're not organized properly. You don't want to add unnecessary stress to your life and lose valuable time trying to find things. With the wide variety of styles and designs for storage and office organizations these days, it's easy to find something you'll find aesthetically pleasing. With your workspace well organized and pleasing to the eye, it'll be more inviting, enabling you to get in your zone quicker and also to take totally candid selfies you can post on Instagram with the caption, "Move over Boss Baby, there's a new Boss Baby in Boss Baby town now!" Nice! Target is a great place to shop for these kinds of items. Once we saw a light-up, neon, koala-shaped pen holder. Who says organization has to be boring!? And once again, don't forget those office furniture discount outlets!

Tech power: Do you have enough outlets in your home office to power your computer, external hard drive, emotional support heating pad, printer, lamp(s), and any other electronics you have? If in doubt, a power strip upgrade may be in order. Good cables are important. Are they up to snuff? You'll want to make sure they're sufficient for carrying the necessary power your devices need or whatever it is that electricity does. The same goes for charging adapters. Do you have another monitor (two screens are better than one) you need to plug in? Is your computer ready to handle the heavy power user you're going to become? You'll want to do what you need to be able to answer "yes" to all of these questions.

Pro Tip: Have a set of laptop, phone, and tablet chargers that can stay in your office, so you don't have to keep moving them around like some sort of normie. You know what they say– "mo' chargers, mo' problems."

The following items are optional. But, they'll make your work from home setup ideal. Ultimately, deciding which of these items to add comes down to your own personal needs, preferences, and budget. If you want to include them all, go for it! Otherwise, consider purchasing them in order to do what makes your home office space work the best for you.

Monitor mount/stand: A monitor arm mount allows you to reclaim some desk space, especially if it has limited capacity. It also helps to reduce neck and eye strain. Another way to make the most of desk space is the use of a dual monitor stand, which also allows for additional space for a keyboard, charging station, jumbo Subway sandwich, and/or documents and notebooks.

Laptop stand: If you're the type of person who likes a change of scene during the course of your workday, then you may want to consider purchasing a stand for your laptop. Not only do they provide stability and protect against damage, but they also promote healthy posture. There are also adjustable laptop stands on wheels that you can move all around your house! Have you ever been a patient in the hospital and eaten gluey mashed potatoes from a table that swings over your bed? They're like that. But for work! And there is no sweeter flavor in this life than when "work" and "hospital" come together. Ohhhhh yeah. That's the sweet spot.

Acoustic treatment: This means making your office space better for recording audio or your next unplugged grunge album. Perhaps you've seen those things that look like egg-crates hanging on the walls in studios? In case you've ever wondered what they are, they're enhancements that minimize reverberation and echo. There are professional kinds you can get, but there are also a lot of options for DIY. Check out both if audio recording is going to be a regular part of your life. Or if you plan on crying a lot but don't want anyone else to hear you!

Whiteboard: This accessory is great for jotting down your thoughts and ideas, brainstorming, maintaining a list of enemies, and planning revenge against said enemies. Or general planning. Both are acceptable. You can choose one that's for your desk or one that hangs on the wall. As Bob Ross would say, it's YOUR WORLD and you can really do anything! Why not get some different colored dry erase markers to make some happy little trees while you're at it?

Creating a home office space that works for you takes a level of investment and putting in place the correct tools and equipment. So, don't rush the process! You'll be adding new features over time as needed and making necessary tweaks and adjustments as you calibrate your work environment according to your own unique needs. Also, don't be afraid to rearrange when you're bored. It sounds weird, but a "new-feeling space" can give you a "new-feeling motivation!" Just remember, lift with your LEGS not your BACK.

STEP #42

HOW DO I CREATE THE RIGHT MOOD IN MY OFFICE SPACE FOR PRODUCTIVE WORK?

The goal of your home office setup is to carve out a dedicated workspace that suits your professional needs and unique personality. A big part of that means creating an environment where you can be your most productive. The most important thing you can do to facilitate this is to establish a workspace that is separate from the rest of your home. You can maintain a better focus on your work when you mentally and physically detach yourself from your home life. You might also try detaching yourself from your corporeal being. You wouldn't believe the quality of work we get done when we're astral projecting!

In the previous section, we focused mostly on elements of your home office setup that support your physical comfort. But your workspace should also be mentally and emotionally supportive as well. You want the design elements you choose to be inspiring and create a mood that makes you feel excited about your work and positively high on the vibez!

Lighting: Even if you're working indoors most of the time, it doesn't mean you can't soak up the sun. If possible, choose a room with a view from your home office space. Natural light can stimulate the mind, boost your creativity, weed out any vampires in your midst, and help reduce stress. So, when thinking about where to set up your home office, try your best to place it near at least one window (unless you're a vampire yourself). In addition to natural light, you'll also want to use task lights, which allow you to adjust the direction your light source is coming from as well as the light's strength (important for controlling glare). LED is energy efficient, but OLED (Organic light-emitting diode) is just as efficient with better image quality. Choose fixture designs that not only reflect your style, but that are both flexible and functional. Also, consider hanging some string lights around your office to create a work atmosphere that is festive and upbeat. Test out how different types of light placements affect your video calls, lest you want to show up on camera looking like one of the aliens from the movie "Cocoon." Not that there's anything wrong with that.

Color Scheme: Design your space with colors that help you focus and feel more energetic. There has been a lot of research on the impact of color on our psychology, so feel free to explore the connection in greater depth if you like. In general, studies show that blue and green colors in a room create a calming feel that reduces stress and increases harmony. Add bright colors like orange, red, and yellow boost energy and foster a sense of optimism. We recommend Pantone shade 448 C for your office space if you're looking to feel a sense of impending doom and cosmic despair! Hey, some people are into that!

When considering colors, think about your personality and needs and choose what resonates with you best. And be sure to avoid overusing colors. You want a nice balance between your color choices and more neutral hues, like gray and white. Try not to base your entire decor on trends either – unless you're a shiplap fan for life! If your heart tells you that an all-art deco design is what you want– go for it! We currently have a collection of limited-edition Jurassic Park action figures sitting on our desk as we write this very sentence! Just do you!

To create the right mood for your office, start with ergonomics. Invest in an office chair that will support your posture. Try to be in a place with plenty of natural light to boost your mood. Use decor, such as large office plants or string lights to boost your mood even further. Make this your safe haven and home for freelancing!

Decorating Tips: You'll be spending a lot of time in this space, so you'll want it to feel warm and inviting. Instead of blank walls, how about hanging a picture of your family, your favorite art, a photo of Ron Howard, and/or a collage of inspirational quotes? There are 'wall' sorts of ways to spruce up your office (sorry, that was a bad pun). Here are a few to think about:

- **Magnets and pins:** Use magnetic linen wallpaper or a piece of cork board to pin a calendar, inspirational items, and important documents on your walls.
- **Vision boards:** Put up vision boards and personal mission statements so that you can see them every day. These have become very popular over the years (We bet Ron Howard has one.) And if you've created one, the home office space for your new business is the perfect place to put it. Right next to your photo of Ron Howard!

- **Shelves:** Add a few strategically placed shelves to maximize the space and help you stay better organized. You can find a variety of sizes and styles online and at places like Lowes and Home Depot. And if you're near an IKEA, that's a perfect place to shop for them.
- **Plants:** Adding a few house plants is strongly encouraged. Not only do they make your workspace look more pleasant, but they also improve air quality and help reduce stress. They also give you someone to talk to outside of your photograph of American auteur Ron Howard.

Positioning for Success/Ergonomics 101: Essentially, ergonomics is the study of supporting the health and productivity of workers. And it is really important for you to consider ergonomic principles when setting up your environment. The benefit of arranging your home office space with ergonomics in mind is that it minimizes physical tension and supports healthy posture, reducing the aches and pains that can negatively impact your health and productivity. To create a workspace that supports your health and comfort while you work, follow the guidelines listed below.

- **Leg space:** Make sure your sitting and/or standing area has plenty of space for your knees, thighs, feet, and tentacles.
- **Back support:** Get a special lumbar pillow or footrest to take pressure off of your spine while sitting. If your chair has armrests, adjust them so your shoulders stay relaxed. Isn't it nuts that we're all walking around with a skeleton inside us? Whattttt?!
- **Posture:** Try to keep your hips, ears, and shoulders in one vertical line, keeping in mind that this may require that you adjust the height of your monitor. Your upper arms should be parallel to your spine and your forearms should

be perpendicular when typing. There are plenty of tools and tips that can help you maintain good posture, so we encourage you to explore and choose what works best for you! Hanging upside down from a coat rack is not ideal but we GET it.

- **Screen positions:** Position your computer screen at eye level and an arm's length away. If you wear bifocals, though, you may need to lower it by 1 or 2 inches to make viewing easier. When working with two computer screens, the one you use the most should be in front of you, with the other off to the side. If you spend an equal amount of time using both screens, place them side by side so that their edges touch (awwwww). Then, angle the outer edges slightly toward you.

- **20-20-20 rule:** Every 20 minutes, look at something 20 feet away for 20 seconds. Staring at your computer for too long hurts your eyes. Following this rule throughout the day protects you from excessive strain on your eye muscles. We recommend gazing into the abyss until the abyss also gazes into you.

- **Breaks:** This really can't be stressed enough. Your muscles can get tired and sore from supporting you when you sit, which can lead to serious problems over time. So, get up, walk around, and do some gentle stretching at least once an hour if you're physically able to. Treat your body well and it will reciprocate. If you inexplicably woke up in the form of a huge cockroach named "Gregor," we're deeply sorry and you should disregard the preceding advice.

Working from home can be so comfortable and convenient. But it also means a more casual, relaxed environment with plenty of potential distractions, which can make being disciplined and establishing a productive daily routine very challenging. A big part of creating the right mood and supporting your own productivity is establishing and sticking to a routine. So, here are some tips to help you do just that!

- **Mornings:** Get up in the mornings at around the same time (this actually helps you sleep better too!), even if you have to set an alarm. While you want to wear comfortable clothes, it helps to shift you into a work mindset to get showered and dressed, instead of leaving on your pajamas. But who are we to judge? If that works better for you, then just go with the flow! We'll admit, sometimes we like to have a shower lunch break just to have that sensory input to shake things up in the middle of the day.

- **Daily schedule:** Establish a daily schedule to keep you accountable and prevent you from being tempted away from your work. Having a daily schedule also puts you in a better position to minimize negative blowback when making any necessary changes to your plans, such as, a "quick" Target run or a "brief" scan of the "Dancing Plague of 1518" Wikipedia article. We'll pause while you look that one up. You're gonna want to.

- **Lunch breaks:** Schedule a real lunch break! Don't eat at your desk. And don't eat underneath it goblin-style either. Take the time to leave your desk and enjoy a meal while doing something relaxing. Even if you don't eat, go for a walk, or do some light stretches. Giving your brain a break and giving your body some movement will boost your energy levels and creativity for the rest of the day.

- **Office hours:** Set your office hours and make sure you and all family members respect them. If necessary, secure your office door with a deadbolt and booby trap. Honor this time by avoiding repetitive scans of social media and excessive texting throughout your workday.

- **Project management software:** If you don't already, strongly consider using some kind of task and project management software. There are plenty of free options to choose from, many of them offering a variety of functions you're sure to find helpful. And no, we do not recommend using a Doodle Bear to jot down important tasks throughout your workday. Adorable? Yes. Functional? Ok, maybe also yes. Is there ANYTHING a Doodle Bear can't do?!

Though it may seem counter-intuitive, establishing a lounge area or other cozy place where you can "escape" from your home office area can be highly restorative. Separation of work and the rest of your life is important for your mental health. Consider creating a reading nook to give yourself a relaxing space to spend some downtime. Nothing is more delightful than hitting the nook at the end of the day with a deep stack of Amelia Bedelia books. Her and her hijinks! Taking care of yourself isn't just important for keeping up with your tasks, it's important for living a long, balanced, pleasant life.

This section has presented you with a variety of ideas and suggestions for creating the kind of mood for your office space that's conducive to productive work. The thing to keep in mind is that ultimately, you simply want your home office to be a space where you *feel* good spending time!

STEP #43

WHERE CAN I WORK IF I CAN'T HAVE A HOME OFFICE SPACE?

If you can't have a dedicated home office space, there are certainly other options. Attractive ones. So much so, that even if you have a "home base" office space, you'll probably want to take advantage of a few of them from time to time. Ever try living in an economy-sized cardboard box that you decorate with puffy paint and cut a window and door into? Well, we HAVE and let us tell you it's…highly flammable. Yet comfortable!

These modern times afford us freelancers options for working all over the world. Or your town or city. Or cardboard box. Now that you're a freelancer, the choice is yours!

Here are some ideas of places to work when you can't or don't feel like being at home:

Your own backyard: Patio furniture isn't that expensive these days and as long as you have access to a good power source, there's no reason you can't have a nice set up right on your porch or deck. And if you're in an apartment, you may be able to create a good workspace on your balcony or patio (remember those portable monitors?). And if your Wi-Fi signal isn't strong enough to work well out there, get a booster or turn your phone into a mobile hotspot (the same goes for any other outdoor locations!). If you're living in a Playskool Playhouse, technically your back-yard could be anywhere! Ok, landowner!

Coworking space: These cozy, yet highly functional places are popping up all over. They can help you feel like a part of a community, offer networking opportunities, and help you fight feelings of isolation. There are often coffee shops and other ame-nities right on sight! But take it easy on the coffee because we all know what happens to our digestive system (we need the coffee aroma to stay)! Even if you're working abroad, options abound. And they are ideal places to meet fellow travelers and a variety of interesting folks working in a wide range of industries. You can find co-working spaces anywhere just by doing a google search of one near you. However, with over 25,000 co-working locations in 172 countries (and growing), co-worker.com is currently one of the best places to find a good co-working space when travel-ing/living internationally. Though they're usually not free, there may be deals out there for solopreneurs.

Coffee shops/cafes: Sometimes it's nice to be around the buzz of activity and unlimited slices of marble loaf. For some people, the background noise and lack of interruptions when working at cafes and coffee shops heighten their focus. Others feel that people-watching boosts their creativity. With the growing popularity of working remotely, a lot of cafes these days are set up for people just like you. There's a variety of food, drinks, Wi-Fi, outlets, and customer loyalty deals galore. Check Yelp before you go and read some reviews to see what you're getting into. There are some coffee shops where it's okay to take a quick call, but you probably don't want to conduct a whole video chat, if only because the internet connection may not be super stable, and your time is better spent scarfing down absolute heaps of marble loaf anyway.

Restaurants and pubs: If you're feeling stifled and want to loosen up a bit to get some inspiration while eating some wings, consider heading to a restaurant or pub with Wi-Fi. Restaurants and pubs usually have pretty good coffee, pleasant music, plug sockets, and great lunch options. Though we don't recommend talking to clients or taking calls while you're there because the noise levels tend to be too high. Especially in the afternoons when your local Creedence Clearwater Revival cover band is playing. Those CCR dudes do NOT mess around. And DO NOT drink and drive. Ever. NOT EVEN ONE DRINK. But you know that you're a responsible human!

The library. Most libraries these days are pretty comfy, with tons of outlets, good lighting, and lots of seating choices. Don't discount this free option! And if you need a bigger workspace to lay out all your stuff, reserve one of their study rooms. ALSO free. Libraries are awesome for times when you need to be hyper-focused and do deep work, free from distractions. Which makes it a bad place to hold business meetings. After all it is a library, and silence is golden. You may also meet your library's resident ghost! They all have one! Ours is named Miss Havisham and she lives in the children's non-fiction section. When she's not moaning, she has great ideas on microlearning!

YOUR LOCAL AREA

If you can't work at home (or if you just want to get out of the house), there are many "work-away-from-home" offices you can check out! With a little imagination, you can pick the environment that suits you best. Try it for a while and rotate to other locations as you desire. Freelance IDs really have it made when it comes to working ANYWHERE you want. This includes campgrounds and RVs!

University/college campus: While some areas may be restricted, there's a wide range of spaces on university campuses where you can be productive working remotely. There are indoor and outdoor areas, private tucked away spots, and wide-open spaces where you can find good places to get your work done and process the post traumatic stress you still carry with you every day of your adult life from the crushing pressure of college! After all, this is in large part what university/college campuses are designed for. Word of warning though, you may find the company of students, who can often be boisterous, to be distracting. On the other hand, it may make you feel more youthful and carefree. We encourage you to give it a try and see for yourself. (Parker loves going to UCONN occasionally to work and bringing a couple of his kids to the library there so they can do their high school homework. Hey, gotta inspire them somehow, right?)

The park and/or your local botanical gardens: Yes, some even have Wi-Fi! But if not, and you need to focus on offline work, these are fun and inspiring to visit. Get your work done while basking in the rejuvenating embrace of governmentally sculpted Mother Nature. You'll probably want to bring a blanket or outdoor chair to prevent your butt from going numb on the picnic tables and benches. At the height of the pandemic, some of us took our car to the parking lot of a park (which was really just a big field) and worked from our backseat with the windows open, tethering to an iPhone for the internet. It was surprisingly glorious!

Museums and art centers: Nothing beats this one! The calm and quiet ambiance you'll find in these buildings make for a fascinating workspace. Many museums also have restaurants with lots of food choices (dino shaped chicken nuggets) so you can get a bite to eat and usually provide plenty of seating. Both museums and art centers offer the opportunity to work in a distinctly creative environment, providing a wonderful way to get your own creative juices flowing. And when it's time to take a break, you can explore the space, take in a bit of culture, or discreetly move into the museum and live out the rest of your days in pure bliss!

Mall and department stores: If you can resist the urge to shop 'til you drop, the mall can be a great place to zone out, people-watch, and get busy. Yes, sometimes they even have Wi-Fi here, too! You may find an outlet in the food court, but that can be a real gamble. Also consider department stores, whose top floors often feature eateries and cafes, giving you a really nice choice of workspaces. Sometimes there's even a pretty good view too! When you've finished your work, hit up "Claire's" for some polyurethane fashion accessories that are all that AND a bag of chips! You know, as a reward.

The gym: If you're finding it challenging to reach your fitness goals, get a workout in and then settle down to work. Or you may prefer to get your work done and then get some time exercising. Many gyms have snack bars and seating areas where you can work without too many distractions. Yadda yadda yadda. We're not totally sure who's actually going to choose this option, but we do agree…technically, it is an option.

Grocery stores: Like the gym, grocery stores offer you the ability to hit two targets with one throw. Most modern food markets have cafes and/or snack bars with seating areas where you can grab a bite to eat and have a seat in a chill spot while getting some work done. Some of them even offer outdoor seating. While the grocery store may not sound as intriguing as some of the other options, it will allow you to work on some business-related tasks and pick up some groceries (candy) and prepared foods (ice cream sandwiches) all in one place.

Your place of worship: While it may be packed during weekend and evening worship services, during weekdays, they're often quiet and fairly empty. It's probably not appropriate to make it your regular office away from home. But there may be times when you find it particularly useful to take advantage of the restorative peace and tranquility to be found in these spaces. We urge you not to take meetings or calls in your place of worship unless your place of worship is actually a Shake Shack.

Hotels: Just because you're not on vacation doesn't mean you can't spend time in a hotel lobby. These spaces have tables and chairs set up to support working away from the office. And there's often good food and beverage options available. If you need some privacy to take a Zoom meeting, a few of the larger hotel chains, like Hilton and Marriott, have day-use room options. So, head to an attractive hotel nearby, tuck yourself into a cozy corner and get your work done in a fresh new environment. If you happen to see two twin girls, dressed in matching blue dresses, holding hands at the end of a long corridor, maybe work somewhere else for the day! And consider choosing a hotel in a touristy part of town. Then after your work is done for the day, you can have a relaxing stroll and take in the sights.

An important thing to remember is that when you're working on any sort of public Wi-Fi, you need to make sure you're taking security measures! This includes making sure sharing is turned off, using a VPN, glaring at busy bodies trying to take a peek at your screen, and using the latest anti-virus software.

While all of the alternatives to working from home are worth exploring, there are a few things to consider when deciding which options may work best for you.

- **Cost:** While co-working spaces are pretty affordable, with all of the great free options available, you want to weigh the pros and cons carefully to make sure it's worth it to add the expense to your budget.
- **Location:** If it's a place you want to go to regularly, it should be quick and easy for you to get there. It might be a great space, but if traveling there isn't convenient, trying to work there on a regular basis will probably be a drain on your productivity. Remember–there are always cardboard boxes!
- **The physical environment:** Does it offer the amenities you need? Does the noise level work for you? Is it a place with minimal distractions? Is it comfortable enough to allow you to work comfortably for at least a few hours? Do you find the space inspiring and energizing or maybe even soothing? How close is the space to your nearest Pizzeria Uno? You want to be able to answer "yes" to these questions.
- **Networking:** Networking is a key ingredient in establishing a thriving business. And while there are plenty of opportunities to network online, making meaningful connections with local freelancers and solopreneurs can also be invaluable. So, if networking is something you're interested in, that's definitely an important reason to consider coworking spaces or sharing your cardboard box with a fellow freelie.

When it comes to finding places to work outside your home, the world really is your oyster. So there's no need to feel limited if you can't work from home. And even if you have a great home office set up, working there all the time will probably feel a bit stale and redundant after a while. So, we encourage you to get out there and experience the big, wide world of work that's location independent!

1 MONTH BEFORE YOU DITCH YOUR CUBICLE

ESTABLISH YOUR DIGITAL PRESENCE

Pause for a moment and take a deep breath. Look back at the last six months. You have put in the work by joining the global ID community, getting your finances in order, finding your niche, and expanding your skills. There is even a foundation for your brand. You deserve a celebratory clap for making it this far, you literal Terminator of productivity. Let's keep the momentum moving, because you are just a few steps away from the finish line! Your next task is beefing up your brand's digital presence.

For a freelancer to go full time, you need a clear and memorable way to attract your future clientele that's not against the law or your moral compass. An all-you-can-eat pizza mukbang is probably not gonna cut it! Establishing yourself as a brand comes down to your story. Well-told stories evoke powerful emotions and can make it easier for potential clients to connect with your brand. In *Building a Storybrand: Clarify Your Message So Customers Will Listen*, author Donald Miller says you should follow a storytelling format, with your client being the "hero" and your business being the "guide." Your client will face a problem, and they will turn to you for a solution and plan. With your expertise, you will guide your client on a journey to success, like a regular Jiminy Cricket or something! Using Miller's storytelling strategy will make it so you are completely focused on the needs of your client, even if that client is a small wooden puppet who wears lederhosen and has a telescoping nose. Hey, we're all consummate professionals here!

STEP #44

HOW DO I ESTABLISH MYSELF AS A BRAND IN THE DIGITAL LANDSCAPE?

Your personal brand story should explain your why, what you do, who you do it for, and how you do it. Let's break this down a bit and go through a few examples.

Your Why: You've already determined how you want to be perceived by the public. The next step is to ensure your potential clients know it. The key to communicating your why is to be clear and authentic. What is the purpose of your business? What is your goal? Remember, your personal brand is not about you (geez not everything is about YOU), it's about how your services can make a difference for others.

Examples:

- I believe that training doesn't have to be boring, and it should be authentic and human centered.
- I hope to improve the work lives of others by helping them to learn the ropes of their jobs efficiently and effectively.
- Learning should never stop and training in any context should immediately show its usefulness and encourage people to want to learn more.

What You Do: You have your "why" crafted, so now it's time to tell your potential clients exactly what you do. Not to be confused with the classic Nickelodeon game show from 1991,

"What Would You Do," this is your big chance to share how you can listen to a client, pinpoint their problem, and then use your specific expertise to provide quality solutions.

Examples:

- I use a human-centered approach to create engaging learning solutions.
- I specialize in "just-in-time" learning for people to access and digest easily while on the job.
- I write and develop realistic scenarios to provide immediate and valuable learning.

Who You Do It For: Let's face it–we're all working our butts off so we can provide a certain amount of comfort and luxury for the special pet(s) in our life. But in this case, we're talking about your target audience (unless you happen to be an ID for dogs, in which case please tell us more immediately.) One freedom of being a freelancer is that you can choose what type of clients and projects you work on. In this step, you will explain who your target audience is and how you can make their lives easier.

Examples:

- I work with small businesses to craft human-centered learning experiences that boost employee performance.
- I work with call centers and the hospitality industry to improve new employee onboarding through just-in-time training.
- I make scenario-based training for customer service and sales enablement at medium-sized corporations.

How You Do It: This is where you get to really show off your skills! Specifically, share the unique strategies you use to solve your clients' problems. This is where you will tap into your niche and show how you are different from others in the field. Don't be shy! This is the time to humblebrag your hiney off. We all know some of those people, don't we? We actually can't relate because we've been told that we're very humble and naturally charming, so…yeah, can't relate.

Examples:

- I craft learning solutions that change staff behaviors using storytelling.
- I am a master of user-friendly job-aids and reference materials for new employees to use during their shifts.
- I work with customer service and sales enablement SMEs to collect information and create realistic scenarios that help employees have better and more productive experiences with customers.

Personal Brand Statement: Now, take your brand story and create a personal brand statement. This will give your audience a summary of who you are and what you do. We know this all feels a bit icky and off putting. It isn't exactly natural to position yourself as a brand but just go for it!

Examples:

- I craft human-centered learning solutions for small businesses, using the power of stories to improve the performance of their employees.
- I am a user experience design and adult learning principles pro who efficiently improves the confidence, ability, and knowledge of hospitality and call center workers.
- I truly believe that practicing realistic scenarios are the key to customer service and sales enablement success, and I can get the information I need from any SME to harness the power of real conversations.

You can use your personal brand statement on your portfolio site, your social media channels, on a novelty t-shirt, and in any marketing materials.

Before you brand yourself in the digital landscape, articulate your WHY. Why are you freelancing? Once you have that figured out, identify what you do, who you do it for, and how you do it. From there, create your brand statement. Finally, do your content marketing - but it needs to be CONSISTENT content marketing around your brand.

Remember, it is essential to have brand clarity. This will ensure you are resonating with the right audience, telling them the right story, so you can provide the best services that go with your purpose. Clarity is what will create impact, but you must be consistent to have longevity. Just look at the Kool-Aid man. Now there's a guy with a consistent brand! Dang, we wonder if he'll ever retire from busting through brick walls. That is the day, we too, will be left in ruins.

Content Marketing: It's time to release your personal brand story to the world through content marketing! A content marketing strategy involves sharing useful and relevant information in blogs, videos, emails, e-books, and other forms of media, to attract ideal clients and grow your brand. Consistency is the key. The more you are active in different online channels, the better your chances of visibility. Good content marketing will bring you more profits, build brand loyalty, and decrease your costs. It will also make you question if you're human any longer or just a vessel for content. Hot tip: it's the latter! Tee hee!

STEP #45

WHAT SOCIAL MEDIA SITES SHOULD I BE ON?

There's no doubt your business needs to be on social media. If you aren't using social media, you're missing out on major growth opportunities. Using social media sites will:

- Build brand awareness
- Help your potential clients find you
- Humanize your brand
- Slowly consume your soul, but in a fun way!

People can't help you if they don't know you exist. According to Pew Research Center, seven in ten Americans use social media every day. That's just in America. Imagine what it's like around the world. The more content you post, the more clients you'll be able to reach. Being on social media sites also helps humanize your brand. If you're quite literally not a human, we recommend using human catchphrases like, "I am definitely a human, I swear," or, "I love typing up content for you guyz with my phalanges on this computing machine YOLO!" Works every time!

Let's take a look at which social media sites you should be on now that you understand the benefits.

LinkedIn: Professional networking website LinkedIn is the G.O.A.T. (Greatest of All Time). This is a reputable site where you can not only spy on your old coworkers but also find jobs,

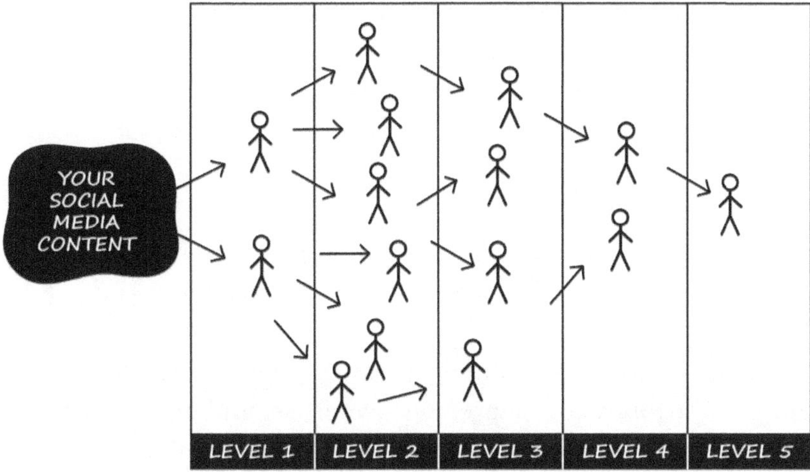

One of the best ways to market yourself as a freelance ID is to do content marketing through your social media channels. LinkedIn, YouTube, and Facebook are great tools to use to promote your content. Be consistent and persistent. Post at least 3-4 times per week for at least 12-18 months. Don't stop. Over time, prospects will come find you to do business!

network with people in your field, encounter incalculable levels of cringe, and take professional development classes. You'll find everything in one place. Out of all the available social media sites, you should set up this account first.

Business and Personal LinkedIn Page: The first thing you should do is create your personal and business profile. Your personal page should include:

- A cover image (not of Neil Diamond)
- Headline highlighting what you do (use your personal brand statement)
- A professional headshot (not of Neil Diamond)
- Featured Work (Highlight your portfolio site and add content you have created)
- Complete background information (relevant work history, education)
- All your certifications and credentials

Your business page should include:

- A cover image (not of Neil Diamond)
- A completed "About" area with links to your website (Not Neil Diamond's)
- Business specialties
- Business hashtags related to learning and development
- Communities you follow (Not the Neil Diamond ones)

You're going to want an official page for your business where you can grow a following, share your expertise, and engage with the online Instructional Design community. Maintaining a business page will give you a competitive marketing edge and show that you're serious about stuff (just not Neil Diamond).

Engage and Network: Your business page is a place where you can grow a following, share your expertise and engage with the online Instructional Design community. If you are consistent with your page, it will give you a competitive marketing edge and show that you are serious about your field.

Follow both thought leaders (aka the big dogs) and members of the L&D community. Comment on other articles and accomplishments, and share blog posts about your experiences in the field. It's probably not a great idea to write a 3,000-word blog on that one time you accidentally set fire to the bathroom at the big L&D convention and gained the unsavory title of "eBurning Poofessional" from your peers. Keep that one to yourself, maybe. These actions will help get your name out there and build your credibility.

Facebook: Since Facebook started in 2004, it has come a long way. Originally designed by a creepy college student for creepy college students, Facebook has grown into a social network that can connect you with billions of people. Literally. Over two billion people use Facebook every day. On Facebook, you can share photos, links, stream videos, chat online, trauma dump on old high school friends, create groups and business pages. Think about what that can mean for your freelance business. You can create a business page and a group for your freelance business.

Facebook Groups: You can build a community around similar interests and topics through Groups. You can create several groups on any topic (again, this is not the time for Neil Diamond), so it is a convenient space for you to connect with your customers. Without purchasing ads, you will have a direct line to the people who use or are interested in your services. There is no worry about pestering or bothering anyone, because people join groups on their own volition. You can miss the noise of getting lost in the abyss of the News Feed or those hyper-specific ads that somehow know you were considering buying a totally random brand of seltzer earlier at the grocery store. Seriously, what's the deal with those?! Is Facebook...sentient? Are they watching us...right now?

Anyway! Here are some super-duper fun ways to use Groups for your business:

- **Market Research:** If you want to launch any new products or services, before you take the plunge, you can get feedback from your audience.
- **Community:** You can build a genuine community with your audience in Groups. One of the best things about creating a Group is you can mark it Private or Public. You can avoid bots by asking admission questions to ensure people join for the right reasons. Once you build your community you can offer livestreams on a Work With Me session, give early access to any courses you built, and you can ask polling questions to find out your audience's needs or their favorite variety of Chex Mix.

Facebook groups are a free way to find out what future or current clients' needs and interests are, and how you can better serve them.

Facebook Pages: Pages provide the same advantages as Groups, except it is always public. The great thing about Pages is that you can provide all the information on your business and give updates about all the fantastic projects you will be working on. While your page is open to all types of audiences, it will give your business exposure, which will mean more clients.

TikTok: In 2016, TikTok was born, and it's still one of the most popular and addictive social networks out there. Seriously, we've opened the TikTok app before and emerged from a fugue state three days later, two towns over. If you are not familiar, it is a 15 second video sharing app. You can make a video about any subject on your phone and share it. Videos use music, collaborations, and dancing to get their audiences excited. Hashtags help get more views to your content on the site. For example, #instructionaldesign might be a great place to start as you work your way up to #thebestIDintheentiregalaxy.

Now, I'm sure you're thinking, "How can this help me with my freelance business?" Simple– exposure. The good kind. TikTok has millions of users every day. Here's how you can leverage that fact:

- Show your business tasks with day-in-the-life videos.
- Music or a dance can be used to share current trends in L&D.
- Make learning videos about simple tasks that Instructional Designers do. For example, how to create job aids.
- Make tutorial videos for Instructional Design software use.
- Give a tour of your home office space while wearing an Arthur the Aardvark costume for no discernible reason. (This is actually a great idea we've just given you for free.)

TikTok can also be used as a micro-learning solution for your clients. Here are some examples:

- Building a community by creating a day-in-the-life video of employees at work.

- Making learning videos for simple tasks, like booking a
  meeting room.
- Short tutorials on how to get off a call when you really need
  to go tell your kids to stop raiding the fridge.

YouTube: YouTube is an oldie but goodie social media site. You can watch and comment on other videos, watch strangers cook hot dogs in their toilets, and create your own videos. The best thing about YouTube is that you can use storytelling to engage and captivate your audience without strict time constraints.

Some ideas for using YouTube in your business are:

- Create work out loud videos. Give your audience a behind-
  the-scenes look at you creating and developing a course
  for a client. Talk through the decisions you are making with
  your reasoning. When you finish, ask the audience to share
  how they would create a similar course.
- Interview people in the field. Reach out to colleagues in
  the L&D space and interview them about an instructional
  design topic of choice.
- Create videos about your freelance journey. It's helpful to
  share videos about the difficulties in your experience as a
  freelancer.
- This actually might be a good place and time to tell that
  "eBurning Poofessional" story of yours! Hey, look at you.

YouTube is a great way to dive into your work process and educate simultaneously.

Instagram: Instagram is a photo and video sharing app where everyone pretends their lives are totally idyllic when in reality, we're all just trying to survive on a tiny rock floating out in space! You can also view other users' content, react, and leave comments. The first thing to do with Instagram is create a professional account. With this type of account, you get access to page analytics, scheduling posts, and creating an Instagram shop for any knowledge products.

Once your profile is all set up, you can create highlights on your page to give your audience quick access to information about your business. In your highlights, you can have:

- A collection of videos of you explaining your business values and your brand.
- Customer testimonials and feedback.
- Frequently Asked Questions can display the most common questions people have asked about your business.
- A collection of services you provide.
- Your very best glamor shots of your bearded dragon "Puff."

Other features of having a professional account are:

- Creating a Q&A with your followers, so they can learn more about your business.
- Conduct live streams that can include interviews, explaining your services, and showing your work videos.
- Create guides to showcase your favorite posts in one location.
- Just generally coming off better than everyone else!

Instagram is a very effective way to give your audience an authentic view of your business.

Social media provides so many opportunities and functions that it may be overwhelming for you. To take things slow, choose one platform to master first. Build your followers on that platform, get into a routine of posting, and then add to another platform. If possible, find a way to clone yourself so you can get all your socials firing at once! If your clone is born with a toxic soul, like many clones are, put that one in charge of X (previously known as Twitter).

STEP #46

WHAT'S THE SECRET TO GET CLIENTS TO FIND ME?

The secret to getting clients to find you is consistency and persistence. That and yelling "OLLY OLLY OXEN FREE!" out your window every day at 10 AM. Keep showing up regularly for your business. Use your social media platforms and blogs to attract new clients by creating content that will show them your valuable services and build a relationship.

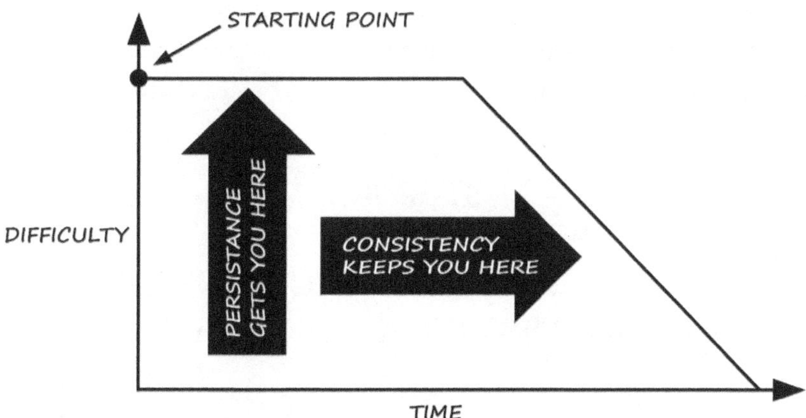

Persistence and consistency are the secrets to getting clients to find you. It's hard to get things started and moving for you. This is where persistence in your self-promotion of your ID skills and services will pay off. But, the only thing that will help you in the long run is the consistency of your efforts. The longer you go, the easier it will be for you to get clients. So, go for it and be patient. It might take a good year or more to really feel the change, but it'll happen!

Be relentless in making your business known. Make contributions to the field by speaking at conferences. The access to snacks, sodies, knowledge, and networking you gain from conference attendance is unmatched. Be a guest on a podcast to discuss industry topics, or maybe even start your own podcast. All the kids are doing it! The bottom line is you have to be consistent and persistent. When you are not getting the traction in your business that you want, do not give up. It will come, and eventually, you will no longer be looking for clients; they will come to you. The way nature intended.

PUT IN YOUR TWO-WEEKS' NOTICE!

Drum roll please! Here we go, (soon to be) freelie. We're really inching toward the finish line now! Don't freak out, but it's time to hand in your two weeks' notice. Holy cats! This is not unlike the moment in Aladdin where Aladdin uses his last wish to set the genie free and the genie's all like, "Whaaa? ME? FREE?!" That's totally your face right now! You should really see it! Let's break down what your two-weeks' notice actually is and the best practices for submitting it.

STEP #47

HOW DO I WRITE AND HAND IN MY TWO-WEEKS' NOTICE?

This is it! Drop everything right now, get out of your seat, and dance like you've never done before. It is time to craft your quit day letter, a.k.a. your two weeks' notice!

A two-weeks' notice is the standard for notifying your employer that you are resigning. It's also the amount of lead time we prefer when making any type of social plans. Although it is not a legal obligation, it's best practice. You do not want to burn any bridges, because you never know when you might meet up professionally. Be sure to check your company's handbook and your contract, if you have one, to ensure that the company does not have protocols on how to tender your resignation.

Your notice should be short and sweet. Keep it simple. It should include:

- An opening address to your manager.
- In your first paragraph, state that you are resigning and give the date of your last day.
- In your second paragraph, thank your employer for the opportunities and experiences provided at the job.
- In your third paragraph, provide your plan for the next steps in relation to your workload. If there are any transitions, you can offer your help.
- Finalize the letter with a formal closing.

Example:

Dear John Doe,

Please consider this letter a formal resignation from my position as _______________. My last day will be _______________.

It has been a pleasure working at _______________. I am grateful for the opportunity to work here and for the mentorship you provided.

I would be happy to assist in the transition period and welcome questions you may have as you are looking for a replacement.

Sincerely,

Your Name

It is best to give two weeks' notice in person or through video conferencing with your manager. Do not attempt to send it by owl courier!

STEP #48

CAN I WORK FOR MY FORMER EMPLOYER AS A FREELANCER?

Of course, you can work for your former employer as a freelancer! The most effective way to do this is by sharing your freelance business with your colleagues after you submit your two-weeks' notice. But, before you do, check the company policy. Ensure there are no bummer waiting periods before a former employee can do consultant work. All companies are different, and some may not have a policy, but it's a good idea to check it out so you can pitch your services accordingly.

COST OF HIRING A FREELANCER	COST OF HIRING AN EMPLOYEE
HOURLY RATE FIXED PROJECT FEE	SALARY HEALTH INSURANCE VACATION TIME RETIREMENT FUNDS PAYROLL TAXES OTHER PERKS

Working as a freelancer for your former employer can be a win-win situation. You get to experience the freedom of being a freelancer and the employer has the potential to access your talents at a lower cost because they won't need to pay your salary, health benefits, vacation time, retirement funds, payroll taxes, and more. Not to worry, freelie, you can get way more income with multiple contracts than working one full-time job as an employee!

Once you get your ideas in order, let them know you are open to working with them on a contract basis, and to keep you in mind if projects come up. Be specific, ask to continue assisting with a project you are working on or for a future project. Give them details about how you can help. If they hire you as a freelancer, then you rock! You've technically landed your first direct client! If you do not get hired, at least you tried. And what the heck do they know anyway?! Keep working on your portfolio and putting yourself out there to various people and organizations. As the saying goes, "There's a lid for every pot!" Except for this one pot that used to belong to our Great Grand-Uncle Bertram.

WHO DO YOU SERVE?!

Unless you happen to be Scottish-American mogul and anthropomorphic duck, Scrooge McDuck, we all gotta serve someone to make a living in this world! That's what this next step is all about– identifying the types of clients you'd like to serve. You may be thinking, "Uhhh isn't any client, the right type of client?" Well, yes. But also, no. Let us explain.

STEP #49

HOW DO I IDENTIFY MY MARKET IN THIS HUGE WORLD OF L&D?

Before you head out and hunt for your perfect market fit, there's some stuff you should know. First of all, hunting humans is considered the most dangerous game and you really should NOT be doing that. We shouldn't really have to tell you that, geez. Secondly, no matter the industry, there are two major ways to find and work with clients:

- **Direct:** You found 'em, you work for 'em…directly (duh). No middle person needed. Cash directly from their hands into your pockets.
- **Indirect:** There's at least one person or organization between you and the client, and your pay usually comes from that middle person. More exposure to various projects, less messy contract stuff for you.

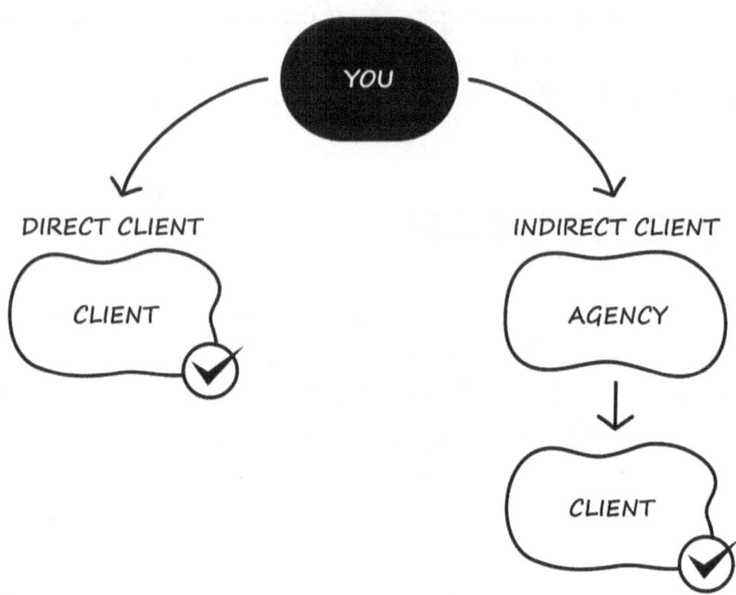

This is a very simplified sketch of a direct client vs. an indirect client. When you're starting out as a few freelancer, it's easier to land gigs with eLearning agencies. They'll have you work on projects for their clients (your indirect clients). As you gain more experience, you can land the direct client gigs. No middle person or agency needed. Then again, you can do BOTH even as an experienced freelancer!

If you are ready to, start with indirect clients first. You can build up your portfolio because you are exposed to different industries and projects. It also minimizes the time you'll need to spend on sales and marketing in the early days. That time can be used to perfect your skills.

It is common for eLearning and instructor-led training providers to outsource Instructional Designers and developers. If you Google your niche (Step #9) plus training providers, you can find out who they are looking for. Make sure you put the name of the industry you are looking for before the search term. For example, if you are interested in healthcare, you can do a Google search for healthcare training providers. Your results will show you the different training providers out there. Just do yourself a favor and do not google, "clown training providers" if you are a fellow sufferer of coulrophobia. Many people do not realize that there are tons of industry-specific training providers out there. (Many people also do not realize that there are tons of menacing clowns just skulking about out there.) A simple Google search focused on your niche can give you a list of potential clients.

For your direct clients, don't forget that small and medium-sized businesses have training needs. Think about companies that involve your niche and see if there are opportunities. Nonprofit organizations, professional organizations, religious institutions, and the government also have training needs. Try taking some time to Google and make a list of the potential opportunities you find, then pitch your services to your future non-clown client.

STEP #50

HOW DO I APPLY FOR GIGS FROM INDIRECT CLIENTS?

Large L&D agencies such as ELB Learning, Clarity Consultants, TrainingFolks, and The Training Associates are a few of the many great places to explore opportunities. Do you see the same industries popping up often in your job searches? If so, be sure to make a note.

Another (awesome) place you can check out is IDLance! We do match ID freelancers to our client projects. So, without hesitation, send us your resume at www.idlance.com/talent-pool. Come swim with us!

Yet another strategy to use when applying for gigs is to do the cold call/email technique. We know this thought has your whole body positively a-quivering with consternation. Remember, it's only awkward if you make it awkward! And it's actually way less weird than it seems. Take some time to research and determine what type of companies you want to work with. Find your ideal company and prepare to give them a cold call/email. It helps call with a script already prepared. We even use this technique when ordering a pizza– like one solitary pizza. Hey, some of us get phone anxiety! When reaching out, keep everything simple. Introduce yourself, use your personal brand statement, and then express your interest in job opportunities.

Here are two sample scripts:

- *"Hi, my name is Amanda Huginkis and I'm a freelance Instructional Designer based in Virginia. I was researching your company, and it looks like you do some really interesting eLearning design and development projects! I was wondering if you had a minute to chat about your company and whether you ever work with freelance IDs."*
- *"Hello! My name is Seymour Buttz and I'm a freelance Instructional Designer. I also specialize in (writing, instructional tech, development, voiceover, video production, etc.). I heard about your company from a colleague and was really intrigued. I'd love to know more about what you do and if you ever work with freelancers."*

There are 3 steps to help you apply for gigs from indirect clients. First, make a list of eLearning content providers. You can Google them or find them on elearning-industry.com. Secondly, reach out to each provider with a personal email to introduce yourself and ask to meet with them on a Zoom call. Lastly, check off your list as you connect with each provider. That list, in itself, is a great motivator!

Keep a spreadsheet or notebook with a list of potential clients, what type of jobs they usually hire for, and when you contact them. This will help you remember who you have contacted and the outcome. After a while, you will have a visual of how far you have come in your freelance journey and can pat yourself on the back.

STEP #51

HOW DO I FIND GIGS WITH OTHER FREELANCERS?

Pay attention to what other freelancers are working on, and you'll get a sense of which industries need consistent help. Join LinkedIn groups, like the Online Network of Independent Learning Professionals or Instructional Design Facebook groups. These groups often share job opportunities for work with indirect clients.

SLACK GROUPS TO CHECK OUT FOR
NEW CONTRACTS!

IDLANCE	ONILP	TLDCHAT
#GIG-ALERTS	#OPPORTUNITIES	#JOBS

There are three good Slack communities you can check out to find ID contract opportunities. IDLance, of course, is one of them! You can also ask to join the ONILP Slack group (start by going to the Online Network of Independent Learning Professionals on LinkedIn). The third group is TLDChat, hosted by TLDC (The Training, Learning and Development Community & Conference). You can find gigs in the #gig-alerts, #opportunities, and #jobs channels, respectively.

Where else can you go? Our own IDLance Slack group, of course! We just need you to submit your name and LinkedIn profile (to make sure you're a human and not a robot!). Just let us know by going to www.idlance.com/slackcommunity. We promise you'll love the vibe there... where you can just be you!

Also, be sure to post in freelance groups. This will let others know you are looking for opportunities, and you can give back by sharing what you come across in your search. Or you can hoard all those opportunities for yourself because the world owes you and you deserve this win for once in your life!!!

Ahem. It's also a great place to make friends! Did you know that having social relationships can help you live longer?!? C'mon, what are you waitin' for??

YOU DITCHED YOUR CUBICLE!

TIME TO CELEBRATE!

As the age old saying goes, "Work Hard. Rub it in thine doubters' faces harder." Wait…maybe that's not the quote. Is it "play harder?" That sounds more right. We like ours better.

ANYWAY, these next steps are some of the most important in this entire book. Why? Because it's time to celebrate YOU and all your extremely hard-earned achievements. Do you suppose Thomas Edison invented the first incandescent electric light with a silent shrug and a, "Meh, I'll just keep this one to myself." No, sir, absolutely not! He probably went out and got…lit.

Speaking of that dude, he also famously said, "I have not failed. I have just found 10,000 ways that do not work." Freelie, we urge you to keep the lessons of Tommy Edison close to your heart as you continue your bizness journey. Not only should you celebrate your wins, but you should also forgive your losses. Heck, maybe celebrate those too! The bottom line is, no matter how busy you get on your new career path– *always* make time to celebrate yourself and *never* let anyone or anything dim your light!

STEP #52

HOW SHOULD I CELEBRATE MY ESCAPE FROM THE 9-5 GRIND?

You did it! The freedom to work in comfortable pajama bottoms, the power to reign from your home office, and the authority to plan your workday are finally in your grasp! You can even gobble down sloppy fistfuls of candy for lunch, free from the side glances of coworkers! Praise be!

You worked hard to set the stage and now revel in the experience of being the master of your work/life balance!

Time to celebrate your car's lower mileage (from lack of commute!) in style.

But how?

You do you, you beautiful, organized, and creative individual. What floats your boat? For us it's upward buoyancy. But that's us!

A fan of fancy caffeinated beverages in the morning? Make a coffee shop in your kitchen with bottles of your favorite flavors to help get you going. You can finally get a sextuple shot of the caramel espresso you've always wanted, but your typical coffee shop couldn't give it to you for cost and health reasons. Seeing that you are making your schedule now, you have the time to make your favorite breakfast how you want. Not a fan of bean juice? You now have the time to make a full course breakfast in the morning. Farm fresh eggs with freshly squeezed orange juice more your speed? Or maybe a raw Pop-Tart, still in its wrapper, eaten hastily over a garbage can is your idea of a good time. You can do it and not worry about rushing out of the door in time to make it to work with traffic!

You even have the time and capacity to plan your vacations, free time, and excursions out into the world or deep into your futon. Always wanted to travel to the local tourist trap but never had the time? Get that dopamine drip by marking it as a meeting in your time management system and do it. Are friends getting together in the afternoon to catch up? You better ask your boss if you can go out to lunch today. Oh, right! You are your boss. We hope that your boss is nice enough to let you go. If your work is completed and submitted to your client in time, take the family or your small army of dogs to see the world's largest duck statue made of rubber bands! What the duck do you have to lose?!

One of the biggest perks of freelance life is having time to do things DURING business hours. Wooo, how terribly naughty! You can make the first available appointment at your doctor's office without checking what days you can take off because of a coworker's vacation. No more checking the carpool rotation to see if you can get the kids into one of the specialist's infrequent time slots. No more stressing about being able to afford the time off work to be healthy. Decreases in stress could also lead to, overall, better health. HA! Another bonus to celebrate! At the end of the day, we all just want the same thing– to spend more time with doctors. Geez, are we lucky or what?

As a full-time freelancer, you can do whatever you want, whenever you want. The time is yours and not someone else's. You can live your dream and not someone else's dream. This is the real celebration that you get to experience for as long as you are an ID freelancer.

Need to go in and talk to a person at a bank (ew)? Maybe you want to upgrade to an all-culottes wardrobe for your new job (spicy)? Maybe grocery shopping for dinner (mmm dinner)? Hint! The banks and stores tend to have fewer people during business hours and zombie apocalypses, so head on in. You can celebrate your freedom via retail therapy without lines or crowds of people or the walking dead.

Not interested in basking in the freedoms of your newfound life? That works, too. Follow your regular work schedule, enjoy working in your office, and feel the satisfaction of completing your tasks and paying bills in the personalized situation you made for yourself. Take some spare time to visit family or invite people over. The elderly or your fellow work from home recluses would love to hear from you during the daytime. Oh! Stop at the easier-to-get-through store and pick them up their favorite high-calorie snack. It'll be a quick stop and help you get in the door of the grumpier family member. Might we be so bold as to suggest Wild Cherry Pepsi and Ring Dings? The combo has a great mouth feel.

Don't want to do any of these things? You might be an introvert, have a delayed sleep phase syndrome, or are just a night owl by nature. That is okay too! Is sleeping in till noon, working until you are done, then playing online games with your friends till 4 AM more your idea of a decent work schedule? Celebrate your coming into a career that fits your natural biology and celebrate with a LAN party or update your rig with a new graphics card.

Your time is now your own. Not being beholden to checking in with a higher authority allows you to be flexible with your time. Straddling the line between work and life is now totally in your hands. Live your life in the order and with the people that you want—even if "people" means a life-size cardboard cutout of Brendan Fraser. Some people do that! It's very healthy and very normal and very cool. Ahh to feel the warm, unblinking gaze of Brendan upon us as we work…

The point is, you've worked hard to make it to this point, and you get to mold it into what you need it to be.

Way to go!

STEP #53

HOW DO I SHARE THE GOOD NEWS WITH MY FAMILY, FRIENDS, AND COLLEAGUES?

Don't sit on this news like a gold-hoarding dragon! Share the good news with your friends and family! You can sing of your victory from the highest local mountain top through a glorious song, have an office warming party, gather friends and family to meet your new coworkers (kids and/or pets), or simply post to your preferred social media outlet.

Or all four.

You have worked hard to reach this goal, and sharing this life change with your friends and family should be a joyous time. You might want to prepare for some to question this career choice or simply not understand the words that are coming out of your mouth.

Most of these questions won't come from a place of malice, just ignorance. Having some jargon-free answers prepared might help your social support net understand your choices. This way, they can celebrate with you, rather than celebrate with you but secretly worry about you (like that one time we married an Edwardian ghost named Egbert. People can really be judgmental.)

Even your best friend forever (BFF) might ask you if you can still pay your bills as a full-time freelancer. And imagine what you can say! "I make twice as much money now. Any other questions?" The point is that your income has no limits in the world of ID freelancing. So, go out there and make it happen. You can do it!

Here are some examples of questions and possible answers.

What is this "Instructional Design"? What do you actually DO? Oh boy. Now's your time to prove you're more useful than Robyn Brown from Sister Wives' nanny. This is a question that we get a lot, especially from those who aren't very familiar with technology. It's hard to relate to those people when you're a computer whiz like we are with the buttons, and the clicking, and the chat rooms, and floppy disks. Your answer could differ depending on your skill set. Learning for some will always default to traditional lectures and note-taking. Here is an opportunity to flash those ID skills you've worked hard to master!

"I build educational interactions that my clients use to train their employees."

"I research and write out the blueprints so others can build a better training program."

"I use my computer skills to bring others' writing to life using animation and graphics."

"I'd like to see YOU try out my job for one SINGLE day Uncle Jim, ya old geezer hag!"

Do you see the people you work for? How do you know that they will pay you what they say? Most people asking this question should know what a contract is and maybe have been short-changed in the past. Digital meetings and messaging programs might not be the same as seeing the person you are working with, but they are definitely easier to schedule and get to than face-to-face meetings.

"The company has a very active online presence. I can get in touch with them anytime I have a question."

"We can schedule video meetings if we need to discuss the project. [company name here] is very good at being available to freelancers."

"I was referred to [company name here] by a [trusted person]. They dealt really well with them in the past."

"You know you can look up this kind of information on the internet, right?"

"I take possession of their personal tamagotchi until I am compensated for my work."

How do your taxes work? WAAH! Math questions make us want to run for the hills. Answer this with as much or as little information as you'd like. We imagine that if you bring out a binder full of notes and tax forms and slap on one of those green money counting visor things, people might not ask you this again, though.

"I file as self-employed."

"I use a financial management software to track my taxes."

"I get a 1099 form from each employer from which I make more than $600."

"I dump chests of tea into the Boston Harbor every year to protest against taxation, and you know that. Try being more sensitive."

Can you really make enough money doing that? Again, you can go into as much or as little detail answering this question as you feel comfortable. Be proud of what you build and the effort you put into your career. You don't have to put a dollar amount to it if it would make you or the question asker uncomfortable.

"Oh, for sure. The job requires a LOT of different skills and the ability to work independently. It can be hard to find people with this kind of skill set."

"Of course. If I get paid [insert math noises here], then I'll have no problem paying my bills."

"Yup."

"I make more than enough money to buy my dog all the puppuccinos she wants. That's what counts in this household."

Aren't you going to get lonely working alone? People need people. We are social creatures, and studies have shown what harm isolation can do to the human mind. Your social needs will differ from others, so respond accordingly. If you suddenly find yourself living in a cave in the Misty Mountains, rattling on about "my precious," it's time to call a friend!

"Yeah, but one of the perks of working for myself is I make my own schedule. That means I can come visit you anytime!"

"Maybe. I'm working on most of my projects with a group of others, so I won't really be alone."

"No way. I'll get to be in my office and focus completely on my work with no distractions. I'll get so much stuff done!"

"I had Chickenpox as a child, so the Shingles virus is already inside me. I am never truly alone."

Isn't it risky to work like that? What about job security? Job security isn't what it used to be. Technology has connected the world like no other time in history. A solid internet connection and the ability to self-manage can secure a job just as well as having reliable transportation and being on time consistently could for brick-and-mortar jobs.

"There is a high demand for Instructional Designers. I don't think I need to worry about that right now."

"The Instructional Design network is awesome. I don't think I could run out of work."

"Honey, I am marvelous! Everyone wants me!"

"I have a home security system and a sock full of pennies that I keep next to my desk, so I'm covered there."

What if they don't like your work? This friend and/or family member cuts right to the quick. I'm sure many of us have this fear lurking in the back of our heads when we are working on a project. Let them see as little or as much of your process for handling this as you are comfortable with.

"The group I'm working with has a great check-in system for the project. If there is a problem with my work, we'll work together early in the process and figure out how to make it work."

"The company I'm working for liked what they saw in my portfolio. I know they like my work."

"I've had that happen before. It was rough and a lot of work to make [employer's name here] happy, but that is part of the job."

*"What if I don't like YOUR work Auntie Joann, ya old busy body! Your green bean and raisin casserole makes me wanna puke!" *runs away crying**

What hours do you normally work? Consider your answer carefully if this question comes from a friend or family member with small children. You might become the defacto babysitter of small, damp, and loud miniature humans. If you are into that kind of thing, plan your work time accordingly, and enjoy your time with the kids.

"11 am to 7 pm. I like sleeping in."

"I tend to keep to business hours unless someone has an appointment or something."

"Normally, I take the kids to school, work until I pick them up, and then work after they're in bed."

Break into line dancing while singing '9 to 5' by Dolly Parton.

How many clients/projects do you have at one time? Once I heard someone answer this question by fluffing their hair, striking a sexy pose, and responding to the questioner in a deep and smoky voice, "As many as I can handle, darlin'." Best video call ever after the laughing died down anyway.

"*I take on [number] of big projects and [number] small projects at one time.*"

"*Depends on the subject. If it is a subject I am familiar with, I don't need too much research time.*"

"*I like having a lot of options to work on at one time. I can jump back and forth between them. This way, I never get bored.*"

"*Like a fire juggler. Deal with the one that burns my hand the hottest.*"

How do you manage your time? Yes! Give your secrets to the world. Let them all know how to manage their time better. Or don't. It can be your little secret if your time management is measured by how many cookies you eat while working, and you don't want anyone to know.

"*I block my time in chunks and schedule tasks as I get them.*"

"*I have a calendar that I write all my tasks down in. It helps me prioritize.*"

"*Poorly, at first, but I've gotten better the more I practice.*"

"*Alarms. A lot of phone alarms.*"

"*I depend on the shadows cast by the giant stone obelisks in my backyard to map out my schedule.*"

Like when planning any eLearning, craft your response with the audience in mind. Remember to think of your audience when answering them. If you are asked a tax question, Uncle Al, the tax accountant, might be looking for different information than teenage cousin Samantha. Why's she asking you about taxes anyway? Samantha is so weird!

Remember to show your excitement! Let your friends and family know how happy you are to go to work. Maybe even show off some of your better builds, or best writing. If printable, slap those bad boys up on the prime fridge real estate and show it off to whoever comes by. You can even use those print outs to cover up the preexisting photos of Samantha, who somehow always manages to suck all the attention from every single person in the room including Great Grandma Ruth who used to consider us her favorite but then one day Samantha showed up with a non-dairy, cherry Dilly bar from DQ for Great Grandma and now it's alllll about Samantha ALL THE TIME and her WEIRD tax questions! *heavy breathing*

STEP #54

HOW DO I CELEBRATE EACH DAY OF MY FREELANCE JOURNEY IN SMALL WAYS?

You can and should celebrate your little victories a little at a time. Our favorite would be picking up a special treat we only get at the end of a project. Be it calorie-heavy, covered in chocolate, pickled in a rusty old can, or in a glass bottle, it's YOUR choice.

Celebrate daily by blocking out some time for any long-neglected hobby during your workday. Start your day like normal, but then take a break to test out that recipe you found while researching ice cream cake. Then, because ice cream cake is tastier when eaten with others, take the time to share the spoils of your crafting with neighbors. This might not seem like a celebration, but there's cake and people around, so naturally it must be. As a second option, you can just eat the entire cake yourself while enjoying the company of your most favoritest pack of raccoon friends. Those little bandits really steal your heart!

Since your time is your own, you can also incorporate your hobbies directly into your workday. Celebrate your freedom by taking breaks to rekindle old hobbies. Before getting out of bed, read a chapter or two of a book series you've wanted to read for years. There's no traffic to wade through, so you don't have to rush out of bed. Wander onto YouTube to repeatedly hit the "dislike" button on Cousin Samantha's new beauty vlog, "Get Glam with Sam," without worrying about getting caught. Practice your knitting while waiting for a meeting to start. (If you can pay attention during a meeting and knit simultaneously, you have a superpower, and we are jealous.) Without the rush, rush, rush of the typical workday, you can enjoy your time at work, and each time you do, it is a little celebration of your new career.

Speaking of time, do you ever notice how sometimes it flies by so fast, yet other times it seems a minute drags on for hours? Have you ever been staring at a clock on the job, trying to find something to do until it's time to leave because the boss wants everyone to work until the last minute? Ever had an old miser make you work on Christmas Eve then he gets visited by three time traveling ghosts and has a total change of heart and surprises you with a giant, prize-winning turkey at your home on Christmas Day? ANNOYING! No more busy work for you. Once your work is done, you are done! Time to celebrate by having movie day with the family or game night with guys. If your family is more outdoorsy (can't relate), visiting the local park for a family hike (can't relate) would be easier to plan if you didn't have to spend all those hours on busy work.

These little celebrations could also help you in your work. Have trouble figuring out how to get a program to do something in particular? If searching for the answer doesn't get you anything useful, and you feel like you are going to smash your desk, take a break and beat up some zombies in your favorite video game or IRL at a local supermarket. Swapping your focus will give your brain a rest, relieve some stress, and save the world all at the same time. Assuming you don't get bitten, anyway. You might even find that in saving the world, you finally remember how to get that program to behave like you know it can.

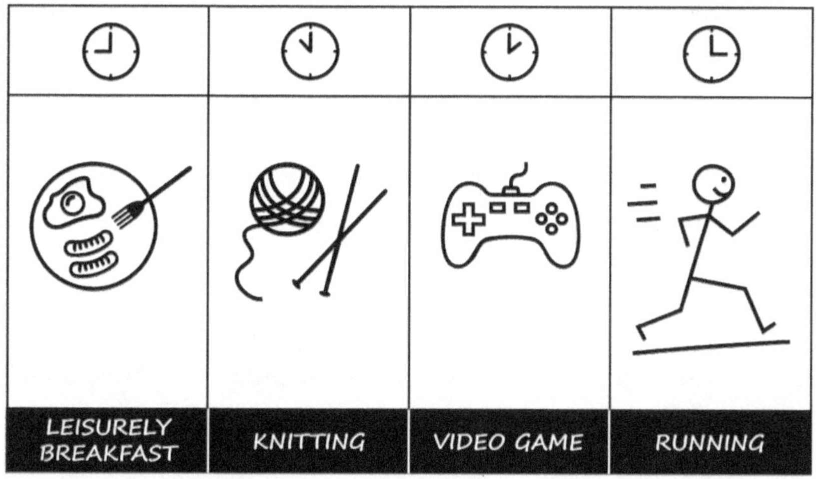

Ditch your cubicle and not your life. On any given freelance day, you can have a leisurely breakfast. Do some knitting mid-morning. Maybe play a video game after lunch. You can even go run on the trail in the middle of the afternoon. These are examples of the small ways you can celebrate each day of your freelancing journey!

With technology being so small, you don't even need to stay at home to work. Those more extroverted can head out to a local coffee shop or library to be around people for a little bit. Those who are more introverted could go to a park or work outside the house or very much inside the safety of one's own car. Outside in the sun, you can synthesize some vitamin D while working. Return to nature for a while and let the growing things revitalize you and celebrate your freedom with the sun, you heliolater you! No more walls or tiny windows. Unless you're into that.

If you're physically able to, working out with a friend is more fun than doing it alone. So they say. How about grabbing that friend that always offers to go to the gym with you and starting up an exercise routine? (Yes, even Parker exercises for fun - by running as far away from his office as possible - after an intense day of storyboarding.) You get a friendly accountability buddy and maybe even a free personal trainer. Not interested in going to the gym but still want to get out from behind that computer screen? You can try grabbing that same gym friend and abandoning them somewhere remote out in "the country" where you don't have to hear from them for a little while! The abduction will definitely help get the blood flowing and your muscles moving. It might even improve the quality of your work by providing you with one less relationship to maintain during the workday!

If friend-napping isn't for you, try some simple chair exercises or any kind of movement you feel safe and comfortable doing. Exercise isn't for everyone and for some people it's just not physically possible. If that's you– that's TOTALLY FINE, DANDY, and GREAT. And if anyone says otherwise, they're a butthead. You can tell 'em IDLance said so.

All of these small things are possible because of your hard work. Your time is your own, so do what you enjoy doing. And don't let anyone yuck your yum either! There's absolutely nothing wrong with bellowing out sea shanties while soaking in the tub every day at 2 PM in the afternoon. It's called self-care, people! Ever heard of it?!

SHARE YOUR NEWS WITH IDLANCE!

We here at IDLance care deeply about your freelance journey and butterfly-esque transformation into an independent, Instructional Design powerhouse. Cousin Samantha could never.

For that reason, it's our sincere hope that you'll let us know how things are going! Whether it's the good, the bad, or the ugly, we genuinely want to hear all about it. We're basically best friends now. Sorry, no take backs! You can expect to receive your BFF locket in the mail in approximately 150 business days.

STEP #55

CAN I WRITE TO THE HEAD HONCHOS?

Do you want to tell someone about what you've done and how you've done it? Venting can help give perspective and maybe even help start the healing process for something traumatic (like that time we married an Edwardian ghost named Egbert). Maybe you have a spicy origin story of why you left your previous employment: a hover-boss or a problematic workspace. We'd like to hear about it.

Why Instructional Design? There are thousands of different career options out there. What drew you to the field? Did you take a class, or are you self-taught? Have you based your entire career on your High School aptitude test result? True story – we got "ferry boat captain." If you are a vicarious learner, what sources did you find helpful? We know about some online classes, and maybe you found a new one we missed. Please help us, help others.

Our IDLance team would LOVE to hear about your journey to freelancing! Drop us an email or chat with us in our social media channels. Tell us about what you're doing and how you got there!

Freelancing is complicated. You got a book to help you with it. Hey, thanks for that, bff! You've always been there for us. Should we sign a friendship contract or...? We just need a notary public. Let us know when you're free! Which should be a LOT more often. The wins just keep on coming!

Why did you decide to do freelance work? Did you network through a friend of a friend, carefully comb through an online platform, or did you get lost down a wiki-rabbit hole? Were you under the impression that "freelance" was a pricing tier at Medieval Times? Turns out those wooden souvenir lances are NOT free. What drew you to Instructional Design freelancing in particular? Did you have a design background and want to do more than just sell a product? Did you discover a love for teaching but didn't really want to do the whole classroom thing?

You've worked and struggled to get this far and made it! You've made it into self-employment for Instructional Design. That's a huge deal! Now what? Are you planning on expanding your client list, or just gonna stick to the clients you know? How will you find new clients? Go to the places where you've found clients before, or seek out possible new pools of clients at your local Monster Mini Golf–like a moth to the flame, we tell ya!

How big do you want to take your Instructional Design business? Any expansion plans? Maybe hire a helper? Maybe two or three? Maybe get SO big that you'll take a flight into sub-orbital space on Jeffrey Bezos's big boy rocket ship? Details! We'd love to hear about your future plans, whether to continue as is or to reveal your eventual Instructional Design (possibly EVIL) Empire.

We really like hearing about how freelancing with Instructional Design has changed your personal life. How did you celebrate your financial freedom from the traditional 9 to 5? A new office in the home, or is your porch your new office? Working outside in the sun is definitely better than working in a sunless box, unless you're a Collyer brother, in which case– you're living the dream! Tell us about the amount of shopping you did for video conference clothing. Maybe some nice tops with absolutely gnarly bottoms you've had since your college years? Ya know, the cozy ones with the permanent toothpaste discoloration spots. Those spots are your family now.

Success stories are the best kind of warm and fuzzy feelings! How has it impacted your family life? How did telling your family and friends about freelancing go? Will you adopt Cousin Samantha into your family for us? Has the job shift helped improve any dusty relationships? Was there soap-opera level drama, or just excited and happy gatherings? We bet your pets were thrilled that you are home more often to say, "Awwww, big streeetttcccchhhh!"

We want to hear all the details! Let's get down to the nitty-gritty! If you have experienced it, we want to hear about it. It'll help us help other Instructional Design freelancers in the future.

Please let us know! Our contact information is:

Email: headhonchos@idlance.com

Facebook: https://www.facebook.com/IDLancealot

Instagram: https://www.instagram.com/idlance_a_lot

LinkedIn: https://www.linkedin.com/company/idlance

YouTube: https://www.youtube.com/@idlance

Incantation: Summon us by saying "IDLance" three times into a mirror in a candlelit room.

STEP #56

IS IT OKAY TO MAKE A QUICK 1-MINUTE VIDEO TO SPREAD THE NEWS?

So excited about your success and want to share, but are unsure how? Want to open up that phone and record some awkward, interpretive dance moves to show how excited you are? Do you want to thank the people who helped you on your journey through the undeniable power of haiku?

We want to see it.

Tell us about your journey.

This was a haiku.

(Hold your applause.)

Your mission, should you choose to accept it, is to submit a 1-minute video about what you liked most about this book. Maybe the tax section was most helpful, or you loved the list of items needed for a freelance Instructional Designer office. Knowing Instructional Designers, how did you pretty up the information and turn it into a work aid? Don't be embarrassed. We knew some of you would do it. Hey, you don't always have time to re-open a book for some information. We'd like to see your designs!

Maybe you want to review the book. That's okay too. Feedback (of any kind) is always welcome! Remember, the goal is to keep it to a 1-minute video. We're sure you have the talent and the skills to create within such rigid restrictions. Isn't that what Instructional Design is all about? Well, that and the VIP status. Do you accept the challenge, freelie?

Let us know that you accept our challenge and that we'll meet at dawn, to face off with swordfish on the second Tuesday of next week, or whatever type of duel (or friendly comment) you'd like to put forth! Unfortunately, we probably can't have a swordfish showdown with EVERY reader of this book; it's not good for the economy or the ocean ecology.

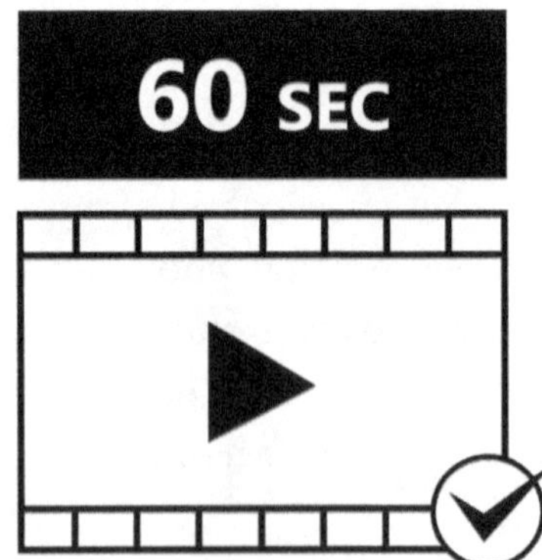

Time to hone your video editing skills, freelies! We'd love to have you send us a 1-minute video of you sharing what you liked most out of the tips you got from this book and how they helped you in your journey to ditch your cubicle!

But! Don't forget to tag us on your preferred social media platform to be sure that we see your video! We WILL watch and treasure them all.

This book was written because we saw a need. We won't say that it took blood, sweat, a few English majors, and tears to write, but it was an effort by many incredibly brave, incredibly good-looking people. Holy Guacamole! We covered a lot of information in this book. From support communities in Step #1 (wow, seems like a lifetime ago) to taxes in Step #36 (if you don't remember that one, you may have disassociated as a survival mechanism), developing your personal brand in Step #26 (you ARE the brand, bb) to planning an office space in Step #42 (don't forget the lava lamp), and computer specs in Step #40 (bleep boop), to how to celebrate your wins in Step #53 (break out the Wild Cherry Pepsi). Wow, look at us. Who'da thunk it.

There is a great deal of information you'll need to keep in your head while freelancing as an Instructional Designer, so off-load some mental data here to clear up a little bit of mental RAM. We'd like to think you'll use it as reference material while transitioning from your previous career to your new one. Or possibly you stumbled onto this while in college because you are rethinking life plans. Maybe you accidentally Freaky Friday'ed with a business professional! That happens! No matter where you are in your grand adventure, it's dangerous to go it alone. Trust us– one time we went on a solo road trip and ended up two states in the wrong direction. That's a true story! So take this book with you. (After paying for it of course! We don't condone stealing here. *aggressively winks at you*)

You don't have to keep this book front and foremost in your collection or display it in a prime coffee table location. We know that spot's reserved for your prized edition of, "Ice Mummies From Around the World."

Maybe you'll pass it on to a coworker and help them out of a similar situation, or maybe it'll end up balancing a table with a short leg. Or maybe, just maybe, you'll meet your twin flame at a local coffee shop where you're both reading this very book. D'awwww! Hey, as long as it helps you successfully transition to Instructional Design freelancing, all the time and effort spent in its creation will be well worth it! And please invite us to the wedding. If it's not clear by now, we love cake-centric events. Unless it's carrot cake. We repeat, do NOT insult us by inviting us to your carrot cake spectacle, sir or madam!

If you haven't started the career-swapping journey yet, you can do it. You might hear things like, "Go big or go home." Actual change isn't always one massive decision that changes your life immediately. You take a few small steps in different directions and test if you like what you see. Let's face it, any movement forward is always a success. You should take the time to celebrate it and be proud! Having to decide what to change can be scary, whether it's big or small. To decide to swap careers or freefall into self-employment can be just as intimidating for some as going back to school or posting on social media or revisiting the movie "The Neverending Story" as an adult. (Don't do it. Seriously.)

We hope this book has given you an idea of the work that lies ahead and some tools to help you get there! And maybe even some giggles and a-ha moments along the way!

Now let's ditch this cubicle and get outta here, boss.

And also, best friend. Seriously, where should we send that friend contract to?

REFERENCES

Holt-Lunstad, J., Smith, T. B., & Layton, J. B. (2010). Social relationships and mortality risk: a meta-analytic review. *PLoS medicine, 7*(7), e1000316.

James, E. L., & Brettschneider, M. (2012). *Fifty shades of Grey: Geheimes Verlangen.* Hörverlag.

Kolb, D. A. (2014). *Experiential learning: Experience as the source of learning and development.* FT press.

Miller, D. (2017). *Building a storybrand: clarify your message so customers will listen.* HarperCollins Leadership.

Williams, R. (2015). *The non-designer's design book: Design and typographic principles for the visual novice.* Pearson Education.